Y0-BCX-350

1.98
CCR
m

(2, 3) BY COURTESY OF THE ART INSTITUTE OF CHICAGO

CHINESE BRONZES

1. Gilt-bronze altar group of Buddha and attendant divinities, six dynasties
(A.D. 386–589), in a private collection in the United States

2. Covered ceremonial dish, Chou dynasty (1125–255 B.C.)
3. Gilt-bronze ceremonial jar, Han dynasty (206 B.C. to A.D. 220)

THE ROMANCE OF
CHINESE ART

BY THE FOLLOWING AUTHORITIES:

R. L. Hobson • Laurence Binyon

Oswald Sirén • Benjamin March

Lt. Col. E. F. Strange • Jiro Harada

Charles F. Kelley • A. F. Kendrick

George F. Kunz • Carl W. Bishop

Kojiro Tomita • Warren E. Cox

*With Many Full Page Plates in Colour
and Halftone*

GARDEN CITY PUBLISHING CO., INC.

Garden City *New York*

N
7340
R62

COPYRIGHT IN ALL COUNTRIES SUBSCRIBING TO THE BERNE CONVENTION
BY THE ENCYCLOPÆDIA BRITANNICA COMPANY, LTD.
COPYRIGHT IN THE UNITED STATES OF AMERICA, 1929, 1930, 1932, 1936
BY THE ENCYCLOPÆDIA BRITANNICA, INC.

Jan '38   Hampshire 1.59

PUBLISHER'S FOREWORD

THE MATERIAL in this book is presented through the courtesy of the publishers of the Encyclopædia Britannica. The text is composed of a selection of articles from its pages, and to its editors we are indebted also for the use of the many colour plates and other illustrations.

Warren E. Cox, Art Director of the Encyclopædia Britannica, in his Preface explains the make-up and comments upon the scope and authority of this volume. We believe it to be the most compact and comprehensive reference book on the various branches of Chinese Art ever made generally available to students and laymen.

We are proud of this opportunity to present such a valuable compilation at a price which nothing but the complete coöperation of the publishers of the Encyclopædia Britannica could have made possible.

PREFACE

As a handbook and general guide for those who enjoy browsing among the exhibits in the museums, this book should prove invaluable, for here in a simple and direct manner one finds much the same comment that the chief curator himself would make, if he were escorting one from case to case. The strange sounding names need no longer be meaningless and one can, with its help, know exactly when the Ming or T'ang dynasties did occur as well as the location of Ching-Tê Chên where the beautiful white porcelain has been made ever since the 15th century, or any of the other dynasties, provinces or cities mentioned on the cards of the exhibits.

The charts under the general article "Periods of Art" should prove particularly helpful, for one can tell at a glance what was happening in the rest of the world at any given time, and trace the influences which spread from one country to another.

Commencing with the brief article on the Aesthetic Development of China, written by Carl W. Bishop of the Freer Gallery at Washington, a general survey can be had of the main influences, religious and other, which changed the characteristics of art as a whole, and these characteristics should be borne in mind as one reads about each of the separate fields in which they manifested themselves. Not always were the various branches of art equally affected by the invading influences; sometimes the changes were felt first in architecture and sculpture; sometimes it was painting which first took on new life and a fresh outlook, to be reflected later in ceramics and lacquer. But whatever the individual changes in the arts may have been, they were

PREFACE

of course dependent upon those major changes in what may be called the great movements, and these should always be borne in mind.

As Chinese Architecture is chiefly known to the student in the West through photographs and small fragments, it is necessary to survey this art with some care, the more so because Chinese Sculpture sprang from Chinese Architecture, and it is in Sculpture that we find a large and ever growing interest today. Museums are constantly adding to their collections of Chinese figures, both stone and wood, and the western world is now beginning to realize that the great masters of Greece and of the Renaissance had their equals in T'ang China. These two branches of Chinese Art have been covered by Mr. Oswald Sirén of the National Museum, Stockholm, author of many books on both subjects and one of the world's greatest authorities. It will be found that he has told the story so simply and so directly that it is fascinating reading.

Everyone who has ever had any interest in Oriental Art at all has heard of Laurence Binyon and many have read some of his works, but nowhere else, so far as I know, can be found, in so few and so well directed words, the history of Chinese Painting. Mr. Binyon has long been Deputy Keeper of Oriental prints and drawings in the British Museum, and his writing tells not only of what was done in different periods but of how it was done and why.

The reader will find the writers of the other articles, on Bronze and Brass, Enamel, Iron, Ivory Carving, Lacquer, Jewellery, Textiles, etc., the greatest living authorities, each of whom in his own way treats of that field which he knows best. The result is that the great pageant of these beautiful arts makes its way through the reader's mind as it has come down through the ages and fills it with that enthusiasm and love for the beautiful which has always been such a commanding force in the lives of men. To understand the arts of a people is to understand the hearts of a people and such understanding is bound to enrich one's own life. Many myths have been told of the arts of the Far East, and much that is untrue has been passed from one to another; it is, however, quite unnecessary to resort to fancy or myth, for there is plenty of human interest, a goodly supply of mystery and ample beauty in Eastern Art, to make the truth itself fascinating, and it is the simple truth which you will find in this book.

PREFACE

One of the most mysterious of the arts, one which Europe has never been able to rival and one which derives its very name—China—from the country of its origin, is treated very fully in the article by R. L. Hobson of the British Museum who has probably written more than any one other man on this subject.   Every word in his article is worth the reading, first because most of the larger museums of the world contain examples of all the wares he describes, and secondly because the artistic rises and falls of China are told more clearly in this one field than in any other.   From the primitive potteries of four or five thousand years ago, through the strong, sturdy modellings of the Han dynasty and the more exquisite ones of the T'ang to the delicate poesy of the Sung and the glorious burst of colour of the Great Ming dynasty, and then on down the ever-declining, ever more refined art of the Kang Hsi, Yung Cheng and Chien Lung periods, there is a perfect reflection of the moods and characteristics of a marvellous people.   We of the Western hemisphere have learned from French and English importations of centuries back to enjoy the beauties of the porcelains of the later Chinese periods, which have had such tremendous influence upon the arts of all countries; and now to strengthen that influence even more, beautiful objects have in recent years come from Chinese tombs, which like those of Egypt are being carefully excavated.   Pottery, provided only it has escaped the careless hand of man, is perhaps the most lasting of all the arts, and through the medium of pottery we now know almost every detail of the lives of the Chinese who lived several thousand years ago: how they built their barns and houses, how they saddled their horses, how the ladies did up their hair, what musical instruments they used, and a thousand other interesting and intimate things.   Is this not mysterious enough?   Could one possibly read a more interesting story than that we are now finding about a strange and fascinating people of thousands of years ago?

But there are other mysteries which are interesting to the student of Chinese Art.   It must be remembered that though some people in our own land think of the Chinese as heathens of little originality and intelligence, they have in fact often been leaders in thought and invention.   To be sure they may find our Western ways difficult to copy or perhaps, to put it another way, they may see little reason to copy them, yet it must not be forgotten that in the field of art no people in the world have ever surpassed them in

PREFACE

technical excellence, in beauty of conception, and feeling of all of the sensitive and strong moods in executions. A little peach bloom vase, a tiny lacquer box, or an embroidered screen offers a problem well nigh as difficult for a Western civilization to solve as the making of a battleship or an airplane was for the Chinese when they first laid eyes on these Western inventions. Our intelligence has produced skyscrapers, fast boats, fast trains, huge guns; their intelligence has produced gun-powder, the glass lens, printing, paper and many other things equally useful; also they have produced probably the most beautiful paintings of nature, certainly the finest porcelains and potteries, superb sculpture, architecture which has stood for thousands of years, and many other things which are an ever-increasing mystery to us as we discover more and more about them. . . .

WARREN E. COX
Art Director, Encyclopædia Britannica.

CONTENTS

xi

CONTENTS

ILLUSTRATIONS

COLOUR PLATES

HALFTONE PLATES

ILLUSTRATIONS

xiv

ILLUSTRATIONS

PERIODS OF ART

An ART period is that duration of time within which the main arts, both fine and applied, show a general recognizable trend or group of characteristics. These characteristics, like those of the human beings who created them, are usually complex and difficult to describe, often being wholly unrecognizable until the observer has equipped himself with a considerable experience in the identification, comparison and classification of various works of art and, even when he is so equipped, these characteristics are sometimes found to be the basis of irreconcilable discussion, so far as details are concerned, by the greatest of experts. That there are, however, specific characteristics upon which the majority of authorities agree and which clearly indicate the time and geographical location on the earth's surface wherein some certain work of art was conceived and made cannot be denied. It is on such expert classification quite as much as upon the deductions of archaeological research that the whole fabric of the history of art, as well as our understanding of the extent and characteristics of the various cultural periods, is based.

As is pointed out in the notes under the first chart in the reference to the period between 500 B.C. and 350 B.C., there seems to occur at times a nearly world-wide stimulus or depression in the field of art. From A.D. 1400 to A.D. 1500 that great movement called the Renaissance prevailed through southern Europe; at the same time the Gothic movement in northern Europe was still productive; western Asia saw perhaps its highest pinnacle in painting, pottery making, rug weaving and the other arts; and in the Far East the great Ming Dynasty (1368 to 1644) was at its height. It seems strangely inexplicable that though the individual causes seem to differ, in some cases being due to religious fervour, in others the pomp resulting from great wealth, the results were nevertheless equally worthy.

Yet when we study that small part of the history of man of which we have records we find that the development of civilization has extended over only a comparatively brief period of time and that it has in the various parts of the earth been parallel and consistent. Thus, though we of the western world may look down upon the civilization of the Far East, perhaps because the East did not produce such efficient battleships, it is evident on closer study that the Chinese are very much like the Westerners. They understood and used bronze at about the same time and, though they have never taken the same interest in iron and steel, it was their invention of the lens and gunpowder which made possible these modern battleships.

Not only were there a number of cultures which originated at about the same time, but it must be kept in mind that from 2,000 years ago (at just the time these cultures began to take on marked individual characteristics) travel, inspired by commerce and war, commenced to bind together the races of man with an ever stronger bond. It is therefore not so surprising that at certain given times man's development in the various parts of the world should be such as to produce simultaneously great artistic achievements.

The tremendous wars which the Mongols waged under Jenghis Khan and which influenced the East and West alike may have dammed the flood of production until it rose to the irresistible pressure which found expression in the courts of the Ming Dynasty as well as in those so similar ones of Renaissance Italy. The religious fervour which made Gothic art possible was not dissimilar to that felt in western Asia and China and both were probably the result of the oppressions of war and at the same time reactions against a too materialistic wealth.

This consideration leads us to question what now seems to be the world trend. What can be hoped for the immediate future? To a remarkable degree the improved methods of travel and communication are bringing together the various peoples. National characteristics are being so blended as to show signs of a loss of identification. The Japanese artist is like the French, influenced by Cézanne, and there are American sky-scrapers in China. Undoubtedly this is going to prove a happy thing for all art as well as for civilization though just now the process is a discouraging one. There is bound, however, to emerge a functional art with a world-wide appeal.

A much more threatening element is that easily perceived interest on man's part in the new toys provided him by a bountiful science. The publics of all countries are becoming so interested in the moving pictures that there is little time to spare for looking at paintings. Similarly, the radio, the automobile and a thousand other inventions bid for man's amusement and time, and compete with all artists. How long it will take the world to adjust itself to this melting down of various characteristics, and to the building up of wider and more profound characteristics; how long it will take artists to adjust themselves to the new competitive demands and learn to make use of the inventions of science rather than combat them or have them make use of art, is a question that cannot yet be answered, but it is certain that until these two obstacles are overcome there can never be great art such as there has been in the past.

Thus we must get out of the habit of thinking that the last art is the best art. There is more loss than gain to be seen when the earlier arts such as those of Egypt or China or Greece are weighed in the scale against the modern, in spite of (or perhaps because of) all the new means available to artists of to-day which these earlier civilizations did not know.

Thanks must be given for their kind assistance in providing the facts upon which the following charts have been constructed to Professor Alfred W. Tozzer, Dr. Herbert J. Spinden, Dr. Ananda K. Coomaraswamy and Alan R. Priest.

	NORTHERN EUROPE		CENTRAL EUROPE		NORTHERN MEDITER-	
	SCANDINAVIA	CELTIC	GOTH TEUTON "HALLSTATT"	RUSSIA	AEGEAN & GREECE	ITALY
B. C. 6000 - 4000	LATER STONE AGE	STONE AGE	NEOLITHIC / LAKE DWELLING CULTURE		NEOLITHIC	
4000 - 2000	LATER STONE AGE	STONE AGE	NEOLITHIC / LAKE DWELLING CULTURE		AEGEAN - CRETAN OR MINOAN	NEOLITHIC
2000 - 1000	BRONZE AGE	BRONZE AGE	BRONZE AGE / "HALLSTATT"		AEGEAN - CRETAN OR MINOAN	NEOLITHIC
1000 - 500	BRONZE AGE	BRONZE AGE	IRON AGE		ARCHAIC	
500 - 350	IRON AGE	IRON AGE		GRAECO - SCYTHIAN	PERICLEAN	ETRUSCAN
350 - 200	PRE-ROMAN	PRE-ROMAN		GRAECO - SCYTHIAN	HELLENISTIC	REPUBLICAN
200 - 0						REPUBLICAN
A. D. 0 - 200		ROMAN - CELTIC				
200 - 300	ROMANO - SCANDINAVIAN	ROMAN - CELTIC			ROMAN	ROMAN IMPERIAL
300 - 350	ROMANO - SCANDINAVIAN					ROMAN IMPERIAL

The chart which extends over the following four pages gives a chronological and geographical outline of the various periods of art throughout the world so that a clea[r] of the country or general area specified at the tops of the columns of the chart. The years, starting at 6000 B.C., or earlier, are grouped into sections indicated at the le[ft] part of the chart to 100 years in extent.

The first part of the chart covers the time from 6000 B.C., or earlier, to A.D. 350, the second, from A.D. 350 to the present time. It should be noted that the ge[o]

In the indication of a given period a solid line shows the length of time during which its influence was felt. If the beginning or end of the line is dotted it show[s] as did many of those in China identified by the dynasties in which they occurred.

The datings of the earliest periods are necessarily vague, often being legendary in character and consequently frequently the field of controversy. But this compilatio[n] by the authors under whose strict supervision each statement was carefully weighed and checked. Under the heading "Goth, Teuton, Hallstatt" are included a numbe[r] Similarly the divisions under the headings "Aegean and Greece" and "Italy" are called by their cultural names without consideration of any of the existing racial diffe[rences]

Civilization seems to have developed from barbarism first in Egypt, in the Tigro-Euphrates Valley, in India or in China, though authorities differ as to which cultu[re] may arise in a consideration of pre-historic India. In China where the bronze age preceded that of Europe the more or less legendary dynasties of Hsia and Shang ha[ve] of the Pueblo area in the southwestern United States.

It is interesting to note that the period between 500 B.C. and 350 B.C., coinciding with the beginning of the iron age in northern Europe, witnessed the excellence [of] and Carthaginian; in Western Asia, the early Persian; and finally in China the Chou Dynasty which produced some of the most beautiful bronzes known to the collecto[r] ous sections of the earth, in a way that would be very difficult otherwise to bring together from various sources of information.

RANEAN / SPAIN	WESTERN ASIA	EGYPT	INDIA	CHINA	JAPAN	SOUTH AMERICA	CENTRAL AMERICA — MEXICO	CENTRAL AMERICA — PUEBLO AREA IN SOUTHWEST U.S.
	CHALDAEAN / SUMERIAN	PRE-DYNASTIC	PALAEO-LITHIC	PRE-LEGENDARY			MAYA	
		PYRAMIDS	NEOLITHIC & CHALCO-LITHIC / EARLY INDUS VALLEY CULTURE	HSIA				BASKET MAKER I
	BABYLONIAN / HITTITE	18TH DYNASTY	INDUS VALLEY CULTURE / EARLY VEDIC			ARCHAIC		BASKET MAKER II
GINIAN	PHOENICIAN / ASSYRIAN	DECLINE FOREIGN DOMINATION	LATE VEDIC	SHANG				BASKET MAKER III
PHOENICIAN AND CARTHA-	PERSIAN		PRE-MAURYA	CHOU				
	HELLENISTIC	PTOLEMAIC	MAURYA	TS'IN				PUEBLO I
		ROMAN	SUNGA		PRE-HISTORIC	ARCHAIC SHELL-HEAPS	ARCHAIC BEGINNINGS	
	PARTHIAN		ANDHRA	HAN		FIRST MAYA EMPIRE	ARCHAIC	
ROMAN	ROMAN	COPTIC	INDO-HELLENISTIC	WEI / SHUH HAN / WU / SIX DYNASTIES				PUEBLO II
	SASSANIAN		GUPTA					

understanding of the time of occurrence, the duration and the relationship of these periods can be gained at a glance. The geographical location is indicated by the name hand side, and it will be noticed that these sections are not constant, the earlier ones being, 2000 years in extent and the later ones being finally reduced on the second

graphical divisions of the second section differ from those of the first, owing to the fact that more definite demarcations politically had been arrived at.
gradual development or decline. If there is an abrupt beginning or end terminated by a small cross-line this shows that the period had a definite beginning or end, such

represents the consensus of the best founded opinions and has been carefully brought together by the authorities enumerated in the latter part of this article, as well as
of European cultural expressions irrespective of their actual racial origins which are still a matter of great doubt; the common names for these cultures are therefore given.
came earlier. It was not thought advisable to attempt to indicate the differing racial elements that created Chaldean and Sumerian culture or such racial questions as
been indicated in accordance with the dating of the Chinese chronicles while the heading "Central America" is used in the broad sense to include also the earliest cultures

the Greco-Scythian period in the territory now known as Russia, while in Greece the Periclean culture was at its height; in Italy, the Etruscan; in Spain, the Phoenician
of to-day. Thus, the reader will find it possible, through the use of this chart, to organize his studies and keep in mind the relative growth and decline of the arts of vari-

A.D.	SCANDINAVIA	GERMANY	FRANCE	ENGLAND	GREECE	ITALY	SPAIN	NORTH AFRICA
350 - 500	ROMANO-SCANDINAVIAN	ROMAN	ROMAN	ROMAN		ROMAN / EARLY CHRISTIAN	ROMAN	ROMAN / COPTIC
500 - 750		CAROLINGIAN	CAROLINGIAN	ANGLO-SAXON				
750 - 1000	VIKING AGE	CAROLINGIAN	CAROLINGIAN	ANGLO-SAXON	BYZANTINE		VISIGOTHIC	
1000 - 1100	SCANDINAVIAN ROMANESQUE	ROMANESQUE	ROMANESQUE			ROMANESQUE	ROMANESQUE	EARLY MUSLIM (EGYPT)
1100 - 1200	SCANDINAVIAN ROMANESQUE	ROMANESQUE	GOTHIC	EARLY ENGLISH / NORMAN ROMANESQUE		ROMANESQUE	HISPANO-MOORISH	EARLY MUSLIM (EGYPT)
1200 - 1300			EARLY AND RAYONNANT GOTHIC	EARLY ENGLISH GOTHIC		GOTHIC	HISPANO-MOORISH	
1300 - 1400	GOTHIC	GOTHIC	EARLY AND RAYONNANT GOTHIC	DECORATED GOTHIC	DOMINANCE	EARLY RENAISSANCE	GOTHIC	TURKISH MUSLIM / MOORISH
1400 - 1500	FLAMBOYANT GOTHIC	FLAMBOYANT GOTHIC	FLAMBOYANT GOTHIC	PERPENDICULAR GOTHIC	DOMINANCE	EARLY RENAISSANCE	GOTHIC / PLATERESQUE	TURKISH MUSLIM / MOORISH
1500 - 1600	RENAISSANCE	EARLY RENAISSANCE	FRANCIS II / HENRY II / HENRY IV	PERPENDICULAR GOTHIC / TUDOR AND JACOBEAN	TURKISH	HIGH RENAISSANCE	CLASSIC REN. / PLATERESQUE	
1600 - 1700	RENAISSANCE	DEVELOPED RENAISSANCE / BAROQUE RENAISSANCE	LOUIS XIV / LOUIS XIII	TUDOR AND JACOBEAN / PALLADIAN (I. JONES)	TURKISH	BAROQUE	BAROQUE	
1700 - 1800	ROCOCO	ROCOCO	LOUIS XIV / LOUIS XV / LOUIS XVI	CLASSIC REN. (WREN)		CLASSIC REVIVAL	CLASSIC REVIVAL	
1800 - 1900	RENAISSANCE REVIVAL / GOTHIC REVIVAL / CLASSIC REVIVAL	EMPIRE / NEO-GREC / GOTHIC REVIVAL / RENAISSANCE REVIVAL	GREEK REVIVAL / GOTHIC REVIVAL	ADAM / CLASSIC REVIVAL / GREEK REVIVAL	GREEK REVIVAL	NEO-BAROQUE		
1900 -	RENAISSANCE REVIVAL / MODERNIST	MODERNIST	RENAISSANCE REVIVAL / MODERNIST	MODERNIST		MODERNIST / NEO-BAROQUE		

It was found necessary in the above second section of the chart on the periods of art, not only to make smaller subdivisions of time ranging from 250 years to 100 the altered, more numerous and more definite national demarcations. The countries of Europe separated, and though there was a strong mutual influence, each began Japan, though closely bound to China, found their own expression, and finally North America which had known only Pueblo culture until the 17th Century became in-title of Romanesque Art and the line between early Christian work and certain work of the Italian Romanesque styles is quite impossible to fix definitely. Both the Coptic casionally called Byzantine. The word Byzantine as used on the chart is confined to that art produced under the direct influence of Constantinople, in Greece and on A new use for these charts is illustrated in this second one: that of the study of one single period of art, such as the Gothic and its development in the various coun-followed almost immediately by its rise in Germany, Spain and England, later in Scandinavia, and still later in Italy where its influence lasted for only a comparatively art soon became flamboyant as indeed it immediately afterwards became in France while in England it was, after the original introduction, first the "decorated" style land, but in America where the original period had never existed. In the same way, the influence of the Roman, the Carolingian and Romanesque, as well as many other

6

WESTERN ASIA	PERSIA	INDIA	CHINA	KOREA	JAPAN	SOUTH AMERICA	CENTRAL AMERICA	NORTH AMERICA
	SYRIAN · SASSANIAN	GUPTA	SIX DYNASTIES		PREHISTORIC			PUEBLO II
		PALLAVA · CHALUKYA	T'ANG	SILLA	SUIKO		FIRST MAYA EMPIRE	
		RASHTRAKUTA	FIVE DYNASTIES		NARA OR TEMPYO	QUIMBAYA (COLOMBIA) · PROTO-ICA (PERU)		
BYZANTINE	ARMENIAN	PALA · RAJPUT · CHOLA · KHMER			HEIAN · FUJIWARA	MANABI (EQUADOR) · ICA (PERU)	SECOND MAYA EMPIRE · TOTONAC · FLORESCENCE	PUEBLO III
		HOYSALA	SUNG	KORAI	MILITARY EPOCH	NASCA (PERU)	ZAPOTEC (S. MEXICO) · CHOROTEGA	
	PERSIAN MUSLIM	PANDYA			KAMAKURA · HOJO	TIAHUANACO	TOLTEC	PUEBLO IV
		VIJAYANAGAR	YUAN			INCA (PERU)	TOLTEC (NORTHERN YUCATAN)	
TURKISH		MOHAMMEDAN	MING	RICHIO	ASHIKAGA	CHIBCHA (COLOMBIA)	AZTEC	PUEBLO V
		MOGUL · RAJPUT PAINTING			MOMOYAMA	SPANISH BAROQUE	SPANISH BAROQUE	EARLY COLONIAL
		KANDYAN · BRITISH	CHING		TOKUGAWA			DEVELOPED COLONIAL · SPANISH COLONIAL
					MEIJI			FUNCTIONALISM · ROMAN REV. · GREEK REV. · GOTHIC REV. · ADAM TYPE · RENAISSANCE REV.

years owing to the continually increasing speed in the development of art periods throughout the world, but to alter and add to the geographical subdivisions because of a more or less individual national development. England, starting with the Roman period, developed partly distinct from, but parallel with, the continent. Korea and habited by Europeans who brought to it and developed an entirely new culture in this area. Many authorities include Carolingian and Romanesque under the general under "North Africa" and the Syrian under "Western Asia" are sometimes considered variant forms of the Byzantine; even the widely divergent Armenian style is oc- both shores of the Adriatic.

tries which felt its influence. With this section it may be seen that Gothic art started between A.D. 1100 and A.D. 1200 in the "Early and Rayonnant" style in France short time, giving way to the Renaissance. In Germany perhaps because of the same national characteristics that made the Baroque so appealing, at a later date, Gothic and later the "perpendicular" style. It may also be seen that there was a revival in Gothic art between A.D. 1800 and A.D. 1900 not only in Germany, France, and Eng- periods, can be traced in the various countries and the approximate dates easily fixed in mind.

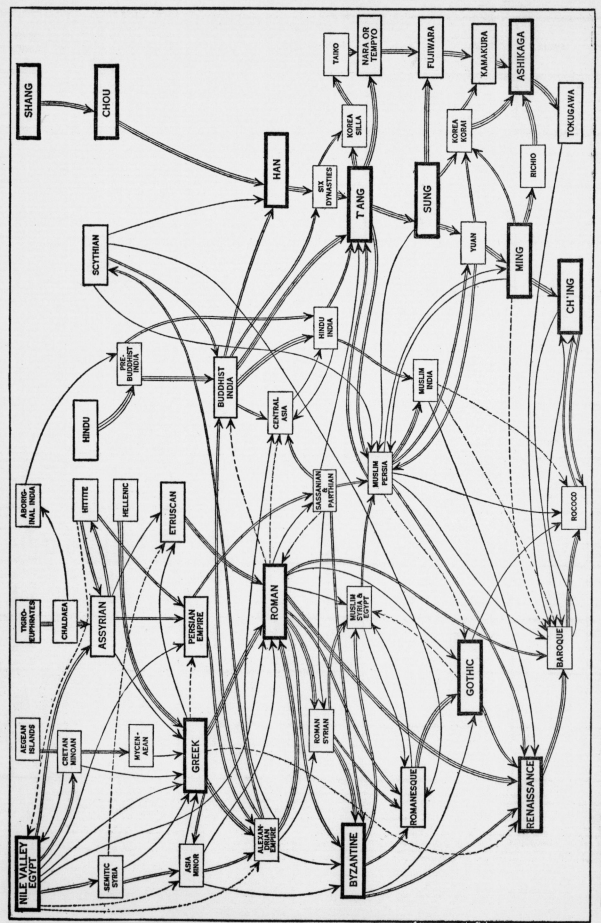

This chart is not designed to show chronological relationships though the earlier civilizations are near the top and the more recent arranged below (for chronological comparisons the charts on the preceding four pages should be consulted)—neither is there any attempt to arrange the countries in which the periods occurred geographically, the primary intention being simply to show those influences which were brought to bear upon the various most

important periods, omitting all question of the original genius of each nation which received, amalgamated and translated these influences as well as added their own contributions. The importance of the period is indicated by the weight of the outline. It will be seen that there are three classifications.

A dotted arrow indicates traces; a single arrow, definite but slight influence; a double arrow strong; and a triple arrow such influence as to be a dominant

factor in the period. Arrows running both ways indicate reciprocal influences such as those between Muslim Persia, and T'ang China. In general the terms used are in their broadest interpretations; thus, "Romanesque" covers Carolingian, as well.

無量壽尊佛

BY COURTESY OF YAMANAKA AND COMPANY

WOVEN BROCADE HANGING

A wall hanging of woven silk brocade attributed to the Ming Dynasty. This hanging, woven entirely in one piece, is said to have come from Jehol, northern China

BY COURTESY OF (1, 2, 4) THE DIRECTOR OF THE VICTORIA AND ALBERT MUSEUM, (3) THE MUSEUM OF FINE ARTS, BOSTON

CHINESE TEXTILES

1. Early 18th century wall-hanging of white satin embroidered with coloured silk

2. One of a series of four panels representing the Dragon Boat Festival in honor of Chü Yüan, statesman and poet, who was drowned in the Mi-lo River, 295 B.C. This panel is of silk tapestry, middle 18th century

3. Eighteenth century Chinese red velvet chair cover. The pattern is in red satin shot with gold thread

4. Ming dynasty (1368–1644) woven damask. The "longevity" character found in the middle of each flower, as well as the design and texture of the material, indicates its Chinese origin

TEXTILES AND EMBROIDERIES

Woven fabrics of China.—The origin of silk-weaving in China is lost in the region of myth and legend, and nothing remains to show what the earliest stuffs were like. The oldest Chinese patterned stuffs known to exist were unearthed by Sir Aurel Stein in the Lop desert, Chinese Turkestan, in 1914. The site lay on the route opened out by the Chinese for the silk trade with western Asia in the 2nd century B.C., and replaced by an easier route in the 4th century A.D. The stuffs are attributed to the 1st century B.C., during the Han dynasty, and they are undoubtedly influenced by earlier traditions. The patterns of dragons, griffins, animals, birds, scrolls and diapers are archaic in form, though at the same time they have a remarkable resemblance to later work. The next Chinese dynasty especially associated with the output of artistic wares is the T'ang (A.D. 618–906). Considerable numbers of textiles attributed to this period have been preserved. The Chinese were then in contact with Persia both by land and sea, and this western intercourse is reflected in the art of the time. It is conspicuously seen in a silk banner said to have been used by the Japanese Prince Shotoku (A.D. 572–623), and now removed from Nara (the old imperial capital) to the Tokyo museum. The design is a typical Sassanian hunting-scene, with the king on horseback attacking a lion; the manner of representation is, however, Chinese and Chinese characters are introduced. Many other silk weavings of this epoch are preserved in the royal treasure-house at Nara in Japan.

A characteristic type of Chinese weaving, done by the tapestry method in fine silks and gold thread, and known as k'o-ssu, is first met with under the T'ang dynasty. The specimens which have been found in the Gobi desert

9

region differ remarkably little from those of modern times. The same very fine silk warp is used, and the weft of bright coloured silk enhanced by the use of gold thread. On the other hand there can be no reasonable doubt that these examples woven more than a thousand years ago were the heirs of a far greater antiquity—perhaps assignable in its origin to the dim period when Chinese handicrafts first assumed a civilized form. The patterns are less archaic than those of the "Han" silks already mentioned, but they are similar in their scope—including dragons, symbolic "lions," phoenixes, and various animals, birds and flowers.

Under the Yüan dynasty, founded by a Mongolian conqueror about 1280, Marco Polo (besides other travellers from Europe) found his way across the Asiatic continent to China. He speaks of the silk brocades woven in many parts of that country. Numbers of Chinese silk and gold fabrics were brought to the West at that time and under the Ming dynasty which followed in the 14th century. Some are at Regensburg and Danzig and in other church treasuries of Europe. Occasionally Arabic inscriptions are inwoven into these stuffs showing that they were intended for the use of a Mohammedan ruler of western Asia.

With the arrival of the Portuguese at Canton in 1517 a new era begins for Chinese textiles. "Chinoiserie" soon came into vogue in Europe, and the trading ships of Portugal, Spain, England, France, Holland and other countries brought home vast quantities of Chinese textiles often made specially for export. During this time the weaving of fine silk fabrics, uninfluenced in design by Western associations, went on as before. Dragons, phoenixes, clouds, waves and symbolical ornaments were reproduced on official garments, temple hangings and other stuffs. In China a landscape or a figure subject becomes a "pattern" almost as naturally as any other kind of ornamentation. Landscapes including rocks, rivers, boats, buildings, trees and figures were rendered by the tapestry-weaving process already described. A panel belonging to a series representing a popular commemorative festival held annually by the Chinese, is here reproduced.

Woven Fabrics of Japan.—Textile art in Japan owes a great deal to the Chinese. The ancient royal treasure at Nara, already mentioned, contains some of the most remarkable early Chinese stuffs in existence. The inference that Japan was then very largely dependent upon the more ancient civilization of her neighbours for the richer sort of textiles is confirmed on more general grounds. In the early centuries of the Christian era large numbers of Chinese weavers settled in Japan. They usually worked under Japanese control; they became distributed through the country.

In the year 1584 a Japanese embassy arrived in Europe, visiting Pope Gregory XIII. in Rome, and King Philip II. in Spain. They brought with them silk weavings as presents, receiving in return velvets and brocades. From this time onwards European influence may be discerned here and there in the textiles of Japan. But before the 17th century was well advanced, Japan closed her doors entirely to the foreigner, until in 1858 the country was reopened to European and American trade by Com. Perry, U. S. Navy.

Japanese textile design displays an acute perception of natural forms, seizing the salient features and transforming them with a light touch to the fabric. Ducks are shown floating on the rippling water, irises growing in the stream, fowls with their chicks, cranes on the wing; with these are landscape effects—lakes and streams, clouds, pine trees, castles and bridges. Symbolic ornaments and small diaper patterns are also common. Different methods of ornamentation are frequently combined in one fabric. A silk stuff may have a woven pattern helped out by printing and completed with a few deft touches of embroidery.

AESTHETIC DEVELOPMENT OF
CHINA

In NORTHERN CHINA, mainly in the basin of the Huang Ho or Yellow River, there slowly emerged in late prehistoric times a focus of civilization destined eventually to make its influence felt in all the neighbouring regions, both continental and insular. Apart from certain well shaped stone implements and fragments of a coarse, unglazed pottery, few vestiges of the Chinese Stone Age culture have thus far been found. An important exception is the recent discovery in northern China of a painted ware with analogies in Turkistan and regions still farther west.

Chinese Bronze Age.—It is only with the acquisition of bronze that a distinctly Chinese civilization first appears. So far no trace has been found of evolution out of an earlier copper period like that which took place in the Occident. On the contrary, the bronze objects found in China are all essentially late forms, identical in principle with types which in other lands appear only toward the close of the Bronze Age. This great advance in civilization seems to have occurred under the mainly legendary Shang dynasty, the date of whose beginning no one knows, but which terminated about the end of the second millennium B.C. It is, however, with the succeeding largely historical Chou period, with its long line of priest-kings and its brilliant feudal aristocracy, that the Chinese Bronze Age is especially linked. In the present fragmentary state of our knowledge of China during the first millennium B.C., it is only possible to reconstruct the civilization of that time very imperfectly. It may be said, however, that although barbarous in many respects, it was distinguished for colour and richness and the lavish

12

PHOTOGRAPH, HERBERT PHOTOS, INC.

GREAT WHITE DAGOBA, PEKING

The great White Dagoba at Peking, China, built in 1652. Its shape is that of a Buddhist reliquary.
Base, body, spire, crown and gilded ball are symbols of the five elements earth, water, fire, air and ether

PHOTOGRAPH, COPR. OSVALD SIREN

THE GREAT WALL OF CHINA

The Great Wall of China at the Nank'ou pass, Chih-li; 228 B.C. It is 1,400 miles long, with square watch-towers at intervals

use not only of bronze but also of gold, ivory, jade, featherwork and ornamental textiles. Its designs are pretty certainly a development of the old Neolithic art, retained because of their traditionally sacred character and the belief that any alteration in them would diminish their magical efficacy.

The high artistic quality of this civilization is best exemplified in the great bronze ceremonial vessels used in connection with the ancestor worship of the nobility. These, for grandeur of form, dignity and ornamentation, and mastery of technique, have never been surpassed, and command the admiration of students and art-lovers the world over.

The Ch'in Dynasty.—The later portion of the Chou period witnessed a great social and economic development, which in time undermined the archaic feudal system. The 3rd century B.C. saw its entire overthrow, along with that of its venerable but long since impotent hieratic dynasty, by the vigorous western fief of Ch'in. The ruler of the latter forcibly united the hitherto loosely federated States into a centralized empire, of which he declared himself first emperor. Of the artistic achievements of his powerful but short-lived dynasty we know but little. A nearly contemporary work states that large bronze statues were then cast, and certain types of vessels of that material have been ascribed to the period, with hardly sufficient reason. That it was an epoch of extraordinary magnificence, there is no doubt. The Ch'in dynasty collapsed little more than a decade after its establishment, having fulfilled, however, its historic mission of assuring once for all the cultural unity of China.

The Han Dynasty.—Out of the general welter of war which followed, there emerged in a few years the great dynasty of the Han, which reigned over the empire, with but one brief interval, from 206 B.C. to A.D. 220. This period of over 400 years is a most important one, in art as in other respects. Then first appeared numerous hitherto unknown culture elements of fundamental importance to the Chinese civilization of later times.

Of its architecture the records have much to say, but nothing has survived save certain foundation mounds and city and boundary walls of rammed earth. Sculpture in stone now first made its appearance, in the form of low reliefs and figures of men and animals set up about tombs; here some connection with the art of western regions may be suspected, for it was just at this time that direct contact with the Occident was first established. Painting underwent a great development, its materials, instruments and technique becoming fundamentally what they have since remained. Of its achievements, only certain archaic delineations of human figures on funerary tiles are known; but it would seem mainly to have depicted scenes of battle, the hunt, and court and domestic life, with but little attempt at landscape. Only in the 2nd century A.D., toward the close of the dynasty, did the names of individual artists begin to be recorded.

The pottery of this period also shared in the great aesthetic evolution then taking place. Glaze, known for millenniums in the Occident, now first appears in China, and the great Han mortuary vessels, sometimes inspired by bronze forms or encircled by bands of vigorous naturalistic scenes in relief, are well known to collectors. The first tentative essays in the direction of porcelain are likewise to be ascribed to this period. Clay figures of men, women, animals, houses and utensils, found buried in tombs, throw much light on the life of the time. The decorative arts, like those of the jeweller and the lapidary, also underwent a rich and striking development; in connection with the latter it may be noted that seals, usually cut in jade or some other hard stone, long known in western lands, now first appeared in China.

The downfall of the Han dynasty, in the 3rd century, led to a condition of disunion and civil war, which lasted for nearly 400 years. Yet, in spite of this, great progress was made in all the arts. In architecture, probably toward the close of the period, arose the practice of uptilting the corners of roofs, regarded by Westerners as so characteristically Chinese. Paintings on silk, still chiefly of human figures but displaying attempts toward landscape, are known to us through copies by later artists. Pottery was further improved and diversified in form, ornamentation and technique, and true porcelain appears, apparently as a direct evolution out of the ware of the Han dynasty.

THE EFFECT OF BUDDHISM

The New Religious Factor.—It was, however, in religious rather than secular art that the period achieved its greatest aesthetic triumphs. This was due to the introduction of Buddhism from India. The effect of this upon China and her neighbours throughout all subsequent history has been incalculable, and may well be compared to the effect on Europe of the introduction of Christianity. The famous early Buddhist sculpture of Gandhara, in northwestern India, reached its maximum development about the 2nd century, but in its pure form spread only as far as eastern Turkistan. The art which now developed in northern China under the Toba Tatar or North Wei dynasty (A.D. 386–534) was no direct outgrowth of this. It must have flowered locally under the stimulus of the new religious faith, although naturally finding inspiration for certain of its elements in Indian, Iranian or even Hellenistic ideas which reached China by the great Central Asiatic caravan-routes. It is best exemplified by the remarkable series of sculptured grottoes of Yün-kang in northern Shansi and Lung-mên in Honan, in regions where the North Wei power successively centred. Its best work is character-ized by slimness of figure, rhythmic grace of curve and that passionless, spiritual calm and benevolence which are the essence of Buddhism.

Very little later, mainly under the local Liang dynasty (502–556), the new influence also reached China by the sea-route through the Straits of Malacca. This latter movement, originating chiefly in southern India, brought with it an art little affected by that of Gandhara, but reflecting rather that of the great Maurya dynasty of the 3rd century B.C. Among the elements which it introduced were the fluted column and great and vigorously executed winged lions; examples of both these still survive, much mutilated, in the vicinity of Nanking, the capital of the Liang dominions. Little is yet known of this southern Buddhist art of China, partly because of the tremendous destruction of its works wrought by the Taiping rebellion of the middle of the 19th century, but partly too because it has hitherto attracted less attention than that of the north.

The heterogeneous mass of animism, folk-lore, and magic which formed the religion of the masses in feudal days was liberated by the destruction of the nobility, and acquired great influence during much of the Ch'in and Han dynasties. Gradually organized into the system known as Taoism, it bor-rowed from Buddhism not merely its temples, festivals and whole parapher-nalia of worship, but also its art, notably its sculpture. Its works, however, are much cruder in every way, and artistic merit of any sort is exceptional.

The T'ang Dynasty.—After this long period of disunion and war, toward the close of the 6th century, China was again united under the brilliant but short-lived Sui dynasty (A.D. 589–618). This in turn was succeeded by that of the T'ang (A.D. 618–906), whose long sway vied with that of the Han as one of the greatest epochs of Chinese history. Under its earlier rulers, China had nothing to fear from comparison with any realm on earth, whether that of Byzantium, of Sassanid Persia or the newly founded power of Islam. Intercourse with the Occident during much of this time was constant and close, and ideas of every sort travelled both east and west.

Buddhist sculpture now attained its highest pitch; naturalism replaced conventionality, and heads, instead of reflecting an impersonal and purely spiritual ideal, became individual portraits. Painting also underwent a noteworthy development. To this period belongs Wu Tao-tzŭ, greatest of all Chinese painters, whose style has exerted enormous influence upon all later times, not only in China, but also in Japan. Two schools appeared, a northern and a southern, and landscape was now seriously developed. Almost all the authentic existing T'ang dynasty paintings are religious in character; but fortunately a very few secular examples survive, while others are known through copies by artists of later periods.

In pottery also the T'ang period reached a higher stage than hitherto. Glazes were increased in range of colour and texture. The forms themselves are predominantly native, although in some cases they reflect western influences, especially that of Sassanid Persia. T'ang grave figures are well known for their artistic merits as well as their great archaeological interest. Bronze, long since displaced by iron for the manufacture of weapons and tools, was in greater favour than ever in the arts, notably for the casting of Buddhist statues and statuettes, often richly gilt. Ivory from southern China and Indo-China and jade from Turkistan were carved into a variety of ornamental shapes. Although probably already known in principle, engraving on wood now makes its first definite appearance. The T'ang period is also noteworthy for the great extension of Chinese culture which then took place into southern China, till then only partially assimilated, and also into Korea and Japan. The dynasty, after a long period of decadence, came to an end early in the 10th century.

The Sung Dynasty.—After another period of turmoil, which however lasted only half a century, China was again united, under the Sung dynasty, which maintained its sway over the whole country for slightly over a century and a half. Then, through Tartar aggression, its power was restricted for a further similar period to that part of the country situated south of the Yangtse River, until it was finally overthrown by the Mongols about 1280.

During the Sung period the influence of Buddhism greatly declined, being replaced by Confucianism, and probably as a result of this, sculpture became decadent. Painting, on the other hand, reached heights never attained before. Landscape underwent its greatest development, the effort being not to depict a scene exactly, but to reveal its inward spirit and arouse a corresponding emotion. Taoism, through its love of solitude and contemplation, provided Sung painting with many of its most romantic concepts. Thus there arose in China an appreciation of the beauties of nature, later imparted to Japan but unknown in Europe until the 19th century. Authentic pictures of this period, while more numerous than those of the T'ang, are nevertheless very rare. During this extremely artistic epoch, pottery also underwent a great development, losing, it is true, something of the strength and vigour of the best T'ang examples, but acquiring nevertheless a characteristic tastefulness in form and delicacy of finish.

Northern China, controlled by successive Tartar powers during much of the 12th century, was conquered soon after the opening of the 13th by the Mongols who overran so much of the Old World at that time. Half a century later they also subdued the realm of the Southern Sungs, and China was thus reunited under their rule. The art of their time has little to distinguish it from that of the periods before or after, although perhaps in some instances their adoption of Lamaistic Buddhism has left a visible impress. It was then that began that tendency to resort to antiquity for models which later became so pronounced. Shortly after the middle of the 14th century an outburst of popular fury drove out the decadent later Mongols and led to the accession of the Ming dynasty, the last native Chinese ruling house.

THE CONFUCIAN REVIVAL

The Ming Period.—The Ming period (1368–1644) is especially noteworthy for its great achievements in architecture, even to-day hardly appreciated at their real worth. Nearly all the city and frontier walls, paved roads, bridges, palaces, temples and pagodas still existing in China were constructed by the great Ming builders. Next to its architecture, probably the most important work of the Ming period, was that accomplished in pot-

17

tery. Here too inspiration was sought from the earlier epochs, especially that of the T'ang. But original work was done, and Ming celadons, polychromes and blue-and-white ware are well known. It was during the latter half of the dynasty that porcelain was first regularly exported to Europe, although isolated examples had reached Mediterranean lands far earlier through Arab traders. The sculpture of this time is dull and uninspired, as shown by its best known examples, the colossal figures of men and animals lining the famous avenue to the Ming tombs just north of Peking. Painting not infrequently displays much excellence, but necessarily lacks the interest always aroused by original creative art. Emphasis was placed chiefly upon landscapes and nature studies, and to the Ming artists who industriously copied earlier works we owe by far the greater part of our knowledge of the secular paintings of the T'ang and Sung times.

In the realm of textiles, embroideries, brocades and damasks of high character were produced, and for the first time, perhaps as a consequence of the contacts opened up with the Near East under the Mongols, Chinese rugs and carpets assume a place of importance. In the minor arts also development attained a high level. Ming cloisonné is characterized by a boldness of design and depth of colour never excelled. Much work of a high technical order was done in the carving of jades and other semi-precious stones and ivory, in dignity and beauty often far superior to later examples. In general, the art of this time, perhaps largely owing to the revival of Confucianism with its worship of antiquity, falls far below that of the earlier and truly great periods. These were spontaneous and creative and had a genuine message; while that of the Mings was consciously imitative and sought its mission in trying to bring back to life a long dead past. Like all its predecessors, the Ming dynasty toward its close underwent a rapid process of degeneration and decadence, the central power becoming weaker and weaker until at last it was overthrown in a great rebellion.

The Ch'ing Dynasty.—The vacant throne was swiftly seized by the warlike Manchus, who proceeded to overrun the entire country, and who gave the Empire an enormous expansion. Their dynasty, known as that of the Ch'ing, produced several rulers of first-rate ability; but their genius displayed itself to better advantage in statecraft and war than in the development of the arts. In architecture they did but little in comparison with their prede-

18

PHOTOGRAPHS, COPR. OSVALD SIRÉN

TWO CITY WALLS

1. Portion of the city wall of Peking; west side, outer view. It is provided with 44 bastions and coated with bricks. The battlements are beginning to crumble. It had been constantly rebuilt or repaired from the end of the 15th to the middle of the 19th century. Its two gates are the Hsi Chih men (north) and Ping Tzu men (south), connecting city and suburbs

2. Portion of the city wall and the double bastion at south gate in Si-an, Shen-si, built at the end of the 14th century, and repaired in places. It encloses an almost square city, and has double gate-towers, square bastions and round corner-towers

PHOTOGRAPHS, COPR. OSVALD SIRÉN

PAGODAS AT SI-AN, SHEN-SI

1. Pai T'a Ssu, small pagoda south of Si-an; 10th–11th centuries

2. Hsiang Chi Ssu near Si-an; erected 681

3. Portion of Hsing Chiao Ssu pagoda near Si-an; about 839

4. Ta Yen T'a, the Great Pagoda of the Wild Geese, Si-an; founded 652; partly rebuilt in the 10th century

cessors the Mings, perhaps because the latter had left so little to be done. In sculpture, China under their rule displayed little originality, development being mainly in the direction of grotesque perversion of taste and excess of ornamentation. In painting almost no original work of consequence was done, although the copying of earlier works was continued. It was in the field of porcelain that the most noteworthy aesthetic achievements of the Manchu period have occurred. A marked development took place in fineness of texture and elaboration of form and decoration. The greatest work was done in the two decades from 1662 to 1683. During the 18th century the tendency toward elaboration of form and decoration became more and more marked, and some of the pieces of the Ch'ien-lung period have never been excelled in these respects. The weaving of textiles and rugs, the execution of objects of personal adornment and household decoration, as well as carving of every sort, also display this elaborating tendency. With it went a steady deterioration in taste for which no intricacy of design could compensate.

Whether the present turmoil in China will lead to another period of artistic greatness, only the future can disclose.

Other Regions.—Chinese culture spread to Korea and Japan (*qq.v.*), but these were not the only regions into which it was carried. During the early centuries of the Christian era it spread over southern China and gradually made that region definitively Chinese. Indo-China and Tibet, although strongly affected, escaped such complete absorption, partly because of the presence in those countries of strong Indian cultural counter-currents. During the T'ang period, and again under the dynasty of the Mings, the influence of China penetrated far and wide through the Indian Archipelago; Formosa was partially subdued and assimilated, Borneo and the Philippines underwent Chinese contacts of which traces still remain, and even distant Ceylon for a time was a tributary of the Ming emperors.

As so often occurs in cases of culture diffusion, the influence of Far Eastern aesthetic development continues to be widely felt, although moribund or dead in the lands which saw its birth. Interest in it grows apace, and collections, researches and publications are multiplied. In the light of recent critical study, largely by Chinese and Japanese scholars themselves, it is being found necessary to reduce greatly the extravagant dates claimed by most Far Eastern nations, with no support from contemporaneous history, for the earlier periods of their culture.

CHINESE ARCHITECTURE

THE ART of building in China has always been closely dependent on the intimate feeling of the Chinese people for the significance and beauty of nature. They arranged their buildings with special regard to the "spirits of earth, water and air," their ambition being not to dominate nature by their creations, as Westerners mostly do, but to co-operate with it, so as to reach a perfect harmony or order of the same kind as that which is reflected in the creations of nature. It was less the outward forms that interested them than the inner meaning, the underlying creative forces. This is most evident in the arrangement of some of the great tombs and shrines or in open-air altars dedicated to the divinities of heaven and earth. But it is also reflected in profane buildings such as the imperial palaces, which were planned and built according to sidereal or cosmological considerations. This appears even from the name used for the present and some earlier imperial palaces: Tzu Chin Ch'eng, the so-called Purple (or Violet) Forbidden City, of astronomical origin: the Heavenly Lord or Ruler Above was supposed to occupy a circum-polar constellation composed of 15 stars called the Purple Protected Enclosure, and as this was situated in the centre of the celestial world, so was the palace of the emperor, the human representative of the highest divine principle, supposed to be in the middle of the human world.

The general arrangement and planning of the Chinese buildings have indeed very little in common with such artistic points of view as have been applied in Western architecture; they result rather from religious and philosophical ideas which have their roots in most ancient traditions. This accounts also for the uniformity, not to say monotony, of early Chinese

20

architecture. The principles of construction have remained the same during many centuries, as have also the plans of the temples and palaces. The modifications of style which have been introduced are of comparatively small importance. It thus becomes possible to draw some conclusions from relatively late examples about the earlier buildings, which unfortunately are practically all destroyed; the wooden material has poorly withstood the

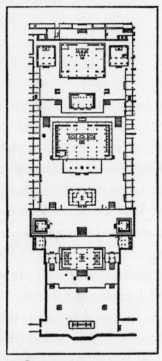

CHINESE TEMPLE PLAN
Showing the usual arrangement of placing the main buildings in a row, the one behind the other.

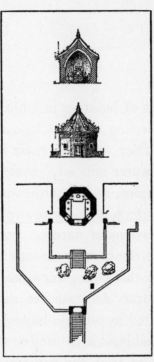

YÜ HUANG MIAO ON PIAO SHAN NEAR TSINANFU

ravages of fire and warfare, and the people have never made any serious efforts to protect their old buildings. It was mainly for the dead that the Chinese created more permanent abodes, and thus the tombs are the most ancient architectural monuments still existing in China. Besides these there are some cave temples hollowed out in the mountain sides and a few stone and brick pagodas of early date which will be mentioned later.

The Walls of China.—The earliest architectural monument above the soil in China is the "Great Wall," a massive fortification running along the northern and northwestern frontier of the country. It was erected by the great Emperor Ch'in Shih Huang Ti shortly after he had reunited the differ-ent parts of the country into an empire (228 B.C.). No doubt minor parts of such a wall had existed before his time, but he planned his defence against the nomadic tribes on a very much larger scale than had any previous ruler. It is stated that nearly 750 km. of the wall were built during his reign. What-ever truth this statement may contain, the fact remains that he laid the foundation of one of the world's grandest constructions, which, after many enlargements and restorations in the course of time, is still of great impor-tance. The structural character of the wall is quite simple. It is built mainly of earth and stone, varies in height between 6 and 10 metres and is mostly covered by a coating of bricks. On the ridge of the wall runs a passage three or four metres wide between crenellated parapets, and at regular intervals square watchtowers rise above the ridge on which fires were lighted as soon as any danger was sighted. In spite of this uniformity, the wall is intimately connected with the landscape, rising in many parts almost like one of nature's own creations, accentuating the sharp ridges of the mountain chains and winding according to the undulations of the ground. It is the greatest and most monumental expression of the absolute faith of the Chinese in walls.

Walls, walls and yet again walls, form the framework of every Chinese city. They surround it, they divide it into lots and compounds, they mark more than any other structures the basic features of the Chinese communi-ties. There is no real city in China without a surrounding wall, a condition which indeed is expressed by the fact that the Chinese used the same word *ch'eng* for a city and a city wall; there is no such thing as a city without a wall. It is just as inconceivable as a house without a roof. These walls belong not only to the provincial capitals or other large cities but to every community, even to small towns and villages. There is hardly a village of any age or size in northern China which has not at least a mud wall or remains of a wall around its huts and stables. No matter how poor and inconspicu-ous the place, however miserable the mud house, however useless the ruined temples, however dirty and ditch-like the sunken roads, the walls are still there and as a rule kept in better condition than any other building. Many a city in northwestern China which has been partly demolished by wars and famine and fire and where no house is left standing and no human being lives,

PHOTOGRAPHS, COPR. OSVALD SIRÉN

EXAMPLES OF THE CHINESE PAGODA, OR TEMPLE-TOWER

1. The Nan t'a (south tower), at Fang Shan, Chih-li; 11th century

2. The Pa Li Chuan pagoda near Peking; 13th century

3. Pagoda of Sung Yueh Ssu, at Sung Shan, Hon-an; A.D. 523

4. Pei t'a (north tower), at Fang Shan, Chih-li; 8th century

PHOTOGRAPHS, COPR. OSVALD SIRÉN

BUDDHIST BUILDINGS

1. Ssu Mên T'a, the Four Gate pagoda at Shen Tung Ssu, Shantung;   2. Wu Liang Tien, a temple in Su-chow, Chakiang; 17th century
    middle of 6th century   3. The Drum Tower in Peking; erected in 1273

still retains its crenellated walls with their gates and watchtowers. These bare brick walls with bastions and towers, sometimes rising over a moat or again simply from the open level ground where the view of the far distance is unblocked by buildings, often tell more of the ancient greatness of the city than the houses or temples. Even when such city walls are not of a very early date (hardly any walls now standing are older than the Ming dynasty) they are nevertheless ancient-looking with their battered brickwork and broken battlements. Repairs and rebuildings have done little to refashion them or to change their proportions. Before the brick walls there were ramparts round a good many of the cities and towns as still may be seen at some out-of-the-way places; before the towns were built there were villages or camps of mud and straw huts surrounded by fences or ramparts of a temporary character.

Types and Construction of Buildings.—Whether the buildings were imperial tombs, Buddhist temples or memorial shrines dedicated to great philosophers or, on the other hand, of a profane nature, such as imperial palaces, dwelling-houses or administration offices, all were arranged within walls and in closed compounds according to similar principles. Characteristic of all these extensive compounds is the clear development of a main central axis running from north to south. The principal buildings, their courts and gateways are all placed in a row, one behind the other, while the secondary buildings are arranged at the sides of the courtyards, the façades, the doors and the gates of the principal buildings all facing south, an orientation which evidently was based on religious traditions. It was not by adding to the height of the buildings but by joining more courts to the compounds that these architectural compositions could be enlarged. There are princes' palaces in Peking which have as many as 20 courtyards and some of the large temples or monasteries have a still larger number of such units. As each compound is enclosed by a high wall it is quite impossible to obtain any idea of the arrangements from the outside, and at the larger palaces the different courtyards are also divided the one from the other by secondary walls with decorative gateways. The courts vary in size and the streets follow along the walls. Through such an arrangement the inner portions of the Purple Forbidden City of Peking became almost labyrinthine.

The types of the principal buildings also remain the same, independently

23

of their use as temples, palaces or dwelling-houses. The most common among these types is the hall, *tien*, *i.e.*, an oblong, rectangular room, usually divided by rows of round pillars or columns into three or more naves of which the foremost is usually arranged as an open portico; in other cases the open colonnade is continued all around the building. The interior is, as a rule, lighted by small windows placed quite low, but exceptionally there may be a second row of windows, giving a brighter effect; these are at a higher level. Very important for the decorative effect of the buildings is the broad sub-structure, the terrace and the far projecting roof. When the substructure

WU-LIANG TIEN, SUCHOW, A 2-STOREYED HALL WITH BARREL VAULTS

is made higher, a so-called *t'ai* is created, *i.e.*, a shorter hall or a centralized building in two storeys on a high terrace with battered walls. Such *t'ai* are often mentioned in the old descriptions of palaces and cities. They seem to have been quite common since earliest times. In the Forbidden City of Peking this type of building is beautifully developed at the outer gates as, for instance, Wu Men, where the great pavilion rises on a monumental terrace. Other characteristic examples of *t'ai* are the drum and bell towers which rise in the centre of many of the old cities in northern China, but similar buildings have also been used as storehouses, watchtowers and observatories. The general name for larger, many storeyed buildings is *lou*, a name which, however, is not used for the pagodas, whereas small buildings of two or more storeys often are called *ko*, and the open small pavilions *t'ing*. Furthermore, one finds in some of the palatial compounds as well as at many private

24

dwelling-houses, particularly where they are connected with gardens, so-called *lang, i.e.,* long open galleries which serve to connect larger buildings.

Considering the most common Chinese buildings such as the *tien*, the *t'ai* and the *t'ing* in their entirety, we may be struck by the fact that the main body of the structures appears much less than in Western buildings. It is, figuratively speaking, pushed into the background by the broad terrace and the far projecting roof which throws a broad shadow over the façade. These two elements are of the greatest importance for the general effect of the structure. The terrace may be developed in various steps and provided with marble balustrades and decorative staircases, as, for instance, at the imperial palace and many large temples, or it may be simply a stone-lined substructure with one or two steps; but it always contributes to lift the building and to form a kind of counterbalance to the projecting roof. It is, however, at the *t'ai* that the substructures become of greatest importance. They may reach a height of 10 or 12 metres and be covered by a hall or pavilion of tower-like effect.

The buildings which rise on the terraces are made of wood; their structural frame is pure carpenters' work. The walls may look massive and appear to support the roof but, practically speaking, they have no structural importance. They are simply filled with brick or clay between the supporting columns. In the larger buildings the outer wall on the façades is usually not placed in the foremost row of columns but this is reserved as an open gallery. In some instances the portico is double, in other cases it is reduced to a few intercolumns in the middle. The building thus consists of a nave and aisles some of which might be completely or partly divided by filled-in walls, by which various rooms are created which indeed may be quite freely increased or decreased, the middle one being, as a rule, the broadest. The intervals between the columns are on the whole quite wide, and sometimes it happens that some columns are excluded in the midst of the building in order to create more free space. But the Chinese hall is not a longitudinal structure like the Greek temples (which also originally were built of wood); it expands transversally to the central axis which is indicated by the entrance door on the middle of the façade. The two short sides with the gables serve no other purpose than to end the hall; they have no decorative importance and no such emphasis as in the classic temples; sometimes they are hardly meant

25

to be seen. The side walls may project as a kind of ante-room to the portico or the corners may be accentuated by columns. The Chinese builders were never so particular or consistent in the placing of the columns as the classical architects. They employed a material which allowed greater freedom than the marble beams and they yielded less to purely artistic considerations than to practical wants. The beauty and strength of their architecture depend mainly on the logical clearness of the constructive framework.

This comparative freedom in the placing of the columns is rendered possible also by the fact that they are not supporting posts as in the classical buildings. They are not provided with capitals and they do not support the entablature, but they are tied both longitudinally and transversally by beams which may cut into, or run through, the posts. The ends of the transverse beams often project in front of the columns, and the longitudinal beams form a kind of architrave which keeps the outer colonnade together. In larger buildings of comparatively late periods brackets or cantilevers are sometimes introduced on the columns below the tie beams but the real bracketing system which serves to support the eaves of the roof is situated above these. The roof brackets are, in their simplest form, two-armed and project in the earlier buildings only from the heads of the columns; but in the later buildings they become manifolded and are placed on the beams as well as on the posts, sometimes so close together that they create the impression of a cornice. It is mainly in the modifications of the bracketing system that one may trace an evolution of Chinese architecture.

The constructive system demanded that the buildings should be developed horizontally rather than vertically. Nevertheless, many of the large halls are erected in two storeys, though the second is often nothing more than a decorative superstructure without floor or windows. The lower storey forms a kind of outer compartment to the building and is covered by a lean-to shed roof while the main span or saddle roof covers the central portion of the building which rises to a greater height. Sometimes there is a coffered or painted ceiling over this portion but more often, particularly in the temples, the trusses and beams of the roof construction are left entirely uncovered.

Roofs.—It is evident that the development of the roof on the Chinese buildings is closely connected with the placing of the entrance door. This is

26

not to be found on the short (gable) ends of the building but in the middle of the southern façade, which usually has also a free-standing row of columns. Most of the important buildings are indeed placed so that they can be appreciated only in full-front view, and their peculiar decorative effect thus becomes dominated by the broad high-towering roof. Whatever the original reason for this particular kind of roof may have been, it was gradually more and more developed from a decorative point of view. The builders may have felt the need of modifying the impression of weight and breadth, inevitably adhering to the enormous roof masses, and this was most successfully done by curving the sides and accentuating the tension and rhythm of the rising lines. This tendency becomes perhaps more evident in minor decorative buildings such as pavilions and pagodas, not to speak of small ornamental works in clay and metal on which the roof appears almost as a crown. The common dwelling-houses in northern China have, on the contrary, much smaller and less curving roofs and, if we may judge from reproductions of earlier buildings, such as the reliefs from the Han tombs in Shantung and some small clay models dating from the Han and Wei dynasties, it seems that the curved roof was then not very far developed. In the T'ang time (7th to 9th century) the characteristic shape of the roof was, however, fully developed.

It is possible that the origin of the far projecting and strongly curved roof may be looked for in primitive thatch-covered huts of a kind similar to those which still are to be seen on the Indo-Chinese islands. If so, it would first have been introduced in southern China (where indeed the curving and projecting roof always was more strongly developed than in the north), and later on, when the whole country became more of a cultural unit, in the northern provinces. When the Chinese once had realized the fine decorative effect of these roofs, they developed them freely at the expense of the main body of the building. The larger the roofs, the stronger becomes the effect of shade under the eaves and the more they seem to be disengaged from the supporting framework and to soar in the air. In many instances the roofs crown the building rather than cover it, and their decorative ornamentation with figures and animals on the ridges and on the corner ribs serve also to strengthen the impression of a decorative superstructure.

When the building has a roof in two storeys the lower one is a lean-to shed roof; the upper one, a span-roof—but the gables of this do not reach down to the eaves: they are cut at one-half or three-fourths of their height. This peculiar combination of the gabled and the hipped-roof is very common both in China and in Japan, but there are also buildings with complete hip-roofs sloping to all four sides. This is, according to the Chinese, the finest form. It is to be found on ceremonial edifices such as the big central hall Tai Ho Tien in the Forbidden City, Peking, and some of the sacrificial halls at the imperial tombs.

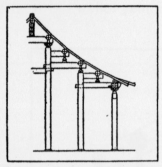

ROOF CONSTRUCTION ACCORDING TO YING TSAO FA SHIH (1103)

ROOF TILES ON A HALL IN THE FORBIDDEN CITY, PEKING

Buildings consisting of two superimposed halls have been in use since very early days, as may be seen on some reliefs of the Han dynasty, and they are also mentioned in many of the old descriptions of the imperial palaces, where such buildings sometimes were connected by flying bridges. Very characteristic and well-developed examples of this type of structure are still to be seen at Yung Ho Kung (the Yellow Temple) in Peking, which was erected in the 17th century as an imperial residence but afterwards consecrated as a Llama temple. Later Llamaistic buildings (from the Ch'ien Lung era) show at times an even further development in height, as for instance the Yu Hua Ko, a temple standing at the northwestern corner of the Forbidden City. In southern China the distribution of storeys seems to have been still freer; there are large temples in Suchow with three superimposed halls and other more centralized structures built in the same way, which indeed may be called towers, particularly if they are placed on terraces. The constructive framework of the main roof consists generally of various beams arranged step-wise one above the other and supporting on their ends the purlins (q.v.). In smaller buildings all the transversal beams may be supported by columns which increase in length towards the middle of the room, the central one reaching up to the main ridge. It is, however, more common that only the lowest or the two lower beams rest directly on pillars, while the upper ones are carried by brackets and small posts rising from the lower beams. The purlins laid on these supports are arranged rather closely, so that the rafters may be stretched in curves, the projecting ones being spliced and bent upwards. The well-developed system of brackets and cantilevers which support this projecting part of the roof will be specially discussed later because it is in this that one may follow the development and decay of Chinese architecture.

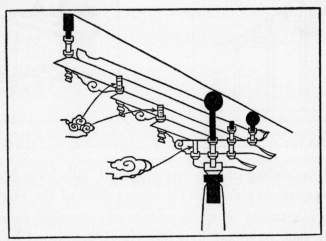

BRACKETING SYSTEM FROM A PAVILION AT THE CONFUCIUS TEMPLE IN CHÜFÜ. YÜAN PERIOD

The outer aspect of the roof is determined by the alternatively convex and concave tiles and the strongly accentuated corner ridges which curve at the ends in a kind of snout and often are provided with series of fantastic human and animal figures, called *k'uei lung tzŭ*. The main ridge-post is very high and decorated at both ends with a kind of fish-tailed owl, called *ch'ih wen*, which had a symbolic significance and served to protect the building against fire and other calamities. On ordinary buildings the roof tiles are of unglazed, lightly baked grey clay, but on the present imperial buildings all the roofs are laid with yellow glazed tiles, while some of the temples and smaller buildings erected for various members of the imperial family have deep-blue roof tiles. Green tiles are sometimes used on pavilions, gates and walls.

29

The columns as well as the filled-in walls between them have usually a warm vermilion tone which becomes most beautiful when softened by dampness and dust. The beams and the brackets below the eaves are painted with conventionalized flower ornaments in blue and green, sometimes with white contours. The door panels of more important buildings are provided with ornaments in gold, but their upper part serves as windows and is fitted only with open lattice-work. On the whole it seems as if later times had tried to gain by decorative elaboration whatever of constructive significance and beauty had been lost.

Minor Pavilions and Gateways.—Besides the longitudinal halls in right angle to the central axis, indicated by the entrance door, there are more centralized structures on a quadrangular, polygonal or round plan, *i.e.*, pavilions or towers, which may be more than two storeys high. The most primitive type of pavilion is a square hut with corner posts which carry a flat or tent-shaped roof. Such pavilions are often seen in pictures representing famous philosophers meditating on nature. Unless they are quite open the walls may be made of bamboo or basket-work. The more elaborate pavilions on a polygonal or round plan developed in connection with the Chinese garden and have been abundantly used in the imperial parks since early times. Such kiosks, tea-houses and pavilions were placed on spots with historical associations or on hills or promontories where the view was particularly beautiful. Their shape and style were developed with a view to the rockeries and the growing trees; how well they fitted into such surroundings may still be seen in the wonderful gardens around the sea palaces in Peking. These small pavilions, half hidden between the trees, clinging on the rocks or rising on stones out of the mirroring water, often give us a more vivid and immediate impression of the charm and naturalness of Chinese architecture than the larger buildings. It was also pre-eminently through such small decorative structures that Chinese architecture became known and appreciated in the 18th century in Europe.

On the larger pavilions the roofs are usually divided into two or three storeys, thus adding greatly to the picturesque effect of the building, particularly when it is erected on a polygonal plan which gives it a number of projecting corner snouts. Beautiful examples of this kind of pavilion may be seen at the "Coal Hill" in Peking as well as in Pei Hai and other imperial

PHOTOGRAPH, COPR. OSVALD SIRÉN

THE CHINESE STYLE IN JAPAN AND CHINA

1. Kodo of Toshodajij, Nara, style of T'ang period; 8th century

2. Wooden pagoda, Hokiji, Nara, Japan; erected in 7th century

3. The Drum Tower, *c.* 1300, on Sung Shan, Hsiao Lin Ssu, Hon-an

4. Stone relief of pagoda of Northern Wei dynasty (6th century), Lung Men

PHOTOGRAPH, COPR. OSVALD SIRÉN

A GATE AND AN OPEN GALLERY, PEKING

1. Wu Mên from the north; the main south gate of the Forbidden City, Peking; reconstructed in 1647, repaired 1801

2. Wan Tzu Lan; an open gallery along a canal in swastika form, at the Sea Palaces. It was erected in the rule of the Empress Dowager, 19th century

parks. They have no walls, simply open colonnades supporting the roof which may give the impression of hovering in the air. When the portions between the successive roofs are enlarged and provided with balconies or colonnades the pavilion becomes a real tower, such as for instance the Fo Hsiang Ko (Buddha's Perfume Tower), which rises above the lake at the Summer palace.

Related to the pavilions by their open decorative effect, yet forming an architectural group of their own, are the *p'ai lou*, *i.e.*, free-standing gateways with three or more openings, which span the streets in many Chinese cities or mark the entrance to some sacred precincts, such as tomb or temple areas. The object of their erection was often to commemorate some outstanding local character or some important event in the history of the place or simply to mark a spot notable for its beauty or its sacredness. The earliest *p'ai lou* were, no doubt, simply large gateways made of wood and provided with inscribed tablets. These could easily be developed into more important structures by adding at the sides more posts and gateways, and they were soon executed in stone as well as in wood. From an architectural point of view they may be divided into two principal groups: the one consisting of *p'ai lou* with very tall side posts reaching above the transversal beams (which may be covered by small roofs); the other, of *p'ai lou* with shorter side posts covered by the roofs, so that the whole gateway has more likeness to a façade or an open flat pavilion. The supporting masts, which may be 4 or 8 or 12 according to the size and importance of the structure, are placed on stone plinths, sometimes decorated with lions, and tied together not only by cross-beams in two or three horizontal rows, but also by carved or painted panels or, in the case of stone *p'ai lou*, by flat slabs decorated with reliefs. Over each one of the openings is a separate small span-roof resting on brackets and usually covered with glazed pan-tiles. The *p'ai lou* thus contain some of the most characteristic features of traditional Chinese architecture, viz., the supporting posts, the curving saddle-roofs on double or triple rows of brackets, and the carved or painted friezes. They are essentially wooden structures. The whole character of these buildings as well as their decoration has been developed with a view to the special requirements of the material, but that has not prevented the Chinese from executing the same type of structure also in brick and in stone. The largest among them stand

31

at the Ming tombs near Nankow and at the tombs of the Ch'ing emperors at Hsi Ling and Tung Ling, but the most elaborately decorated marble *p'ai lou* may be seen in some of the old cities in Shantung, such as Chüfu and Weih-sien.

Closely connected with the *p'ai lou* are those highly decorative sham façades which used to be erected in front of important shops. They also consist of tall masts tied by cross-beams with manifold rows of brackets which support small roofs in one or two storeys. Under these are panels decorated with human figures in relief or with brightly coloured floral designs

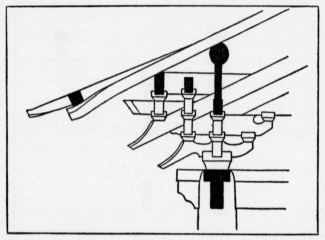

BRACKETING SYSTEM ON BELL-TOWER AT SHAO LIN SSU. YÜAN PERIOD

in open-work into which the signboards of the shops are inserted. High masts or pillars are indeed much in favour in China; they are mostly used pair-wise, either free-standing in front of palaces (as the *hua piao*) or at the gateways of the dwelling compounds. Another type of gateway which is quite common consists of broad pillars made of masonry and coated with glazed tiles, often with ornaments in various colours. When a span-roof connects the deep pillars a kind of small gatehouse may be created.

Of considerable importance also for the outward effect of the Chinese buildings are the balustrades which line the terraces and staircases in front of the buildings. They are in northern China mostly made of white marble and composed of square posts ending in sculptured finials between which ornamented panels and moulded railings are inserted. Such marble balustrades may be seen at most of the important temples and, in their richest

32

development, on the terraces of the Three Great Halls (San Ta T'ien) in the Forbidden City in Peking. Here they are repeated in three different tiers and broken in many angles, according to the shape of the terraces, producing a splendid decorative effect, particularly as the white marble stands out in contrast to the red colour of the buildings.

Stone and Brick Buildings.—Although Chinese architecture is principally wood construction, it should not be forgotten that a great number of stone and brick buildings have been made in China, including bridges, for which the Chinese since earliest times have used brick and stone. The great

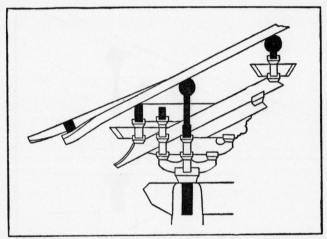

BRACKETING SYSTEM FROM THE CH'U TZU AN, SHAO LIN SSU, SUNG STYLE

majority of the still existing buildings in masonry are of comparatively late periods; very few indeed can be dated before the Wan Li era (1573–1619). The only important exceptions to this general rule are the pagodas made of brick and mud, several of which may be ascribed to the T'ang period (618–906) and a few to even earlier times. On the whole, it seems, however, that the Chinese regarded brick and stone work as material fitted for storehouses, walls, substructures and the like, but hardly for real architecture in the same sense as wood construction. It is a characteristic fact that brick buildings are not even mentioned in the standard work on architecture which was published by imperial order in the year 1103 under the title *Ying Tsao Fa Shih* (The Method of Architecture). This beautifully illustrated work in eight volumes (which has been issued in a modern reprint) is founded on the practical experience of architects and decorators, which the author, Li

15116

33

Chieh, collected from various sources. It gives everything that an educated Chinese towards the end of the Sung period considered the fundamentals of architecture. No stone or brick houses are mentioned, not even columns, door-frames or floors of stone. The only stoneworks particularly described are the plinths and corner pilasters, stairs, balustrades, dragon heads on staircases, thresholds and stones for the door-posts, besides canals, sluices, platforms, terraces, etc. The measures and instructions for the execution of all these various kinds of stonework are very accurate, but they are of no great importance for the architectural style. The constructive methods are treated only in the third part of the book, which contains "Rules for large work in wood," *i.e.*, framework of buildings, posts, trusses, rafters, etc. Then follows a chapter called "Rules for smaller works in wood," *i.e.*, doors, windows, partition walls, coffered ceilings, screens, cornices, gutters, staircases, door-panels, balustrades, besides Buddhist and Taoist house shrines, or *Fa yüeh*, decorative gate-façades erected in front of important houses, etc. Then follow "Rules for works in carved wood," concerning decorative details, and at the end of the book, "Rules for exterior roofing," also concerning the ornamental figures on the roofs, etc. The author devotes some paragraphs to bricks and to roof tiles but he gives no rules for construction in such materials.

Turning to the existing monuments in China, we may notice the Ssu Men Ta, at the temple Shen Tung Ssu in Shantung, as the earliest and most important example of architectural masonry work. The building, which in spite of its name—the Four-Gate pagoda—is no tower but a one-storeyed square house (each side about 7.35 metres), was erected A.D. 534. It is coated with finely cut and fluted limestone slabs, but the interior body of the walls may be partly of mud. It has an arched entrance on each side and a cornice consisting of five corbelled tiers but no other architectural divisions. The pyramidal roof is made of corbelled stone slabs and supported by a large square centre pillar crowned by a small stūpa. The solid and self-contained aspect of the building together with its fine proportions make it one of the most remarkable of Chinese architectural monuments. It is possible that similar buildings existed in earlier times when stone and brick may have been more freely used; the type may be observed, for instance, in the more or less house-shaped tomb pillars of the Han dynasty in Szechuan and Honan.

PHOTOGRAPHS, COPR. OSVALD SIRÉN

TWO HALLS IN PEKING

1. Pao Ho Tien, one of the Three Great Halls, in the Purple Forbidden City, Peking; built 1627, repaired 1765

2. The Hall of Classics, at the Confucius Temple, Peking. The upturned lines of roof corners suggest aspiration, as, in another form, the Gothic is said to do. The tent form is sometimes regarded as the possible origin of the characteristic shape of Chinese roofs

PHOTOGRAPHS, COPR. OSVALD SIRÉN

CHINESE TOWERS AND PAVILIONS

1. One of the pavilions on the Coal Hill, Peking
2. Yu Hua Ko, a Taoistic building in the Forbidden City, Peking

3. The Drum Tower, Haien Yang, Shen-si. Drums were ordinarily beaten to give directions for the change of night watches and, in rare instances, to warn the citizens of some disaster

The next in date among the masonry buildings are some real towers or pagodas of the Sui and T'ang periods which will be mentioned later; most of them are made of packed clay or dirt in combination with stone or brick. Still more common is the combination of brick and wood construction. It can be carried out in different ways, either by lining a real wooden structure with brick walls or by placing a bracketed span-roof on strong brick walls, eventually adding pillars for interior support if the walls are too wide apart. This method of construction has been used in most of the outer city gate-towers, of which the oldest now preserved are from the beginning of the Ming period, and also in numerous watchtowers and storehouses on the walls that enclose the cities of northern China. A particularly fine example is the famous bell tower at Peking, often considered as a monument of the Yuan dynasty, though it was completely renewed during the reign of Chi'en Lung. All these buildings exhibit on the outside massive brick walls more or less regularly divided by windows or by rows of square loopholes which give to the battered façades of the big gate-towers a fortress-like appearance. The shape of the high roofs is, however, the same as on ordinary wooden structures, and if one examines these masonry buildings more closely, one usually finds wooden columns inserted in the walls as well as detached in the interiors.

The substructures of the gate and bell towers are in most cases pierced by tunnels or barrel vaults serving as passages. These may be either round or somewhat pointed, as for instance on the drum tower in Peking which actually dates from the Yuan period. The vaults are constructed with great care and precision, sometimes reaching a span of nearly 15 metres. Vaulting (but not the system of voussoirs) was undoubtedly known in China in early times; it was used in the tomb chambers which were covered with bricks, in the tunnels leading to these; when heavy brick walls were erected around the cities, barrel vaults followed suit for the entrances. The step from such constructions in brick to the building of cupolas is not a very long one. We do not know exactly when cupolas first came into use, but we have reason to assume that they were well developed in the T'ang period. As an evidence of this the mosque in Hangchow may be mentioned because the farthest rooms of this building are covered by three cupolas on pendentives (*q.v.*). The mosque may have been renewed in later times but in close

35

adherence to the original model which, of course, was of Persian origin. Another kind of cupola is to be found over the hall of the big bronze elephant on the Omi mountain in Szechuan erected during the reign of Wan Li (1573–1619). The transition of the square room into a round cupola is here also accomplished by means of pendentives but outwardly the building is covered by a tent-shaped roof. One of the small sanctuaries on Piao Shan near Tsinanfu is an example of a more pointed cupola.

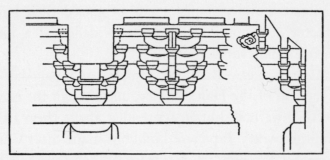

BRACKETING SYSTEM OF CHIEN CH'ING KUNG, FORBIDDEN CITY, PEKING

At the end of the Ming period buildings with classical orders in one or two storeys began to appear. Internally these were covered by longitudinal or transversal barrel vaults, but outwardly they were provided with the usual span and shed-roofs. Among the best examples of this kind of building may be mentioned the Wu Liang Tien in Suchow and Shuan Ta Ssu in Tai-yuanfu, besides the two halls on Wu Tai Shan. The façades are divided by arches and columns, but these are partly inserted in the wall and the capitals are stunted or turned into cantilevers, the entablature reduced to an architrave, the cornice replaced by rows of brackets above which the upturned eaves project in the usual manner. This combination of classical orders and Chinese brackets is indeed characteristic evidence of how foreign the principles of Greek architecture always remained to the Chinese. Such buildings may have been inspired by Indian models, but the Chinese modified them quite freely by grafting on the pseudo-classical models elements inherited from their indigenous wooden architecture.

An entirely different type of masonry work is illustrated by the buildings made after Tibetan models mostly as late as in Ch'ien Lung's reign. The towers and sham fortresses on the slopes of the Western hills in Peking, which were erected in order to give the Chinese soldiers an opportunity to practise assaults, are well known by all tourists. Still larger and more important Tibetan buildings may be seen at Jehol, the famous summer resort of the Manchu emperors in northern Chihli, where an entire Llama cloister was erected after the model of the famous Potala in Lassa, the residence of the Tibetan pope-kings. This enormous brick façade in some nine or ten storeys must in its absolute bareness have appeared quite dreary to the Chinese. They have tried to give it some life or colour by surrounding the windows with pilasters and canopies made of glazed tiles, but the sombre and solid character still dominates, giving evidence of a foreign culture transplanted into Chinese surroundings.

Historical Development.—Buddhist temples and pagodas have existed in China since the end of the Han dynasty, and though the earliest ones are no longer preserved, we may obtain some idea about them from old reproductions and contemporary Japanese buildings made after Chinese models. The first messages of the new religion were brought to the Chinese at the beginning of our era, but it was not until the 2nd century A.D. that it became more widely spread, largely due to the pilgrims who journeyed between China and India. They brought news not only of the writings and images of the new religion but also of its buildings. It has been reported that small bronze models of the famous stūpa of Kanishka at Peshawar (erected in the 1st century A.D.) were brought to China by Hui Sheng, a monk who took part in a mission to India in the year 518. No doubt other pilgrims did the same, and there may have been many small models of this much admired religious monument in China. As far as one may judge by later Indian reproductions, reverting more or less directly to the famous pagoda of Kanishka, it was built on a square platform, but the main section of it seems to have been round or bottle-shaped and divided by projecting cornices into three or more storeys. Very characteristic of this pagoda was the high mast with its nine superposed metal disks and crowning lotus bud. At present there are no such pagodas preserved in China, but ancient engravings on stone give us reason to believe that they have existed.

The oldest pagoda in China still standing is at Sung Yüeh Ssu, a temple on the sacred mountain Sung Shan in Honan. According to historical records, it was built about 523, when the palace previously existing here was consecrated as a temple. The tower is made of mud and brick on an octagonal base and reaches a height of nearly 30 metres. The lowest section consists of a plain plinth above which follows a main storey divided by pilasters and windows in a kind of aedicula (*q.v.*). The upper section of the tower has the shape of a convex cone, divided by narrow cornices into 15 low, blind storeys. It is crowned by a large bud or cone with nine rings, an equivalent to the mast with the metal disks which is usually found in the wooden pagodas. The early date of the building is verified by the style of the lion reliefs and the mouldings of the main storey.

The character of the whole structure is solid and severe, at the same time the incurvation of the outline prevents any impression of rigidity.

There is no other pagoda of as early date but the type returns with some modifications in some later pagodas, as for instance, the Pei T'a (the North tower) and the Nan T'a (the South tower) at Fang Shan in Chihli. The former, which was built at the beginning of the 8th century, shows a more typically Indian style with its bottle-shaped top, part being on a terraced substructure while the latter, which was built at the beginning of the 12th century, has a stiffer appearance without any incurvation of the outline or narrowing towards the top. It is divided by bracketed cornices into 11 storeys and reveals by its form and details a closer connection with traditional Chinese constructions. To the same group of buildings belong also the pagodas at Chêngtingfu, Mu T'a (T'ien Ning Ssu) built about 1078 in nine storeys with wooden cornices, and the Ching T'a built at a somewhat later period, and furthermore the two big pagodas near Peking, known as Pa Li Chuan and T'ien Ning Ssu, which were erected during the Chin and Yüan dynasties (in the 12th and 13th centuries). They show some likeness to the Nan T'a at Fang Shan, but their dimensions are much larger and their high plinths are richly decorated with figure reliefs in baked clay. Both have 13 low blind storeys and make quite an imposing effect by their great height, but they lack the elastic incurvation which gives to the pagoda at Sung Yüeh Ssu such an harmonious character.

Many of the early pagodas in China were, no doubt, constructed of wood and have perished, because of the unresisting material. There are records of a very large wooden pagoda erected in A.D. 516 at Lo-yang at the order of the Empress Dowager Hu. According to Chinese chronicles this was 1,000 ft. high (a statement which must not be taken literally but

38

PHOTOGRAPHS, COPR. OSVALD SIREN

BUDDHA'S PERFUME TOWER, AND TWO GATEWAYS

1. View of the Fo Hsiang Ko (Buddha's perfume tower) and the buildings in front of it at the Summer Palace, Peking; 19th century

2. Portion of the bell tower in Si-an, Shensi; erected 15th century

3. Portion of Nandaimon gate, temple of Todai-ji, Nara, Japan; c. 1199

merely as a general indication of unusual height) and consisted of nine
storeys. Above the tower rose a mast 100 ft. high carrying 30 gilt metal
discs which, as well as the chains by which the mast was tied to the four
corners, were hung with no less than 500 gilt bells. This noble edifice became, however, the prey of fire in 534. The description must have been
based on hearsay, but it nevertheless has some interest as testimony of the
existence of wooden pagodas in China at an early date. It is also confirmed
by several reproductions of pagodas found among the cave sculptures from
the beginning of the 6th century at Yun Kang and Lung Men. Here one

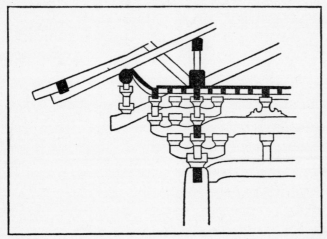

BRACKETING SYSTEM ON THE KONDO OF TOSHODAIJI. T'ANG STYLE

may see executed in relief pagodas with three as well as with five storeys
illustrating exactly the same architectural type as found in the earliest
Japanese pagodas from the beginning of the following century. They are
built on a square plan with corner posts and projecting roofs over the successive storeys and crowned by high masts carrying discs and ending in the
form of large buds or small stūpas. In the successive storeys on some of
these pagodas are placed Buddhist statues.

Excellent examples of the same type of pagoda may be seen at some of
the old temples near Nara in Japan, as, for instance, Horyuji and Hokkiji
which were erected at the beginning of the 7th century in the Suiko period
by builders from Korea or China. The pagoda at Hokkiji has five storeys;
the bracketed roofs project quite far but narrow gradually towards the top
so that the appearance of heaviness is avoided. Each side has four carrying

39

posts with projecting cantilevers, which at the corners are placed diagonally and cut into the shape of clouds, a motif which is particularly characteristic of this period. The rafters are square and rather substantial; the far projection of the eaves is produced by a very clever construction which no doubt was developed in China before it was introduced in Japan, although the earliest Chinese examples no longer exist. The principle of this system consists in the redoubling of the rafters below the eaves: instead of placing the outermost purlins directly on the cantilevers, which project from the posts, supporting shorter rafters are introduced which are fastened in the beams and trusses of the roof and which carry by means of vertical struts or cushions the further projecting upper rafters. These may be made longer and the roof is lifted higher, the effect becoming lighter than in buildings where the purlins rest directly on cantilevers or beams. This constructive system with redoubled rafters remained in use until the Yüan period, perhaps even later, though the form of the lower rafters as well as other details becomes modified. Furthermore one may notice in these early buildings the very solid and broad shape of the various members, as, for instance, the comparatively short columns with entasis (*q.v.*) and the very broad and heavy cantilevers cut into the shape of clouds at their lower side. The trusses and beams of the roof, to which the rafters are tied, are solid and strong, the various parts being tied together with consummate skill.

The essential parts of the buildings and the method of construction are the same in the pagodas and in the temple halls of this period, as may be learned from a closer study of the Golden Hall or Kondo of Horyuji, an oblong, quadrangular room with a colonnade and a roof in two storeys. A very important member added to the pagodas is, however, the mast which runs through the whole height of the tower. The purpose of this mast is not really constructive, it is not meant to support the tower, but simply to form a spire rising high above the roof and carrying the nine metal rings or discs. The builders usually did not tie the mast very tightly to the framework of the tower, because if the whole structure were suspended on the mast, the security of the tower would be jeopardized by the unavoidable swaying of the mast. In some comparatively recent examples one may find the mast suspended in the beams of the tower, but here the intention evidently was to lift it a little above the ground in order to avoid the still greater danger that might arise through the gradual sinking of the tower which would then, so to speak, be carried by the mast or hang on it. In the oldest pagodas which for the longest time have withstood storms and earthquakes the mast is a relatively free-standing post within the structure, always with plenty of room for its swayings, which thus do not really affect the security of the tower.

Quite a number of pagodas and temple halls of the 7th and 8th centuries are to be found in Japan, but it is our purpose here simply to point out certain general principles of construction borrowed from China. The five-storeyed pagoda at Horyuji is, in spite of the verandah which was added later round the ground storey, the most important example, but characteristic of the same style (which was developed in China, during the northern Wei dynasty and in Japan during the Suiko dynasty) are also the three-storeyed pagodas at Hokkiji and Horinji, which remind us of the stone reliefs representing pagodas in the grottoes at Lung Men and Yun Kang.

Important modifications of the old style may be observed on the beautiful pagoda of Yakushiji which was erected at the beginning of the 8th century in close adherence to Chinese constructions from the beginning of the T'ang period. It is a three-storeyed tower, but each one of the storeys is provided with a closed balcony carried on cantilevers, so that the pagoda at first sight gives the impression of a six-storeyed building. The intermediate shed-roofs are of the same shape, though smaller than those which cover the main storeys; a kind of rhythmic division is thus created, and the decorative effect becomes more interesting than in the earlier pagodas. Of great importance for the horizontal articulation are also the far-projecting carrying beams of the balconies, as well as the repetition of the three-armed brackets in double tiers under the eaves of the six successive roofs. The bracketing system has here attained its highest development, the lower brackets being used as supports for the upper ones which reach farther out and are provided with cushions. Their transversal arms replace the formerly used cantilevers, and on the top of them may be one more tier of similarly shaped brackets, as on other buildings of the same period. It should be observed that all the brackets are complete, the lower ones being so arranged that they carry a continuous beam and also the transversal arms of the upper brackets, while these serve as supports for the upper beams

41

under the eaves and for the rafters. In order to strengthen the vertical construction, struts with cushions are often placed on the hammer-beams in the intervals between the brackets.

The same characteristic forms and constructive features return in some contemporary temples and pagodas which thus also testify that the parts to which we have paid special attention are typical features of the architecture of this period. Interesting in this connection are the two large temple halls at Toshodaiji, another temple not far from Nara, i.e., the Kodo (Hall of Teaching) and the Kondo (the Golden Hall). The former once formed a part of the imperial palace at Nara but was moved to its present place when the temple was erected in 759. The building is quite simple, an oblong, one-storeyed hall with double rows of columns all around, the inner row standing free in the room, the outer being filled out to form a wall. The columns are not quite as heavy as on the buildings of the preceding period and the inter-columns are very long. The brackets are introduced only in one tier but between them are struts which contribute to support the roof.

The same principles of construction are still further developed on the Kondo of Toshodaiji which, with the exception of its entirely rebuilt roof, is an unusually imposing example of T'ang architecture. The building stands on a comparatively broad and high platform, but it is provided with a colonnade only on the front. The columns have a slight entasis and rest on moulded plinths. They are tied together, as usual, by a long architrave-beam and provided with quadrangular cushions from which the three-armed brackets project. These carry the upper longitudinal beam and a second tier of brackets. Above this follows a third row of brackets which is almost hidden below the far projecting eaves. The rafters project between the arms of the uppermost brackets and abut against the tranversal arms of the second row of brackets. The rafters are doubled, the upper ones being supported by struts which also carry the outermost purlins, and the two layers are furthermore tied by braces. The whole system is carried out with perfect logic in a method which may be termed the highest perfection of wooden construction.

How closely this building depends on Chinese models is proved by the reproduction of a similar temple hall on a large stone gable above one of the

42

gateways to the Ta Yen T'a pagoda at Sianfu. This remarkable engraving which we reproduce from a copy executed by a Japanese artist for Prof. Sekino, is of great historical importance, because it evidently reproduces a Chinese temple on which we may observe the same constructive details as pointed out on the Kondo of Toshodaiji. It matters little that the columns have been made spiky and the roof too small, as long as we recognize the principle of the whole constructive system, *i.e.*, the brackets and the struts, of which the lower ones have the same kind of curving legs as may be seen on some Japanese buildings of the 9th and 10th centuries.

Before following the further development of the traditional wooden construction during the Sung and the Yüan dynasties it is necessary to mention a group of buildings which illustrates another side of T'ang architecture. These are pagodas in what is popularly called the "Indian style," that is to say, buildings made of packed mud and brickwork which rise in terraces on a square plan. The most important among these pagodas stand in the neighbourhood of Sianfu within or just outside the district which once was occupied by Ch'angan, the capital of the T'ang emperors. In the first place should be mentioned the Ta Yen T'a (the Large Pagoda of the Wild Geese) which was founded in the year 652 by the great Buddhist pilgrim and teacher, Hsüan Chuang. It was then made of clay and brick in five storeys; later on, though still in the T'ang period, some storeys were added, and after some vicissitudes, the tower was rebuilt between 931 and 933. Later repairs have been carried out in the Ming and Ch'ing periods. The present pagoda, which has five storeys, seems however to correspond quite well to the T'ang building. It stands on a fairly high terrace and is at the base about 25.5 metres square, its full height being almost 60 metres. Its general shape reminds us of an elongated pyramid with truncated top. The successive storeys, which are accentuated by corbelled cornices, grow lower and narrower towards the top. The uppermost has a pyramidal roof crowned by a glazed cone which is now well covered by small trees and bushes. The coating of the walls is made of yellowish, lightly burnt bricks. They are quite plain except for some very thin pilasters and the arched gateways and a window on each side. The interior division is made by beams and wooden floors and the staircase which still exists makes it possible to ascend to the top. The imposing effect of this tower depends on its fine proportions and

43

well balanced, massive form, which is strengthened by its position on a natural elevation.

Not far from this stands a smaller pagoda called Hsiao Yen T'a (the Small Tower of the Wild Geese), erected 707–709. This tower had originally 15 storeys but of these hardly 13 are now preserved. The storeys are very low but, as in the previous instance, accentuated by corbelled cornices.

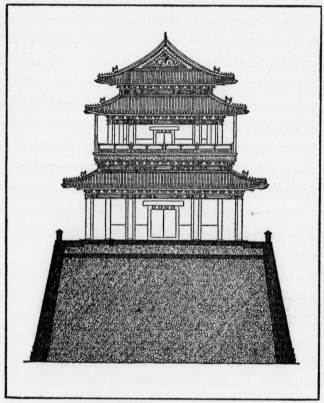

P'ING TZU MEN, INNER GATE-TOWER, PEKING

Only the ground floor is a little higher and on the northern and southern side provided with vaulted entrances. The upper storeys have small vaulted windows on the façade but otherwise no openings or divisions, and it is impossible to know whether they ever had any floors because there is no longer any staircase. Externally the tower differs from the Ta Yen T'a by the fact that it is not a stepped pyramid but a square tower with a slight curve on its middle part.

In still worse repair is the Hsiang Chi Ssu, situated a little farther south-

44

ward from Sianfu. It was erected in 681 according to the same general design as Hsiao Yen T'a, probably in 11 or more storeys, of which, however, only ten remain. The outline is not curved but rises straight towards the top which is largely ruined. The storeys are quite low but provided with an horizontal and vertical moulding possibly suggested by wooden buildings. The dependence on wooden architecture is still more evident in another pagoda situated in the same neighbourhood called Hsing Chiao Ssu, which was erected in 839 at the place where the remains of the great pilgrim, Hsüan Chuang, were removed in 669. It is a comparatively small tower measuring only about 20 metres in height and 5.35 on each side, but it presents an unusual historical interest by the fact that some of the most characteristic elements of wooden architecture have here been faithfully reproduced in brickwork. The storeys are not only marked by corbelled cornices but also with rows of three-armed brackets which rise from a kind of horizontal beam and provided furthermore, in the two upper storeys, with carrying posts in the shape of half columns. This close adherence to wood constructions may also be taken as an evidence of the greater age of the wooden pagodas in China as compared with the brick pagodas, which probably were developed through influence from India.

On each side of the Hsing Chia Ssu are smaller three-storeyed pagodas erected to the memory of other monks, both having three divisions without any cornices. Such minor quadrangular towers of three to five storeys dating from the T'ang, Sung and Yüan dynasties are often to be found on tombs or other memorable places. One of the largest and most beautiful among them is the Pai T'a Ssu in the same neighbourhood south of Sianfu; others are to be found at Shen Tung Ssu in Shantung and at Fang Shan in Chihli. The same architectural shape may also be observed in the celebrated pagoda Pai Ma Ssu near Honanfu which was not built until the Sung period, though it often has been mentioned as one of the oldest pagodas in China, probably owing to the legend connected with the Pai Ma Ssu temple. It is supposed to have been founded by Indian missionaries, who carried the first *sutras* to China, but as a matter of fact, the present pagoda was preceded by an earlier one in wood, which perished by fire in 1126. Other characteristic buildings are the Chiu T'a Ssu, or Nine-towered Pagoda, near Lin Cheng in Shantung, and the Lung Kung T'a at Shen Tung Ssu, an

CHINESE ART

impressive square tower in three high divisions, which are encumbered by sculptural decoration.

Although the greater part of the buildings which still remain in China from the T'ang and Sung dynasties are pagodas made of mud and brick

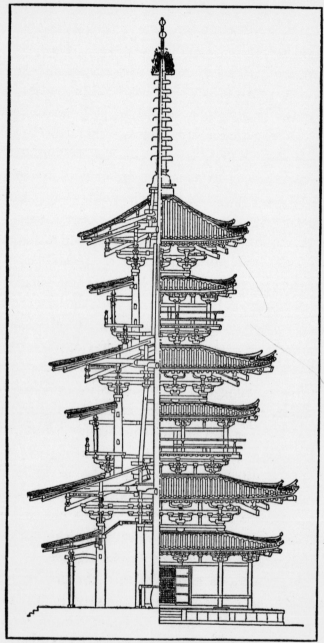

CROSS SECTION AND ELEVATION OF YAKUSHIJI PAGODA. 8TH CENTURY

PHOTOGRAPH, COPR. OSVALD SIRÉN

CHINESE MEMORIAL GATEWAYS

1. P'ai-lou or memorial gateway built of wood, at the lake of the Summer Palace, Peking. These characteristic structures, usually of wood, mark the entrance to a sacred or beautiful spot or commemorate some event or person

2. Marble P'ai-lou at the Altar of Heaven, Peking. This illustrates the type

of p'ai-lous with tall side-posts reaching above the transverse beams

3. Marble P'ai-lou over the main street in Wei-hsien, Shantung. In this type of p'ai-lous, the shorter side-posts are covered by roofs, making the gateway resemble an open pavilion. This is one of the more elaborate examples, with three openings and storeyed roofs

there are also some examples of temples constructed at least in part of wood, dating from the end of the Sung period. The most authentic and important of these is the Ch'u Tzu An hall at Shao Lin Ssu, the famous temple on the slope of Sung Shan in Honan, where the miraculous Bhodidharma, the founder of the Dhyana or Zen Buddhism, is said to have remained several years. According to an inscription, the Ch'u Tzu An was erected about the year 1125 or shortly before. It is a small, square building (measuring about 11 metres on each side) standing, as usual, on a stone terrace. Each side has four hexagonal stone pillars but only those of the façade are even partly visible, the others being completely embedded in the brick walls. In the room are two pairs of smaller and two pairs of larger hexagonal pillars, all decorated with Buddhist reliefs, and the gateway is framed by carved stone beams. Thanks to these solid stone supports the building still stands, but the roof, which is made of wood, threatens to fall in (if it has not already done so). At the writer's visit to the place in 1921 large pieces of the eaves were missing, and perhaps now the building has no other roof than the sky. The most interesting parts of this structure, however, are not the carved stone pillars but the brackets under the eaves which illustrate how these were used in the Sung period. The modifications in comparison with the bracketing system of the T'ang dynasty are quite noteworthy. Thus we find that the brackets emerge not only from the pillars but also, between these, from the horizontal beam. They are placed more closely together than previously, forming a kind of cornice. In the lower tier the brackets have three arms but in the upper tier the transversal arms have been cut by the under rafters, which are pointed and project like beaks or long paws. They are tied by means of braces to the brackets and carry at both ends struts (vertical posts) on which the purlins or corresponding beams rest. This change may be said to imply that the lower rafters have lost their original character and become a sloping cantilever transversing the lower brackets which they lengthen, thus making them better fitted to support the far projecting roof. The modification has evidently a practical purpose, though it hardly improves the original bracketing system, as exemplified on the T'ang buildings.

The evolution continued in this same direction; the three-armed constructive brackets gave place to two-armed ones transversed by thin sloping

47

beams or rafters, cut like beaks at the end. These project successively, the one tier reaching beyond the other, each one carrying its row of brackets which serve to support the longitudinal beams or a kind of struts for the purlins. The former system may be observed on the Bell Tower at Hsiao Lin Ssu, which according to an inscription was erected about the year 1300, where the third storey has no less than four tiers of gradually projecting brackets with beaks. The latter method is quite common; as an example may be mentioned one of the pavilions at the Confucius temple at Chüfu, also of the Yüan dynasty, where the horizontal pieces form a support for

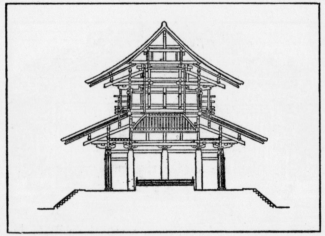

CROSS SECTION OF THE KONDO OF HORYUJI, BUILT IN 7TH CENTURY

several sloping cantilevers (or rudimentary lower rafters) which have been joined into a kind of bed for the struts and purlins of the roof.

Chinese buildings dating from the Sung and Yüan dynasties are scarce indeed, but our knowledge of the architecture of these times may be supplemented by observations on Japanese buildings from the 12th and 13th centuries, i.e., the Kamakura period. In Japan this was a time of great building activity, and according to the best informed Japanese authorities, remarkable for its close imitation of the contemporary Chinese models. Quite important in this respect is the Shariden (Chu Tsu An) of the Zen temple Engakuji in Kamakura, built according to the same principles as the above-mentioned Chinese hall, though with an extraordinarily large and high roof covered with straw. This is carried by brackets of the same type as those which were observed at Chu Tsu An of Hsiao Lin Ssu. The brackets are placed so

48

closely together that they form a continuous cornice. The purely Chinese origin of the constructive system of the Shariden of Engakuji may be confirmed through a comparison with some of the illustrations in the above-mentioned architectural treatise *Ying Tsao Fa Shih* published in 1103. On the buildings or schematic designs reproduced here we find brackets of exactly the same type as those described above, though their significance is partly obscured by the addition of some large transverse beams which probably have their origin in the imagination of the draughtsman.

The Japanese called this constructive system which they have borrowed from northern China, "karayo," while another somewhat different contem-

A STONE ENGRAVING ON THE DOOR GABLE AT TA YAN T'A, SIANFU

porary method was called "tenjiku," because it was considered to have been derived from India via southern China. It was used principally at large gates and temple buildings, to which one desired to give a particularly imposing appearance by the development of their upper portions. This was achieved by multiplying the brackets and transforming them into straight arms or cantilevers projecting stepwise from the posts. A good example of the *tenjiku* style is the Nandaimon gate at Todaiji, which was erected in 1199. It has five spans of columns on the long sides and a roof in two storeys, of which the lower one is supported by seven tiers and the upper by six tiers of cantilevers projecting from each column. At the corners are added diagonal cantilevers to form a support for the corner beaks. This kind of construction seems, however, never to have won much popularity in northern China; it is so simple and natural that it hardly can be credited with particular artistic importance. Projecting roof beams have indeed been used in many countries to support the eaves, but the characteristic feature of the *tenjiku* buildings is that the cantilevers are multiplied or massed together by the insertion of intermediate pieces into large composite brackets.

The further development of the wood construction in China after the end of the Yüan dynasty is a question which hardly needs to be discussed, because no real progress can be observed, but rather a gradual decline, which becomes evident in the more and more arbitrary treatment of the bracketing

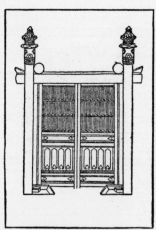

OUTER GATEWAY ACCORDING TO
YING TSAO FA SHIH (1103)

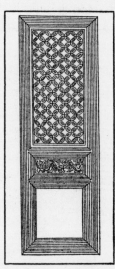

DOOR PANEL ACCORDING
TO YING TSAO FA SHIH
(1103)

system. At the beginning of the Ming dynasty one may still find buildings constructed in the same style as those of the Yüan period, *i.e.*, with beak-formed pieces laid transversally across the brackets, but the projecting pieces become often clumsy and out of proportion to the brackets. A fine example of early Ming architecture is the Bell Tower in Sianfu, the lower roof of which rests on a double row of brackets of the same type as those of the Yüan buildings. On the other hand, the tower of the eastern gate of T'a Tung Fu, erected in 1371, shows beak-shaped pieces projecting from very feeble brackets.

The question how long a really constructive bracketing system remained in use in China is difficult to answer without more detailed investigations than have hitherto been made. It is evident however, that already during the latter half of the Ming period simpler methods were applied, as may be seen for instance on the earliest buildings in the Forbidden City in Peking. It is true that the outer appearance was kept up by fixing multiple rows of brackets and pointed beaks below the eaves, but these have no real constructive function. The purlins rest on projecting beams or on struts standing on the columns. The closely arranged and freely multiplied brackets and beaks which we find on the big palace halls and imposing gate towers in Peking are nothing but ornamental cornices, the decorative effect of which nobody will deny. The roof would indeed rest just as well on the building even if these sham brackets were taken away. The forms are still the same as before but they have lost much of their significance because they lack inner necessity. The particular quality and importance of the old architecture of China depended on its firm and clearly developed wood construction. It was purely carpenters' art, and based on the special requirements of the material. Each part had a definite function which was not concealed by any superimposed decoration. This architecture was logical and purposeful and it remained a living art as long as the original principles of construction were kept up, but once these were encroached upon by purely decorative tendencies, both vitality and further growth were at an end.

CHINESE PAINTING

THE FIRST thing to be said about Chinese painting is that very little is known of its actual achievements. We have indeed ample records of the lives and works of innumerable painters, from the first centuries of our era onwards, and a mass of criticism. Chinese paintings also exist in vast quantities. But it must be realized that of genuine, or probably genuine, works of the great masters of the best periods, very few indeed remain. It is impossible to doubt, from the evidence of what has survived, and from literary records, that Chinese painting, with its majestic and continuous tradition of more than 1,500 years, is one of the greatest schools of painting that the world has seen. But we are without the means of comparing Chinese painting as a whole with the paintings of Italy, or other European schools, the successive masterpieces of which are known and accessible.

It is true that during the 20th century the almost complete ignorance which prevailed on the subject till the end of the 19th century has been greatly lessened. Important discoveries have been made, and it is impossible to predict what may yet be discovered. The fundamental difficulties, however, of the study of Chinese painting are likely to remain; the extreme rarity, namely, of certain and documented works, on which an accurate conception of the greater masters' style can be based. The practice of repeating famous designs with variations, of copying ancient works, which has prevailed in all ages, makes it possible to have a general idea of the styles of certain periods and certain masters. But immense and repeated destruction accounts for the rarity of ancient pictures in China itself. In Japan collections have been made, centuries ago, and religiously preserved;

and these paintings form the best foundation for study, though in many cases the traditional attributions have been abandoned by modern criticism.

General Characteristics.—Painting is the pre-eminent art of China. It is right that the art of any nation should be judged by a world standard, not merely from a national point of view. In spite of all differences and peculiarities, Chinese painting takes its place with the other pictorial arts of the world, for there is a fundamental affinity between all successful works of art.

Painting, for the Chinese, is a branch of handwriting. Both for writing and painting a brush is used; and to acquire a fine hand in writing demands a mastery in manipulating the brush and modulating its strokes such as few European painters attain. Ink is the favourite medium; but Chinese ink is a wonderful substance, capable of an immense range and an extraordinary beauty of tone. Many Chinese masterpieces are in monochrome. Coloured paintings are either light-coloured or full-coloured; but the ink-drawing remains almost always the foundation of the design. Fresco-painting, technically a different method from the fresco-painting of Europe (*see* Church's *Chemistry of Paints and Painting*, p. 307, 1915), was largely practised—and probably the grandest art of China was in this form—but the frescoes of the finest period seem all to have been destroyed. The great mass of Chinese pictures, however, are paintings on silk, or, less commonly, absorbent paper, the pigments being water-colours or body-colours (*see* R. Petrucci, *Encyclopédie de la Peinture Chinoise*, 1918, a translation of a well-known treatise illustrated with woodcuts called the *Mustard Seed Garden*. *See* also Ferguson's *Chinese Painting*). Paintings are usually in the form of hanging pictures or of horizontal scrolls, in both cases normally kept rolled up. The latter form involves a mode of composition peculiar to Chinese art, though imitated by the Japanese. These paintings, often of great length, are unrolled bit by bit and enjoyed as a reader enjoys reading a manuscript. A succession of pictures is presented, though the composition is continuous. Thus, in the case of landscape, for which this form has been used with most felicity, one seems to be actually passing through the country depicted. Other forms are the framed picture and the small album picture.

Chinese technique admits of no correction. The artist closely observes and stores his observations in his memory. He conceives his design, and having completed the mental image of what he intends to paint, he transfers it swiftly and with sure strokes to the silk. The communication through the sensitive and powerful strokes of the brush of something personal and unique must, in such an art, count for much in the spectator's appreciation. The qualities prized by the Chinese in a small ink-painting of bamboos, a favourite subject alike with beginners and masters, are those prized in a piece of fine handwriting, only there is added a keen appreciation of the simultaneous seizure of life and natural character in the subject. In the *Mustard Seed Garden* treatise cited above, it is said that in a master's work "the idea is present even where the brush has not passed." And this emphasis on the value of suggestion, of reserves and silences, is important to notice, because no other art has understood, like the Chinese, how to make empty space a potent factor in the design. It may be that Chinese painting relies too much on suggestion, presuming in the spectator a sensibility and a fineness of organization which are found but in choice societies; on the other hand it avoids that laborious accumulation of unessential phenomena which in European art has proved the death of so many pictures by accomplished hands. A certain slightness, comparatively speaking, is inevitable in Chinese paintings, partly because of the water-colour medium, partly because suggestion is preferred to statement, partly because so many of the artists were amateurs and not professionals. It is remarkable, however, how solid and structural a Chinese landscape can be. The greater painters gave much thought and pains to elaborating a convention by which the sense of shape and mass can be given to rock forms, for instance, without losing directness and vitality of brush stroke, the sense of handwriting. Each successful convention was preserved, handed down and imitated. Mountains could be painted in the manner of this old master or of that. And the Chinese, with their passion for codification, have carefully tabulated all these various methods. The painter's art is also saturated with literary associations. Certain flowers and birds are painted together because their association is consecrated by a poem. Many painters were poets; some, like Wang Wei, distinguished in both arts. But it is less the direct illustration of a poem or story that is normally aimed at, than the evocation of a mood similar to that expressed in the poem.

When we turn to the subject-matter of Chinese painting, we are struck

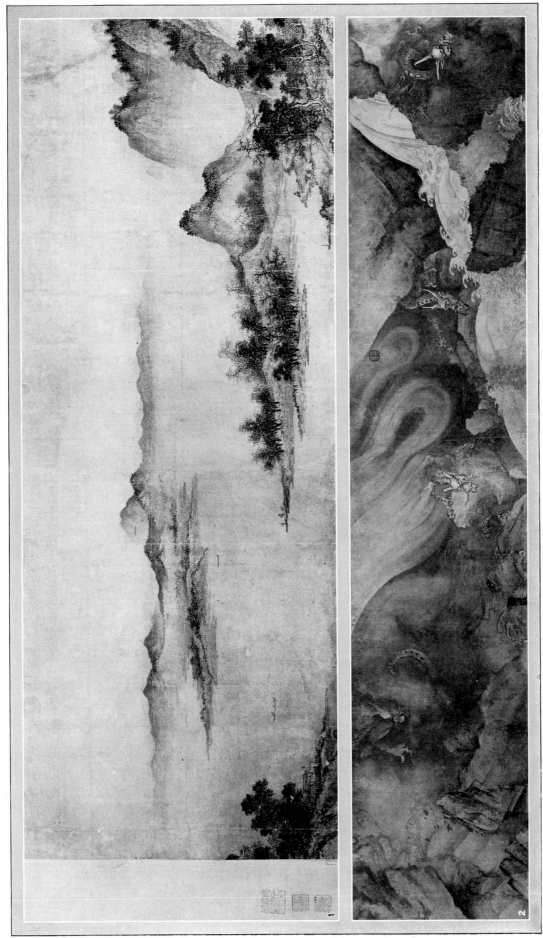

BY COURTESY OF THE MUSEUM OF FINE ARTS, BOSTON

LANDSCAPES OF THE SUNG PERIOD (960–1260)

1. A landscape scroll by Tung Yuan, 10th century, Southern Sung school. Painted with the graceful, gentle brush strokes characteristic of this artist
2. Dragons and a waterfall among cavernous rocks, by Chen Jung (960–1127), Southern Sung school. Chen Jung was especially skilled in painting dragons, symbolic of the powers of nature

BY COURTESY OF (1, 2, 3, 4) THE MUSEUM OF FINE ARTS, BOSTON, (5, 6) THE TRUSTEES. THE BRITISH MUSEUM

SIX CHARACTERISTIC PAINTINGS, 4TH TO 14TH CENTURY

1. Chinese herdsman, a painting of the mid-12th century, Sung period. 2. A man on a water-buffalo attributed to Li T'ang (c. 1100), of the Northern Sung school. 3. Landscape with bridge and willows, by Ma Yuan, a landscape painter of the late 12th and early 13th century. His work shows the vigor of the Northern Sung school combined with delicacy and sensitiveness. 4. Detail, from "Ladies Beating and Preparing Silk," a genre painting attributed to the artist-emperor, Hui Tsung (1082–1135), Sung dynasty. It probably preserves a T'ang design. 5. Portrait of a Buddhist priest, a Chinese fresco of the 14th century. 6. "Harmonious Family Life," part of "The Admonitions of the Instructress in the Palace," attributed to Ku K'ai-chih (4th century), one of China's earliest painters

by the early appearance of landscape art and its actual predominance. Landscape is accounted the most important of subjects because it includes man and all living things; the whole is greater than the part. Man does not play the central and heroic part that he plays in the art of Europe, for which the nude human form is the most significant and expressive of motives. Flowers are quite as important as figures. This difference in the fundamental conception of life and the universe makes itself felt in design. Instead of the symmetry which contemplation of the human body has made the basis of Western composition, the Chinese prefer the principle of balance. They contemplated trees and saw that they were unsymmetrical but perfectly poised. Where in Europe we have Christian themes, in China we have Buddhist themes; instead of the stories of classic mythology we have the stories of Taoist legend and the fairy tale. Genre-painting (*q.v.*) is as common as in the West, though portraiture is perhaps less common. But always the life of the world outside man—the life of animals, birds and plants —plays a much larger part than in Western art. The life of action counts for less, and the contemplative life for more.

Early Periods.—From literary references we can infer that painting was practised in China several centuries at least before Christ, chiefly in the form of portraiture. It is not till we come to the Han dynasty that we have any more tangible evidence, though there exist some rude designs in red on jade which may be a thousand years earlier. Designs on lacquer of the 1st century A.D., found in Korea by Mr. Umehara, and in Chinese Turkistan by Sir Aurel Stein; some rough paintings on tiles (Eumorfopoulos collection), and other decorations; outline drawings on vases of rather later date, give some hint of what painting in the Han period was like. We see that a Chinese type of decorative design, animated by movement in the forms, was already matured. The incised stone friezes of the period are clearly translations of paintings, and these give an idea of the character of pictorial design and the range of subject—scenes from history and legend, ceremonies, dances, mythical creatures, and all the fairy world of Taoism.

In the 4th century, however, flourished an artist who ranks among China's most famous masters: Ku K'ai-chih. There exist two rolls attributed to him: one, *The Admonitions of the Instructress in the Palace*, is in the British Museum; the other, illustrating a poem on a river nymph, is in the Freer collection at Washington. These paintings are by different hands. The one in the Freer collection is altogether drier in handling, and may be a Sung copy. The British Museum roll is of a marvellous subtlety and distinction; the line is intimately expressive. Its actual date is disputed, but it is generally thought to be, if not an original, a T'ang copy. In any case there is no doubt that both of these paintings represent the design of the Chin dynasty (A.D. 265–420). They are, therefore, extremely precious documents, and their value is increased by the fact that while the British Museum roll depicts scenes of court life, with all the details of dress and accessories of singular refinement, the Freer roll, with its dragon chariot and floating fairies, gives the imaginative or fanciful side of the art of the period. In both cases the landscape element is quite primitive. The landscape introduced into the London painting is indeed in strong contrast with the consummate grace and expressiveness of the tall and slender figures, and the air of a mature and fine civilization which they seem to breathe. Far from being primitive, the figure-drawing seems to belong to the close of a tradition rather than its beginning; and we may conjecture behind it the ruder, masculine style of Han gradually subtilized and transformed in the direction of elegance and charm. Ku K'ai-chih, famed especially for his portraits, painted all kinds of subjects, including Buddhist themes. But if we may take these two pictures attributed to him as typical of the period, we find no trace of Indian influence in them.

Of about the 6th century are some of the earliest wall paintings in the rock temples at Tun-huang, on China's western frontier (*see* Pelliot, *Grottes de Touen-houang*, vol. iv.) full of animated movement, containing figures of the same elegant type as those in the Ku K'ai-chih roll. But these are provincial in manner.

It was in the 6th century that the famous six canons of Hsieh Ho, himself a painter, were formulated. The exact meaning of the first and most important of these has been disputed, but it is clear that the emphasis is laid on creative inspiration, conceived not as a personal gift but as the spirit of the cosmos entering into the artist and enabling him to produce the movement of life.

The legends of the great masters tell, not of the deceptive appearance of reality in their paintings, but of their being so informed with passionate life that they assumed material existence and motion. The emphasis on movement is significant. Even in decorative designs the forms seem to move and flow.

The T'ang Dynasty (A.D. 618–905).—In the 7th century the empire, after a period of division, was consolidated under the great T'ang dynasty, which lasted for 300 years. This was undoubtedly the period of China's grandest art. It is true that almost all the painting of the time has perished; but all the available evidence confirms the testimony of the Chinese historians and critics to the greatness of the T'ang masters. Some fragments of a painting of a spring festival, found by Sir Aurel Stein in 1914 at Turfan, and some other paintings found in the same locality by the Otani expedition, are precious relics of early T'ang art, for they show us something of the pictorial style of the early 8th century. Here we find the new T'ang ideal of feminine beauty: a more massive form, compared with the slender elegance of preceding periods; a full, rounded face, with hair heaped around and above the head, and an air of smiling health. Precisely the same types and the same pictorial motives are found in the few pictures surviving from this period in Japan. And it is from the early painting of Japan, closely modelled on Chinese prototypes, that we can most safely infer the great style of T'ang. This kind of painting is mostly Buddhistic, and the grandest T'ang works were of Buddhist inspiration. Supreme among them, according to all testimony, were the works of Wu Tao-tzǔ, acknowledged to be the greatest of all Chinese painters.

China, during this epoch, was open to foreign influences as she has never been since. Her empire expanded westward; her suzerainty extended as far as the Caspian. Envoys and tribute-bearers were constantly coming or going; there was a great interest in foreign ways, dresses and customs; Indians, Persians, Turks and Syrians met in the capital, which was truly a world centre. But the influence of greatest moment was Buddhism, now accepted with fervour. Great numbers of Indian monks, some of them doubtless artists, were settled in China. Chinese pilgrims journeyed to India and brought back sacred manuscripts and images. But Chinese art, strong in its own traditions, was able to assimilate the Indian formulae and create a Buddhist art of extraordinary splendour. Among the earliest of the T'ang masters may be mentioned Wei-ch'ih I-sēng, who came from Khotan to China about 630. A copy of a picture of Vaisravana by this artist is in the Freer collection at Washington; and his style is perhaps to be discerned in a remarkable roll in Mr. Berenson's collection. Yen Li-pēn (born *c.* 600) was famous for his portraits of national worthies, foreign envoys and Buddhist pictures. We know his work only through copies. With Wu Tao-tzŭ, T'ang painting underwent a transformation. His early style was fine and delicate; later, it became broad and of amazing power. He painted over 300 Buddhist frescoes, as well as paintings of all kinds of subjects on silk. All have perished. One or two of his designs have been preserved by being engraved on stone, and some paintings and drawings are extant which may be copies from his work. The majestic fresco *Three Bodhisattvas*, given to the British Museum by Mr. Eumorfopoulos, dating probably from the 12th century, presumably preserves the T'ang tradition, and from it we may infer the yet grander and more magnificent creation of Wu Tao-tzŭ and his followers. All records agree in emphasizing the overwhelming power of his creations and also the almost sculptural character of his figures. Of actual and authenticated work by a known T'ang artist we have only five portraits of priests (much damaged) painted about 800 by Li Chēn and preserved in Japan. These are in a contained and rather austere style. But our chief documents for T'ang Buddhist painting are the pictures recovered from Tun-huang, on the western frontier of China, by Sir Aurel Stein and Prof. Pelliot. These are now in the British Museum, at Delhi and in Paris. A certain number are dated, with dates of the 9th and 10th centuries. Those which are in Chinese style may be taken to reflect the central tradition of Buddhist painting, though in a more or less provincial form. Of much the same character is a large Buddhist picture of the 9th century in the Boston Museum.

The Tun-huang pictures are largely devoted to the cult of Amitabha Buddha, who presides over the Western Paradise, and of his spiritual son Avalokitesvara, or Kuan-yin, the genius of Compassion, who in later times assumes a feminine form. There are many pictures of the Paradise, in which we see a host of blessed beings presided over by a Buddha (usually, but not always, Amitabha) gathered round a sacred concert, where a dancer performs to music on a terrace raised above the lotus-lake. Some of these complex compositions, containing a great number of figures, are remarkable

58

for the harmonious serenity of the design—there is no confusion or awkwardness in the arrangement—and the varied beauty of the colouring. Other votive pictures portray the great Bodhisattvas, especially Kuan-yin, or scenes from the Buddha legend. In the former case, the forms, draperies and ornaments are closely modelled on Indian prototypes; in the latter, types, dress and architecture are purely Chinese. From the small scenes sometimes painted at the sides of the large pictures we get a hint of the secular style of the period both in figure and landscape. The figures of donors, which are also fairly frequent, give us contemporary costume. Though mostly the work of artisans rather than artists, the value of these paintings as documents is very great, and a few are of real beauty.

In this era landscape became important as an independent art. The character of Chinese landscape is seen in the word for landscape, *shan-sui*, mountain and water. Li Ssŭ-hsün (b. 651) was the first eminent painter who devoted himself mainly to landscape. He painted in greens and blues, with gold outline. None of his works exist, but copies preserve the characteristics of his style. His son, Li Chao-tao, developed this technique. A small picture in the Boston Museum, ascribed to him but probably of later date, gives a good idea of this "miniature" kind of landscape-painting. A very different tradition in landscape was founded by Wang Wei (b. 699), who was equally famous as a poet. He matured a style of ink-painting, in which the landscape became the counterpart of an emotion, more subjective and more "impressionist" in method than the work of Li Ssŭ-hsün and his school. Copies exist (one is in the British Museum, and an earlier one in the Freer collection) of a famous roll by Wang Wei, *Scenery of the Wang Ch'uan*. The painting was engraved on stone when it began to decay. Rubbings have been published by Dr. B. Laufer in *Ostasiatische Zeitschrift* (April 1912).

Ts'ao Pa and his greater pupil, Han Kan, were especially famous for their paintings of horses. Han Kan found endless subjects in the fine horses sent as tribute from central Asia. He worked in the 8th century for the emperor Ming Huang. A contemporary, Han Huang, painted buffaloes and rustic scenes. The splendidly modelled pottery figures of horses and camels found in T'ang tombs give us a clue to the vigour and breadth of the animal painting of these masters, whose work has perished.

CHINESE ART

Admirable *genre* pictures and scenes from court life were also painted in this era. Chou Fang is known by versions (one in China and one in a New York private collection) of his *Listeners to Music*, a design in which the Chinese genius for eloquent spacing is conspicuous. The beautiful picture in the Boston Museum of *Ladies Beating and Preparing Silk* probably preserves a T'ang design.

The Five Dynasties (A.D. 900–960).—In this short period a great many artists are recorded, of whom Hsü Hsi was famous as a flower-painter and Chou Wēn-chü for his pictures of women. Still more celebrated was Huang Ch'uan, who painted landscape, birds, flowers, etc., and who is said to have started what is called the "boneless method"; *i.e.*, painting without a drawn outline.

The Sung Period (A.D. 960–1260).—Under the emperors of the Sung dynasty China was re-united. The emperor Hui Tsung was himself a painter and a great collector. In his reign the Academy of Painting became very prominent and attracted artists from all parts. A certain realism was inculcated, but in style a fastidious simplicity was to be aimed at. The small album-painting of a bird in a bough in the Eumorfopoulos collection, and similar paintings in famous albums in Japan, some of which are attributed to Hui Tsung, illustrate the ideals of the time. Flower-painting, hardly existent in the T'ang period, was now a favourite theme, and some painters, like Wēn T'ung, specialized in ink-painting of the bamboo. Of the flower-painters Chao Ch'ang was the most celebrated. The most eminent master in landscape of Northern Sung was Kuo Hsi, who wrote an essay on landscape, partly translated by Waley (*Chinese Painting*, pp. 189–194). Mi Fei invented a new style in landscape, without outline and with boldy brushed-in wooded peaks rising above rain and mist. His style is preserved in many pictures, though again few or none are actually by his hand. Chao Ta-nien painted autumn and winter scenes; Fan K'uan was famous for his snow-scenes.

But the most famous name in the art of Northern Sung is Li Lung-mien (*c.* 1040–1106). Much of his work consisted of copies from earlier masters. He had a reverential passion for tradition. At first he painted horses, but soon abandoned such subjects for Buddhist themes. Rarely using colour, he drew with a delicate, nervous line. Copies of his works are numerous, and a few originals have been reproduced in the *Kokka*. He is revered by the Chinese as a perfect type of Chinese culture; judged purely as an artist, he would not have so great a fame.

In 1127 the Tatars occupied northern China. The emperor Hui Tsung was taken prisoner and died in exile. Hang-chow became the new capital of what is known as Southern Sung. The changed temper of the times is reflected in the art of a people no longer greatly interested in external events which they were helpless to transform. The passion for romantic solitudes, for soaring peaks and plunging torrents, which had always haunted certain minds, eager to escape from the pressure of official life and ceremonious routine, became a mastering inspiration. The Zen sect of Buddhism, now dominant, with its reliance on intuition, its contempt for all outward forms, replaced the votive picture of single or assembled Bodhisattvas, glowing with colour and gold, by pictures of Arhats, in intense contemplation, or by swift ink-sketches of Zen saints; even a poising bird or blossoming spray could become in this mode of thought as "religious" a theme as the glorified Buddha. The emphasis was all on the interior mind. This temper, to which Taoist love of freedom and fluidity contributed much, gives a peculiar poetic character to the art of Southern Sung. Some there were, like Li Sung-nien, who kept to the older traditions and painted scenes from history and legend, and sets of pictures on weaving and agriculture. But the genius of the age is seen rather in Li T'ang (to whom are attributed a roll in a Japanese collection and a beautiful small picture in the Boston Museum), and still more in his famous pupils, Hsia Kuei and Ma Yüan. Owing to the enthusiasm with which the landscapes of this school were collected in Japan, we are able to judge of its productions from concrete examples. Though this school soon fell out of favour in China, it represents to Europe Chinese landscape at its finest; synthetic in conception, impassioned in execution, it unites simplicity with grandeur. Hills and high places had always been regarded with reverence as the abode of spirits. We find no counterpart to the feeling of aversion or disgust which the Alps inspired in Europeans down to so late a period. And though the Chinese have always been an agricultural people, it is not the relation of toiling man to the fruitful earth which inspires their typical landscape art. It is a more cosmic inspiration; a feeling of affinity between the human spirit and the energies of the elements,

—the winds, the mists, the soaring peaks, the plunging torrents. Technically, Chinese landscape design differs from European. The high horizon precludes the need for uniting sky and ground, divided by the natural horizon of sight, by means of vertical lines and masses. The eye passes from the foreground, so often a source of trial to the European painter, to the central motive, usually a mountain form.

The Yuan or Mongol Period (A.D. 1260–1368).—In this comparatively short period there was a tendency to go back to the style of ancient masters. Chao Mêng-fu is perhaps the most famous painter of the time. Countless pictures of horses now in Western collections are attributed to him, few of them with any probability. He also painted landscapes and flowers. Another fine painter was Jên Jên-fa, of whom there is a good example in the Eumorfopoulos collection, and others in Japan. The four chief landscape masters were: Huang Kung-wang, Wang Mêng, Ni Tsan, and Wu Chên. The two latter led roaming lives and had nothing of the professional about them. Ni Tsan painted suggestions of landscape in ink, in a reticent, delicate manner. Wu Chên, known as the "Priest of the Plum-blossom," excelled in paintings of bamboos. Ch'ien Hsüan is a master whose name is very frequently forged on paintings; he painted birds, flowers, also figures. Wang Yo-shui was famous for flowers. Yen Hui is admired in Japan for his Taoist sages, but is less known in China.

The Ming Dynasty (A.D. 1368–1644).—The art of the Ming period is characterized as a whole by a gradual fading out of the interior glow which under Buddhist and Taoist inspiration had suffused the creations of earlier periods. Concentrated in herself, China had no longer any stimulating contact with the world without; and her art became concerned rather with the beauty of material things than with the expression of the interior spirit. At the same time a reverential conservatism prescribed for the painter both subject and manner of treatment. The painters of this period are so numerous that only a few outstanding masters can be mentioned. The first Ming emperor re-established the Academy of Painting, with the aim of emulating the glories of Sung art. Gifted painters flocked to his court. Lin Liang painted ink-pictures of eagles, wild geese, flowers, etc., in a style of extraordinary breadth and power. A good example is in the British Museum, which also has a fine *Fairy and Phoenix* ascribed to Wu Wei, a master who

BY COURTESY OF THE MUSEUM OF FINE ARTS, BOSTON

THE ARHANT RAKAN BESTOWING ALMS

Sung painting, 12th century, one of a set of one hundred, representing the Five Hundred
Arhant. It was executed at Ming Chao in 1178, as a pious dedication. The paintings are in
colours on silk and mounted as panels

A SNOW SCENE

Painting, probably early Ming period, by an unknown artist—a typical landscape composition

strove to recapture something of the strong brush-work of Wu Tao-tzŭ. Very typical of early Ming art are the bird and flower pictures of Pien Ching-chao (Pien Wēn-chin) and of Lü Chi, in which a certain solidity and a decorative richness of colour combine with powerful drawing in a large design. In landscape, Tai Chin, accounted one of the foremost Ming painters, led a new movement and had many followers. His style was broad and free, with little or no colour. Another school preferred minuteness of detail, with an ornamental use of colour, especially a rich blue. Of this school were Chou Ch'ēn and T'ang Yin, who also excelled in figures.

Tung Ch'i-ch'ang (1554–1636), eminent as a critic as well as a painter and calligrapher, despised these "professionals" and their laborious technique. He is associated with the "Learned Man's Painting," in which refined taste and literary associations counted for much more than mere accomplishment. Tung Ch'i-ch'ang claimed that this style originated with Wang Wei in the 8th century, the founder of the Southern school. (In distinguishing the Northern and Southern schools, he tried to give these rather shadowy terms a geographical foundation which does not really, however, as a fine example of early Chinese animal sculpture, exist.) The Southern school, adorned in the earlier part of this period by Shên Chou and Wên Chêng-ming, two much-admired masters, had by the close of the dynasty become triumphant and supreme. Among bird and flower painters of the 16th century, Chou Chih-mien may be mentioned as one of the most distinguished, though his work is rare.

The Ch'ing (Manchu) Dynasty (A.D. 1644–1911).—Painting in the 17th and 18th centuries is very largely devoted to landscape in the style of the Southern school, which in the later developments of the literary man's style becomes loose, slight, capricious and eccentric. Among gifted amateurs of the beginning of the dynasty, Chu Ta is much admired for his ink-sketches of flowers, rocks, etc. More important artists of the K'ang Hsi period are "the four Wangs," Wang Shih-min, Wang Chien, Wang Hui and Wang Yuan-ch'i.

Another great figure in the 17th century is Yün Shou-p'ing, also called Nan-t'ien, the most famous flower painter of the Ch'ing period. Wu Li, who was converted to Christianity and became known as Father Acunha, painted landscapes. The influence of the Jesuits was considerable for a time in

63

China, but had no lasting effect on the arts. The Jesuit Giuseppe Castiglione was made to learn the Chinese style of painting under the name Lang Shih-ning. Chiao Ping-chēng, however, learnt something of European perspective and taught it to Lēng Mei and other artists. Chiao Ping-chēng's sets of pictures of agriculture and weaving were engraved in 1696. Shēn Nan-pin went to Japan and stayed at Nagasaki (1731–33); his work had a very stimulating effect on the naturalistic movement in Japan. Apart from this naturalistic movement, the modern painting of China seems to show little new life, and though good painters flourished in the 19th century, they were mostly content with exercises in the various manners consecrated by the past.

WOOD–CARVING

Splendid examples of Japanese 8th century wood-carving may be found in the phoenix and musical angels adorning the canopy hung in the Kondō of Hōryuji and in the *gigaku* masks carved in paulownia wood and preserved in the Imperial treasure-house Shōsōin, the Hōryuji monastery and other ancient temples in Japan. The *gigaku* masks in the Shōsōin, numbering 164, the majority of which are in wood, the most of which are in paulownia, if not all, the rest being in dry-lacquer, are believed to have been used in connection with religious services observed at Tōdaiji, especially at the inauguration ceremony of the Great Buddha which took place on April 9, 752. The belief is substantiated by the carvers' signatures and dates written on the inside of the masks, and also on the original bags which contained them. Inscriptions on some of the masks indicate the number of days spent in carving the mask, some being 5 and 7 and others 9 days. The wooden masks used in *bugaku*, the music of which is still preserved and occasionally performed in the Palace, are smaller and less grotesque in appearance, as may be seen from the old masks scheduled as "national treasures" and preserved in some temples. The *no* masks, all carved in wood, which came into existence in the 16th century, taxed the resources of the talented carvers, and a large number of masterpieces are now in possession of the head families of the different schools of *no* drama.

Up to the 15th century, the work of the wood-carver was confined to the embellishment of the temples: carvings on the pedestals, nimbus, and baldachins of Buddhist figures, and some slight ornamentations on the building itself, such as the carving of the beam-ends into animal heads and the use

65

of the *kaeru-mata*, a simple decoration between the beams. But in the second half of the 16th century, the decorative wood-carving came to assume an importance in palatial mansions of the shōguns and in shrines where wood-carvings were inserted into the *kaeru-mata* between the beams, attached under the rafters, used as the panels of the gate, etc., a large number of which may still be seen at Kitano Jinsha and Nishi Hongwanji of Kyoto, Chiku-bushima Jinsha in Lake Biwa, etc. The predominance of wood-carving as an architectural decoration in the 17th century may be seen at the mausoleums of the Tokugawa shōguns at Shiba, Tokyo, and at Nikko, where both the interior and exterior of the buildings are profusely covered with wood-carvings ranging over a wide variety of subjects faithfully executed and realistically coloured.

The taste for simplicity has not tolerated wood-carving in the architecture of dwelling houses. The only place the carver could display his art was in *ramma*, the ventilating panel in the narrow partition wall over the sliding screens that separate one room from another. The *ramma* carving has made a special development of its own, all sorts of subjects being treated: flowers and birds, animals and insects, figures in history and romance, landscapes and mists, etc., carved on board to give, together with the decoration on the sliding screens, a character to the room.

Some fine carving in wood, the temple decoration in miniature scale, may be seen in the family shrine (*butsu-dan*) where the ancestral tablets are kept, generally fitted into a recess in the room. In their profuse and minute decoration some of the portable shrines (*mikoshi*), used in the procession at the festival, are also beautiful examples of the art of wood-carving. So also are the small ornaments for cabinet decoration or for the *tokonoma*, the recess in the guest room for objects of art. Some wonderful workmanship in wood has been produced by the *netsuke* (ornamental button for suspending a pouch or medicine case) carvers when many of the talented sculptors in wood turned from carving Buddhist figures to smaller objects in greater demand.

The Chinese have utilized the wood-carving more lavishly than the Japanese in their home architecture. They have carved their heavy beams on the ceiling and the massive pillars as well with delicate tracery. The simplest of their chairs and tables are invariably carved in the "key"-pattern, some simpler than others, and the doors are in delicate trelliswork design or

BY COURTESY OF (1, 2, 3, 5, 6) THE DIRECTOR OF THE VICTORIA AND ALBERT MUSEUM

EXAMPLES OF FAR EASTERN WOOD-CARVING

1, 2, 3. Chinese shop front
4. Carved ramma in the crane room of the Nishi Hongwanji, Kyoto
5, 6. Carved beam from a Chinese house
7. Wood-carving under the eave of Kitano Jinsha, Kyoto
8. Chinese screen with carving

9. A Chinese temple
10. Wood-carving on the famous gateway (Yōmeimon) of the Nikko Shrine, Japan
11. Wood-carving on the wall of the Nikko Shrine
12. Sleeping cat at the Nikko Shrine carved by the left-handed Jingoro
13. Carved ramma in the wave room of the Nishi Hongwanji, Kyoto

FROM (1) THE OPPENHEIM COLLECTION, (2) THE WANNIECK COLLECTION, (4) THE GARDNER COLLECTION, (5) "MISSION ARCHÉOLOGIQUE EN CHINE" BY SEGALEN-VOISINS AND LARTIGUE (PAUL GEUTHNER); PHOTOGRAPHS, (3) COPR. OSVALD SIRÉN

ANIMALS IN EARLY CHINESE SCULPTURE

1. Bear in gilt bronze; Han dynasty (206 B.C.–A.D. 220)
2. Reclining bull, bronze; North Wei dynasty (A.D. 386–534)
3. Dog, in clay; Han dynasty (206 B.C.–A.D. 220)
4. Two bears, gilt bronze; Han dynasty (206 B.C.–A.D. 220)
5. Reclining horse, from the tomb of General Ho Ch'iu P'ing, Shen-si, (c. 117 B.C.)

ornamented with carvings in low relief. Lanterns with diapers or some other interesting designs in pierced work are held by brackets or arms carved in forms of dragon heads. Although rich in variety, the designs used in the wood-carving show a fondness for geometric patterns that is distinctly Chinese. The following are some of the other motives resorted to by the wood-carvers emblems of richness and happiness, clouds and thunder patterns, the curious mask of a creature "TaoTieh," "The Eight Trigrams" or "Pa Kwa," "The Four Quadrants," "The Five Elements," etc. Sacred scenes and figures incised in floral scrolls, intermingled with series of conventional emblems of one religion or another, form subjects for wood-carvers in decorating the Buddhist, Taoist and Confucian temples. Sacred to Buddhism are the eight symbols, the chief among which is the lotus, an emblem of purity, chosen because the lotus lifts out of the mud its rosy or white blossoms unsullied, forming a fitting resting place for the Buddha. Taoists have their symbols of eight immortals and derive many floral emblems of longevity from sacred plants, the most prominent among which is the peach, the tree of life of their paradise, bearing fruits ripening but once in 3,000 years which confer immortality to those who partake of them. While Confucianism has no distinct emblem of its own, the symbol of culture and examples of filial piety, such as the well known 24 examples of filial piety, are sometimes attributed to it.

Artistic vitality characterizes even the highly conventionalized designs of the Japanese wood-carvers, but the bulk of the Chinese work reveals a sense of laborious and mechanical execution. On the whole, the Chinese wood-carvings are more effective as a design and ornament compared with the Japanese work, which, while the thing carved on is well decorated, carry a far less decorative value. The former aims more for the effect, while the latter pays much greater attention to the mode of execution and technical skill. The former covers the carving with paint or lacquer, while the latter delights in appreciating, whenever possible, the clear-cut chisel marks in natural wood. Even the decorative panels in the temples and shrines which are coloured, show traces of the Japanese wood-carver's pleasure derived from the clear cuts of his chisel. There is a tendency in both for an effort to surmount difficulties in design and execution, defying time and labour, with little regard for the artistic merit in the result achieved.

67

CHINESE SCULPTURE

The HISTORICAL records about sculptural works in China do not begin until the Ch'in dynasty (221–206 B.C.); the earliest refer to the 12 colossal statues of "the giant barbarians" and the bell-frames in the shape of monsters "with stags' heads and dragons' bodies," which the great emperor Ch'in Shih Huang Ti ordered to be cast from the weapons of war collected throughout the kingdom. These enormous bronze statues which were placed before one of the imperial palaces near Hsien Yang, on the Wei River in Shensi, are mentioned by Lu Chia, an author who lived from the Ch'in to the Han dynasty, and by several later chroniclers such as Chang Heng (d. A.D. 139) who speaks of "the metal barbarians sitting in a row." At the end of the later Han dynasty Tung Chow melted "ten bronze men into small cash, also the bell-frames"; the two remaining ones he set up inside the Ch'ing Ming gate at Ch'angan but these were also lost during the 4th century, when a local ruler tried to remove them but found them too heavy for the muddy roads, the result being that one was melted down into cash, the other thrown into the river. Nothing is known about the artistic character of these statues, but their recorded history proves that they were considered extraordinary for their motives and size.

Ch'in Dynasty.—The only sculptures now remaining which possibly might be attributed to the Ch'in dynasty are some decorative animals in bronze. Most of these are of small size and placed on the lids of sacrificial vessels, but nevertheless with a well developed sculptural character. A larger example—sometimes ascribed to the Ch'in period—is a statuette that represents a reclining bull (now in the possession of L. Wannieck, Paris).

68

It is said to have been found together with some bronze vessels, decorated in Ch'in style, at Li Yü in northern Shansi, but to judge by its style, it can hardly have been executed before the 6th century A.D. (Northern Wei dynasty). We illustrate it, however, as a fine example of early Chinese animal sculpture.

Among other bronze animals which have been ascribed to the Ch'in period should be mentioned a large dragon or hydra with crested neck and flame-like wings at the shoulders and the loins, in the collection of A. Stoclet, Brussels. It is in marked contrast to the bull, fierce, fantastic, grotesque to the utmost without any connections with nature, and must, indeed, be earlier in date, though hardly of the Ch'in period. Other fantastic animals appear at the handles of some large bells in Ch'in style.

New efforts were evidently made in different directions during this short period which, in the field of art, was simply an introduction to the classic age of the Hans. The rigid ceremonial art of earlier times is gradually modified by a more direct and vivid interest in nature. The Chou art (1122–256 B.C.) was preëminently symbolic and geometrical. The art of the Ch'in and the Han periods aimed at the presentation of the actual rhythm of things, the inherent life and significance of the artistic forms.

The Han Dynasty.—Most of the Han monuments have evidently been destroyed; yet, to judge from those which remain as well as from minor plastic creations in bronze and clay, Chinese sculpture was at this early period much better fitted to treat animal motives than human shapes. It is only in the reliefs that the human figures reach an importance comparable to that of the animals, and these are, on the whole, more like paintings translated into stone than real sculptures. With the exception of the small tomb statuettes made as substitutes for real people, human representations are quite rare and artistically much inferior to the representations of animals. The Chinese have never considered the human figure an artistic motive in itself, but simply used it for expressing an action or a state of consciousness. They have taken greater interest in types, postures and motives of drapery than in the bodily form or the muscular organism. The case is quite different with the animal sculptures. They may adhere to certain types or formulae characteristic of the period to which they belong but their artistic importance depends mainly on the rendering of their organic form and vitality. The

69

best among them are monumental creations, hardly inferior to animal sculptures of any other period or nation. The conventionalization, which is more or less preponderant during the early epochs, does not convey an element of immaterial abstraction but serves to accentuate the muscular organism, the energy of movement, the monumentality of the form, all that makes the animals great and convincing as works of art.

Bronze, Clay and Stone Work of the Han.—Among the great number of wild and domestic animals represented in bronze, clay and stone during the Han period we may choose as examples some bears executed in bronze. The majority of these bears are quite small, intended to serve as feet for sacrificial vessels, but there are also some of a larger size which have the character of free standing sculptures. The two best are in the Gardner Museum in Boston. These are represented in a squatting posture, stretching their heads forward with a friendly roar. The modelling of the limbs is not carried very far, yet it is sufficient to awake an impression of suppleness and force. The artist has not been afraid of exaggerations in the characterization of the lumpy forms or the telling postures. The heavy weight of the body supported by the broadly placed forepaws, the elastic power of the enormous legs, the softness of the bulky paws and the long nose which seems to form a direct continuation of the ears, are rendered with a power of conviction and a sense of monumental unity that are rarely found in later animal sculptures.

It should also be noticed that in their representations of animals the Chinese have quite often combined two or more into a group. They have composed them in the most intricate positions and built up groups which satisfy the highest requirements of plastic art. Most of these groups are on a relatively small scale, but they are nevertheless truly monumental. The finest results are achieved in groups of fighting animals, because the bodies are here represented in their highest tension, in the full development of their muscular effort, and so closely interlaced that they complete each other perfectly in the expression of the plastic idea. The same is also true of some of the animals which are composed into an architectural unity with monuments such as the tomb pillars in Szechuan (which will be mentioned below).

Tomb Statuettes of the Han.—The greatest variety of animal types may however be found among the clay statuettes made for the tombs. The material was most easily handled and thus invited all sorts of individual vari-

PHOTOGRAPHS, COPR. OSVALD SIRÉN

SCULPTURES AT THE TOMB OF WU LIANG TZU, SHANTUNG

1. Men coming in carts and on horseback to a festival in a house; stone relief from the tomb shrine of Wu Liang Tzu; A.D. 147

2. Two tigers; stone relief from the same tomb
3. Statue of a guardian lion at entrance of the same tomb

BY COURTESY OF (3, 4) THE MUSEUM OF THE UNIVERSITY OF PENNSYLVANIA, FROM (2) "MISSION ARCHÉOLOGIQUE EN CHINE" BY SEGALEN-VOISINS AND LARTIGUE (PAUL GEUTHNER); PHOTOGRAPHS, (1, 5) COPR. OSVALD SIRÉN

MONSTERS IN CHINESE SCULPTURE

1. Winged lion; statue at the tomb of Prince Hsiao Hsiu (d. A.D. 518), near Nanking. 2. Chimaera; statue at the tomb of the Emperor Ch'i Wu Ti (d. A.D. 493), near Nanking. Chimaeras usually guarded the tombs of emperors; lions those of princes and dukes; the largest are 10–12 ft. long. 3. Chimaera; statue from an imperial tomb of the 6th century A.D. 4. Chimaera; statue from an imperial tomb. 5. Statue of winged lion at the tomb of Duke Hsiao Ching (d. A.D. 523), near Nanking

ations, and as these clay sculptures were executed as substitutes for living animals, which in earlier times followed their dead masters into their tombs, it was natural that they should be made as lifelike as possible. The majority are domestic animals such as horses, sheep, dogs, pigs, hens and ducks in various sizes, the smallest hardly more than two or three inches high, the largest measuring a foot or more. They were usually executed in clay moulds but sometimes modelled by hand, and the best among them have retained a spontaneous freshness and vivacity which make them very entertaining. Proportions and shapes are treated with a great deal of freedom. The dogs have enormous heads, the horses have necks which curve like high arches, and the pigs have snouts like bowsprits, yet the exaggerations serve simply to accentuate the typical features of the various animals.

Besides the animals there are human *ming ch'i*, or tomb statuettes, made as substitutes for living people, such as servants, and wives who formerly were buried alive with the husbands. Most common amongst these statuettes from the Han period are the slender ladies in long robes with wide sleeves reminding one of the Japanese kimonos. They stand usually in very quiet postures simply with a slight inclination of the large round head, but occasionally we find them represented in a dancing movement, though with closed feet, swinging their bodies and their arms in a rhythmic fashion.

Stone Sculptures of the Han.—Stone sculptures on a large scale were, no doubt, also executed in steadily increasing numbers during the Han period, though comparatively few of them have been preserved. Among the earliest which can be approximately dated are the animals at the tomb of General Ho Ch'ü Ping, situated at the Wei River some 20 m. N.W. of Sianfu. They were discovered by Ségalen and Lartigue during their explorations in 1914 and more completely dug out by the latter in 1923. Lartigue has also published them in an article in the German magazine *Artibus Asiae* (1927) in which he presents some evidence for the supposition that these statues were executed about 117 B.C., the year of the death of the famous general. He thinks that the statues, which represent a horse standing over a fallen warrior, a reclining horse and a buffalo, were placed in front of the mound, and that their present quite irregular positions have been caused by the shifting of the mud. Besides these, complete sculptures may, however, be seen in the neighbourhood of the mound, a large block with a mythological figure, executed in relief, and fragments of some animal sculptures which seem to indicate that this large composition never was completely finished. It is difficult to appreciate the artistic importance of these large statues without seeing the originals, but if we may draw some conclusions from the reproductions, the sculptures are comparatively undeveloped from an artistic point of view. This is particularly true of the main statue, the horse standing over a fallen warrior. The composition is indeed significant but the formal treatment does not seem to do justice to the motive. The short-legged horse with an enormous head is more bulky than monumental, and the figure under its belly is simply a large block. Here is little of that intrinsic energy which is so prominent in some of the minor sculptures already mentioned. This impression is, however, to some extent counteracted by the reclining horse and the buffalo which, even if they are heavy and bulky with stumpy legs, reveal a very sensitive artistic treatment, particularly in their expressive heads. Here one may discover a touch of that excellent animal psychology which is one of the greatest assets of Han art, a characterization which, to some extent, makes up for the shortcomings in other directions.

Sculpture Developed for the Dead.—Other stone sculptures from the beginning of the Han dynasty which might serve for comparison have not come to light, though it is more than probable that they have existed, because this tomb was hardly an isolated case, and broadly speaking sculpture in stone as well as in clay had its origin in the decoration and the arrangement of the tombs. It was for the dead rather than for the living that the Chinese developed their creative activity in the field of the plastic arts. As proof of this may be quoted not only the various classes of clay and stone sculptures mentioned above, but also numerous reliefs executed for the decoration of the "spirit chambers" of the tombs and the sculptural pillars placed in front of the mounds. These monuments marked as a rule the beginning of the "shen tao" (spirit path) which led up to the tomb and which in later times was farther and farther extended in a straight line from the mound towards the south. The interior of the tomb consisted often of two or more chambers (as also may be observed in contemporary Korean tombs), the first being a kind of ante-room called the "spirit chamber," where the soul of the deceased was supposed to dwell, while the coffin was placed, together with various vessels and other paraphernalia of bronze or clay, in the back room. The main decoration, be it in sculpture or painting, was concentrated in the ante-room where the walls often were covered with representations from ancient history and mythology or with illustrations with a moral import.

Tomb Pillars.—Quite a number of the decorative pillars which formed the gateway to the "spirit road" are known from central and western China, particularly the provinces of Honan, Shantung and Szechuan. They are usually constructed on a rectangular plan of large and well-fitted stone blocks reaching a total height of 15 to 18 feet. When completely preserved they consist of a moulded pedestal, a very broad shaft and a cornice over which

BY COURTESY OF THE METRO-
POLITAN MUSEUM OF ART
SCULPTURE OF THE SUI
PERIOD

SCULPTURE OF THE NORTHERN WEI
PERIOD

the roof projects quite far. But the form varies somewhat in the different provinces; thus the pillars in Honan, of which the best known stand at Têng Fung Hsien on Sung Shan, are very broad and provided with projecting buttresses. Otherwise they are quite simple without any particular development of the cornices and decorated with ornaments and figures in very low relief. The earliest of these Honan pillars is dated A.D. 118, the latest A.D. 175.

The pillars in Szechuan have usually no buttresses, but they are higher and characterized by a richer architectural composition; their upper parts, the cornices and friezes under the projecting roof, are particularly well developed. We find here, reproduced in stone, the beam ends and brackets so

73

characteristic of Chinese wooden architecture, and between these are sculptural decorations executed in high relief, sometimes almost in the round. These pillars are all from the later Han dynasty, but only one of them, the pillar of Fung Huan at Ch'iu Hsien, is dated by an inscription which contains the year A.D. 121.

Symbolic Decorations of the Han.—More important for their sculptural decorations are, however, two pillars in the same neighbourhood erected at the tomb of a man called Shen. On their shafts are representations of the symbols of the four directions; *i.e.*, the red bird of the South, the white tiger of the East, the blue dragon of the West and the black tortoise of the North, animal representations which, with regard to energetic rhythm of line and grand decorative stylization, may be compared to the best works in bronze or clay known from this classic epoch. At the corners of the entablature are seated human figures which seem to carry the projecting beams on their shoulders, and, on the middle of the south side, a kind of *t'ao t'ie* (glutton) appears between the beams. All these figures are executed practically in the round and most skilfully composed into the architectural scheme of the monument. The very high frieze is divided into two sections, of which the lower one is decorated with hunting scenes in quite low relief and the upper one with some larger figures in high relief. One may observe here men riding on stags, horse-like animals running along with the swiftness of the wind, and hunters who aim with their bows above their heads or grasp the passing leopard by its tail. Here is the same free-play with animal and human forms as may be observed on some of the inlaid bronze vessels or on the glazed Han urns with relief friezes. The motives seem to have some reference to the life beyond the tomb, though they represent this with a naturalness and an intensity of movement which make them appear like scenes from real life. The style reveals something of the same energy and nervous tension that characterizes the small bronze ornaments of this period, and it can hardly be explained without accepting an influence from west Asiatic sources, though the Chinese transformation of the west Asiatic tradition is more complete in the large stone sculptures than in most of the minor bronze ornaments.

Dramatic Expression of the Pillars.—The majority of the tomb pillars in Szechuan, of which at least a score were discovered by Ségalen and Lartigue

74

during their exploration in 1914, show the above-mentioned combination of friezes with flat reliefs and tri-dimensional representations of animals and human figures on the entablature. The motives vary, some being historical or legendary, others religious or mythological, but they are all more or less imbued with a dramatic expression, and executed in a form of high decorative beauty.

Much simpler than these are the pillars whcih stood at the entrance to the tomb of the Wu family at Ch'ia Hsiang in Shantung. They were erected about the year A.D. 147 and they are still in their original place, although the tomb-area has become a large pit, usually filled with water. The pillars are provided with buttresses and a small superior storey on the projecting roof, but their sculptural decoration consists simply of quite low reliefs representing dragons, tigers and birds, in decorative translation, besides legendary illustrations with a moral import, framed by geometrical ornaments of the same kind as may be found for instance on the mirrors of the Han period.

Reliefs of the Han.—The same kind of motive, executed in a strictly conventionalized linear style, appears also on the large stone slabs which used to be arranged along the walls of the ante-chamber in the tomb, but which are now transferred to a primitive little store-room where they stand without any kind of order. These reliefs from the Wu Liang Tzu tomb have become known all over the world through numerous series of rubbings taken of them since the 18th century, and reproduced in many Chinese and European publications. Two or three of the reliefs have found their way into Western collections, though it should be noticed that the majority of the stone reliefs, said to come from Wu Liang Tzu, are simply modern imitations, made on the basis of rubbings.

Legendary Motives.—Nothing is more entertaining than to follow, with the aid of Chavannes interpretations, the legendary motives represented in these reliefs and thus to learn something about classical Chinese examples of filial piety, matrimonial fidelity, the faithfulness of loyal citizens, the valour of great heroes, not to mention the quasi-historical traditions about the great Yü and Ch'in Shih Huang Ti or the mythological stories about the king of the East, Tung Wang Kung, and the queen of the West, Hsi Wang Mu. Very common motives in these reliefs are the long processions of riders and carriages and the rows of men on horseback escorting a carriage, which may be representations of the journey of the deceased to Hades.

The compositions are arranged in horizontal storeys, with single rows of figures, animals, trees, houses and the like, appearing as silhouettes against a neutral background. The artistic expression lies mainly in the contours, and in the engraved lines; the modelling of the forms is very slight. These reliefs may thus hardly be called sculpture in the real sense of the word, but rather paintings or drawings translated into stone. We have reason to suppose that they were made after such patterns and reproduce popular wall paintings which existed in some contemporary palaces, a supposition which is supported by the poet Wang Yen Shou, who describes the wall paintings in the Ling Kuang palace executed about the middle of the 2nd century A.D. He mentions in his description mythological illustrations of the same kind as may be seen in the Wu Liang Tzu reliefs besides "many riotous damsels and turbulent lords, loyal knights, dutiful sons, mighty scholars, faithful wives, victors and vanquished, wise men and fools," motives which correspond more or less to those appearing on the stone reliefs from Wu Liang Tzu and other places in Shantung.

Bactrian Types.—It has been claimed that the proud horses of these reliefs were of Bactrian origin. This is possible but the Chinese sculptors were certainly less guided by observation of nature than by artistic models, be it in bronze, clay or textile. They have accepted and further developed a definite type of horse which probably existed in the art of the Hellenized west-Asiatic countries.

Less Hellenistic and more definitely Scytho-Iranian in character are the winding dragons and heraldically placed tigers which appear in one or two of these reliefs. They belong to the same great family of ornamental animals which we also met on the stone pillars in Szechuan, and may thus be said to form some additional proofs of the general acceptance of this kind of animal sculpture during the Han period.

Still more remarkable examples of the same stylistic current are the two lions which stood at the entrance to the tomb of the Wu family (at the sides of the above-mentioned pillars) but which are now more or less buried in the mud. The anatomical character of the only visible one is rather free. It is, indeed, no common lion but a descendant of those proud animals which stood at the royal palaces in Susa and Persepolis and whose artistic pedigree may be traced to Chaldean and Assyrian art. The form is supple, the body is thin, the whole animal is dominated by the broad curving neck which comes so far to the front that the head almost disappears and the neck continues in the enormous jaws. At the shoulders one may observe traces of small wings, though they have been practically worn off by time. Such a creation has hardly been shaped from nature. Even if single lions now and then were sent as tributes from western Asiatic nations to the Chinese emperor, these were hardly known by the people in the provinces, and as there were no other lions in China, we may well suppose that the inspiration for such animal representation was drawn from examples of Iranian art rather than from living models.

Animal Statues.—To the same group of animal statues from the end of the Han epoch may also be assigned two-winged tigers at the tomb of K'ao Yi at Ya Chou Fu in Szechuan, which have been published by Ségalen and Lartigue, and the enormous seated lion—which has served as a plinth for a pillar in the Okura Museum in Tokyo. There are furthermore some minor animal statuettes of the same type but they hardly need detain us as they only verify what has already been said about the artistic style and derivation of these sculptures. Nor do we need to stop at the human figures executed in stone on a large scale, because their artistic importance is much inferior to that of the animals.

Animal Sculptures of the Six Dynasties Period.—During the centuries which followed the fall of the Eastern Han dynasty (A.D. 214) artistic activity in China lost some of its intensity. The times were restless, filled with war and political upheaval. The empire was again divided into several minor States, to begin with, the Three Kingdoms, Wu, Shu and Wei, and later on, after 223, into a northern and a southern half, the former being under the domination of the Tartars, among whom the Toba tribe came out the strongest and took the name of the Northern Wei dynasty, while the latter was ruled over by a number of short-lived native dynasties—Sung, Ch'i, Liang and Ch'en—which had their headquarters at Nanking. We know very little about the artistic activity during these times but it seems that the stylistic traditions of the Han period remained in force also during the 3rd and 4th centuries of our era. Some tomb reliefs, mainly from Shantung, executed in a kind of coarser Han style, may well be of this transition period, and the same may be said of a number of minor plastic works in bronze and clay.

The general evolution can be followed most closely through the small tomb statuettes; they reflect the variations in taste and fashion better than the large stone sculptures. Among them are real *genre* figures represented in various occupations such as music-making, feeding the hens, or with children in their arms, and we may observe how the fashion is changed from the simple "kimono" to an elegantly draped mantle over a tightly-fitting undergarment and how the head-dress becomes higher and more decorative. These tomb statuettes and minor animals in terracotta originate mainly from Honan, whereas the larger stone sculptures of this same period are executed for the reigning dynasties in Nanking. These monuments which form one of the most important groups within the domain of Chinese sculpture, have been more or less identified and reproduced by various explorers.

The largest among these lions and chimaeras measure up to 10 or 12 ft. in length and may still be seen at their original places, but some smaller ones, 4 to 6 ft. long, have found their way to Western collections. They all represent winged, lion-like animals but it is possible to distinguish two main types, *i.e.*, the chimaeras, which are a kind of cross between dragons and lions, and the real lions which have wings on their shoulders but no feathers or scales on their bodies and no ornamental beard. The former seem to have been considered the nobler, because they were employed as guardians at the tombs of emperors, whereas the lions stood at the tombs of princes and dukes.

Early Chimaeras.—The earliest chimaera which can be dated stands at the tomb of Emperor Sung Wen Ti (d. 453). It is a colossal and, in spite of its dilapidation, still imposing animal, largely covered up by a heap of refuse, so that the statue had to be dug out whenever it was photographed. The upper part of the head is lost and the surface of the grey limestone is very much worn but it is still possible to see that the body as well as the legs have been covered by ornamental scales or feathers and that the animal had wings not only at the shoulders but also at the ears.

The second earliest in date of the chimaeras which still remain at their original sites is the one at the tomb of Emperor Ch'i Wu Ti (d. 493). The

78

BY COURTESY OF (4) THE MUSEUM OF FINE ARTS, BOSTON; FROM (2, 3) "MISSION ARCHÉOLOGIQUE EN CHINE" BY SEGALEN-VOISINS AND LARTIGUE (PAUL GEUTHNER); PHOTOGRAPHS, (1, 5, 6) COPR. OSVALD SIRÉN

LARGE AND SMALL WORKS OF CHINESE SCULPTURE

1. Pillars forming the entrance to the tomb-area of Wu Liang Tzu, Shantung, A.D. 147
2. Pillar at the tomb of Fung Huan, Sze-Ch'uen, A.D. 121
3. Pillars at tomb of Shen, Sze-Ch'uen

4. Seated Bodhisattva, marble statue, late T'ang dynasty
5. Tomb-statuettes in clay, Han dynasty, in a private collection in Berlin
6. Praying monk, a marble statue, 12th–13th century A.D.

PHOTOGRAPHS, (1, 3, 4) COPR. OSVALD SIRÉN, (2) H. C. ELLIS

DIVINITIES IN CHINESE SCULPTURE

1. Seated Buddha, colossal statue at Yun Kang, Shan-si, 6th century. 2. Seated Bodhisattva, early 6th century, from Yun Kang, Shan-si. 3. Hindu divinities and a guardian at entrance to a cave, Yun Kang, 6th century. The sculptures of the cave temples (5th—6th centuries) show strong influences from the art of Central and Western Asia. 4. Portion of a wall in the Lao Chun cave, Lung-Men, Ho-nan, early 6th century

dimensions are somewhat smaller but the animal is more completely preserved. The long body has a more dragonlike character, the legs are comparatively short and the tail well developed. The most imposing part is, however, the enormous head with the open jaws from which the ornamental beard hangs like a long tongue. One may here observe three pairs of wings as well as feathers drawn in spirals over the whole body.

Sixth-century Chimaeras.—The same proud bearing characterizes the chimaera at the tomb of Emperor Liang Wu Ti (d. 549). The movement of the long and supple body is still better developed and it receives a most effective continuation in the enormous curve of the neck. The animal is moving forward in an ambling fashion; we feel its vigour and suppleness. The wings and the feathers are indicated in quite low relief or simply engraved.

This nobility and energy are carried still further in the two large chimaeras which now stand in the University Museum at Philadelphia. We have no information whence they come, but they illustrate a further evolution of the style of the chimaeras at the tomb of Emperor Liang Wu Ti, which would date them shortly after the middle of the 6th century. It is possible that they stood at the tomb of some of the emperors of the short Ch'en dynasty which followed after the Liang, such as Ch'en Wu Ti (d. 559) or Ch'en Wen Ti (d. 566). In comparison with these beasts, the earlier chimaeras appear almost like domestic animals. The fantastic wildness and the seething energy are here given free outlet. The legs are stretched, the bodies drawn, the head is wildly thrown backwards, the chest pushed forward into a large curve, and all these movements are accentuated by engraved lines which give the impression of taut steel springs. Besides these large ones several minor chimaeras are known but none of them reaches the extraordinary expressiveness of the last-mentioned.

Winged Lions.—The largest of the winged lions still remain *in situ*, not far from Nanking; their weight and colossal dimensions have made their removal impossible, but some of them are so far decayed that, if nothing is done to protect them, they will soon disappear. The earliest and most important stand at tombs of various members of the Liang family, *i.e.*, the brothers of the Emperor Wu Ti, Prince Hsiao Hsiu (d. 518), Prince Hsiao Tan (d. 522) and the cousin of the emperor, Duke Hsiao Ching (d. 523).

Besides these, two or three pairs of large lions are in the same neighbourhood, at Yao Hua Men, to the east of Nanking, but they are later and artistically inferior. The anatomical difference between the lions and the chimaeras is, as already said, not very important. The former as well as the latter are feline animals with an enormous curving neck and wings, but they are not provided with scales or feathers, nor do they have any ornamental beard like the chimaeras, only a large tongue which hangs down from the open jaws over the projecting chest. They are all represented in an ambling posture, majestically walking or coming to a sudden standstill, when the fore-legs are strained and the hind-legs bent. The head is lifted high on the proudly curving neck, the forms are full, the limbs heavier than in the chimaeras. Their massiveness is at least as imposing as the concentration of power in their enormous limbs. Most eaten by frost and water are the lions at the tomb of Duke Hsiao Ching which is now covered by a watery rice field in which the lions sink up to their shoulders.

Lions of Hsiao Hsiu Tombs.—Better preserved and more completely visible are the two colossal lions at the tomb area of Hsiao Hsiu, now covered by the village Kan Yu Hsiang, and here remains one row of the other monuments which flanked the "spirit road," *i.e.*, two large tablets with inscriptions carried by tortoises and a fluted column on a plinth composed of winding dragons. This seems to be the earliest preserved "tomb alley" in China, an arrangement known from a great number of later tombs. The lions are of the same family as those already described, the fact that they have wings is in itself a proof of their dependence on Persian art. It should, however, be remembered that the Achaemenian and Sassanian animals were descendants of the Assyrian which must be regarded as the fore-fathers of all the greatest Asiatic and a good many European lion sculptures. To what extent the Chinese really knew such models is a question which cannot be discussed here; it is in any case evident that they transformed the foreign models quite freely, not to say fantastically, in harmony with their native traditions. These animal sculptures form stylistically a direct continuation of the plastic art of the Han period. Yet, they indicate that a new wave of Western influence reached China at this time on a more southern route than through the northwestern nomads. These lion sculptures do not appear in the northern provinces which were dominated by the Tartars. They belong to the more

80

southern provinces where the old Chinese civilization and the creative spirit of the "Han people" never were completely subdued by foreign elements.

Religious Sculpture of the Six Dynasties.—When Buddhist sculpture was introduced into China it had passed through a long evolution in India and Central Asia; the principal iconographic motives, symbols and attributes were all developed into definite forms; the Chinese took them over just as they took over Buddhist scriptures; and whatever modifications they may have introduced concerned more the artistic interpretation than the motives themselves. It should never be forgotten that they were greater artists than any other people of the Far East, and when Buddhist art took root in China, the country was by no means devoid of sculptural monuments. There were (as we have previously seen) artistic traditions which could not be forgotten, only modified when applied to Buddhist motives. The Buddhas and Bodhisattvas were, of course, represented in human shapes but the artists could not enhance their significance by accentuating their physical organisms or their likeness to ordinary human beings, nor could they change their general shapes or postures if they wanted to be understood. The iconographic rules are indeed much more exacting in Buddhist than in Christian art, and the motives are more limited in their artistic scope.

Religious Symbolism.—The great majority of the Buddhist sculptures represent isolated figures, seated or standing in very quiet postures without any attempt at movement, except certain symbolic gestures. The heads are made according to quite definite types, somewhat changing with the periods and localities, but it is rare to meet heads with individual expression or portraitlike features. The bodies are as a rule entirely covered by long mantles or rich garments according to the rôle or meaning of the figure; they have hardly any importance of their own but serve simply as a substratum for the rich flow of the mantle folds which, particularly in the early sculptures, conceal the forms much more than they accentuate them. Even in figures which are represented almost nude, such as the guardians at the gate (*Dvarapalas*), the representation is not really naturalistic; their Herculean forms and muscular movements are altogether exaggerated and their significance is symbolic.

The earliest dated Buddhist sculptures in China, known to us, are small bronze statuettes of a greater historical than artistic importance. Some of them are provided with inscriptions which make it possible to fix their date, the earliest being of the years 437 and 444, whereas the earliest dated Buddha in stone is of the year 457. These small statuettes represent standing or seated Buddhas or Bodhisattvas against a leaf-shaped nimbus decorated with engraved flame-ornaments. The figures are mostly of a very moderate artistic importance recalling by their types and draperies the Graeco-Buddhist art of north India. The large nimbuses behind these small figures constitute, however, a feature which is not known in Gandahara sculpture.

Yün Kang Cave Temples.—The greatest *ensemble* of early Buddhist sculptures in China is to be found at the Yün Kang cave temples near Ta Tung Fu in Shansi where the Northern Wei dynasty had its capital until 494, when it was removed to Loyang in Honan. The work at these cave sculptures started about the middle of the 5th century and was continued towards the latter part of the 6th century. Amongst the rich material displayed at this place one may observe different stylistic currents, some originating from Central Asia and India, others more closely connected with earlier forms of Chinese art. Here are ornaments of a distinctly Iranian character, and architectural forms of the same type as on reliefs from Taxila and Peshawar, but also some decorative motives recalling the art of the Han period. Among the figures there are some curious examples which form a link with Central Asiatic art, *e.g.*, the five-headed and six-armed god who sits on a large bird with a pearl in its beak. This is no doubt the Garuda-raja, the bird of Vishnu, which also may be seen in some paintings from Tun Huang. This and other Hindu divinities of a similar kind, which appear in the Buddhist pantheon at Yün Kang, testify that artistic influence from central and western Asia reached China in connection with the introduction of Buddhism.

Artistic Expression.—Most famous among the figures here are the colossal Buddhas and Bodhisattvas which, however, seem to us artistically least interesting. A certain conventional type and fold design have in these figures been enormously enlarged without any intensification of the rhythmic motives or the artistic expression. More artistic expression and beauty may be found in some other figures at Yün Kang which are less closely allied to Indian models and more imbued with the traditional Chinese feeling for rhythmic lines and elegant form. The figures themselves are quite thin and

BY COURTESY OF (1) THE MUSEUM OF FINE ARTS, BOSTON; PHOTOGRAPHS, (2, 3) COPR. OSVALD SIRÉN

BUDDHAS OF THE EARLY 6TH CENTURY

1. Buddhist votive stela, dated A.D. 529. The interlacing dragons at the top are of the same character as those on the slabs raised at tombs in the Han period, but their fierceness and energy of movement reveal some influence from Sibero-Asiatic art

2. Seated Buddha in a niche at Yün Kang, Shan-si; early 6th century

3. Standing Buddha accompanied by two Bodhisattvas; early 6th century, Yün Kang, Shan-si

BY COURTESY OF (2) GRENVILLE WINTHROP, (3) THE MUSEUM OF THE UNIVERSITY OF PENNSYLVANIA; PHOTOGRAPHS, (1, 4) COPR. OSVALD SIRÉN

RELIGIOUS SCULPTURES OF THE 6TH CENTURY A.D.

1. Buddha accompanied by two Bodhisattvas, Cave 2 at T'ien Lung Shan, Shan-si, middle 6th century. 2. Standing Bodhisattva, marble statue of Sui period, about 600. 3. Standing Buddha; statuette in gilt bronze, dated 537. 4. Guardian at entrance of Cave 8, T'ien Lung Shan, Shan-si, North Ch'i period, middle of the 6th century

flat, sometimes hardly modelled into full cubic volume, and they are entirely covered up by very long and heavy garments. The folds of these are pressed and pleated on the very thin shapes and uniformly arranged on both sides of the figures in long concave curves, forming a kind of zigzag pattern at the border; the contours are very tense, with the elasticity of drawn bow-strings. When this type of draping is fully developed the drawn-out, curving mantle folds may suggest wings.

Temple Grottoes at Lung Men.—The same energetic style as in the best Yün Kang sculptures may also be observed in some of the statues in the famous temple grottoes at Lung Men in Honan which were begun shortly after the Northern Wei dynasty had transferred its capital to Loyang (494). During the last decade these caves have been so badly destroyed that hardly 10% of the original sculpture still remains; all the rest is either smashed or beheaded, some of the heads being replaced by clay substitutes of a very provincial type. The most beautiful and earliest sculptures at Lung Men are to be found in the so-called Lao Chun Tung cave which is decorated from ceiling to floor with a great number of niches of varying sizes in which Buddhas and Bodhisattvas are grouped, either alone or together with adoring bikshus or other attendants. The majority of these sculptures were executed in the 3rd or 4th decade of the 6th century, but only some of the minor reliefs remain still in a fair condition. Yet some characteristic positions may be observed, for instance the cross-ankled Bodhisattvas which represent Maitreya, the coming Buddha, while the Buddha Sakyamuni is seated with legs straight down. The stylization of the folds is carried out according to the same patterns as in the Yün Kang caves, but the stone is harder and the technique is superior to that of the earlier Yün Kang sculptures. Some of these Lung Men sculptures have certainly been among the finest works of their kind in China.

Another variation of the Northern Wei period style may be observed in the sculptures which decorate the temple caves at Shih Ku Ssu, near Kung Hsien in Honan. The work was here started about the same time as at Lung Men but the material is of a softer kind and the technique is not quite so fine. The large central Buddha at this place, which now stands up to its knees in mud, is a broad and block-like figure modelled in very large planes, with a remarkable cubistic tendency, which also may be observed in several minor

83

heads from the same place, now dispersed in various European and American museums.

Buddhist Stelae.—Besides these cave sculptures of the Northern Wei period should be mentioned a large number of Buddhist stelae, *i.e.*, slabs with figures in high relief, varying in size, some up to 12 ft. high, others quite small. Their decoration consists generally of a combination of niches with Buddhist figures and ornamental borders. On the back of these slabs are often found long rows of figures in flat relief representing the donors of the monuments. This form of stelae was probably developed from the earlier type of inscribed memorial stones, as used in China since the Han dynasty. It is worth noticing that we find at the top of the Buddhist stelae the same kind of winding and interlacing dragons as on the slabs which were raised at the tombs; their fierceness and energy of movement seem to reveal their derivation from the Sibero-Asiatic art, based on Scythian traditions which, indeed, had a great influence on the development of the ornamental style of this period.

Transition Period.—The stylistic ideals of the Northern Wei period retained their importance until the middle of the 6th century. About this time a new wave of artistic influence reached China from northern India. It may be quite clearly observed in some of the monuments which were executed during the Northern Ch'i and Northern Chou dynasties (550–581). The best cave sculptures from this time existed, at least a few years ago, at T'ien Lung Shan not far from Taiyuan-fu in Shansi. They were started in the Northern Ch'i period and continued, with some intermissions, during the Sui and T'ang dynasties.

Sculptures at T'ien Lung Shan.—The earliest sculptures at T'ien Lung Shan are to be found in the caves no. 2, 3, 10 and 16, probably executed between 560 and 580. The system of decoration in the first two caves consists of three large groups, one on each wall representing a seated Buddha accompanied by two Bodhisattvas and, in some instances, also by adoring monks and donors, characterized with striking realism. The main figures are executed in very high relief, giving almost the impression of free-standing forms, yet there is a certain flatness about them, noticeable particularly in the Bodhisattvas which stand turned half-way towards the central Buddha and whose garments—arranged in pleated folds—spread out in wing-like fashion at the sides. They are not very far removed stylistically from corresponding figures on later Wei monuments, though their heads are less archaic both in shape and expression.

The maturest examples of this transition period—possibly executed as late as 580—are to be found in the 16th cave at T'ien Lung Shan, where all the three walls are decorated with large groups of Buddhas with Bodhisattvas and other attendants placed on raised platforms, the fronts of which were decorated with representations of dwarf musicians. The central Buddhas are lifted into commanding positions on high pedestals in the form of lotus-flowers or altars; their shapes are full and well rounded, their heads comparatively small for the strong bodies. They are all seated in the same cross-legged posture, with bare feet and hands in the *abhaya* and *vara mudra* (gestures signifying "without fear" and "charity"). Their mantles, which are made of a very thin material, are draped only over the left shoulder, leaving the right bare, and the folds have practically no relief. Buddhas clothed in this fashion are very rare in Chinese art; they may occasionally be found in later T'ang sculpture but at this early period they are certainly surprises.

Foreign Influence.—The most probable explanation of this apparent anachronism in the style of the Buddhas seems to be that they were made from foreign models or by foreign artists while the less important side figures were carved in accordance with the indigenous principles of style. The figures are altogether Indian in spirit and form. It is hard to believe that Chinese artists would have been able to reproduce Mathura models so faithfully as we find them here, and it may at least be claimed that they have never done it better, either before or after. Possibly some Indian artist, well acquainted with the Mathura school, worked for some time at T'ien Lung Shan.

The same general types and principles of style which characterize the sculpture at T'ien Lung Shan may also be found in some isolated statues coming from this or a similar centre of sculptural activity. The most characteristic feature of all these figures is the cylindrical shape indicated in the legs and arms, as well as in the shape of the whole body, which often stands like a column on the lotus pedestal. Nothing can be more unlike the comparatively flat and angular shapes of the Northern Wei figures, which even when they have a more developed plastic form are linear rather than rounded.

Sculptures from Chihli Province.—Another provincial variation of the transition style may be seen in the sculptures from Chihli, the present metropolitan province, and particularly from Ting Chou where the supply of a beautiful white marble was abundant. The artistic quality of these sculptures is however quite uneven; the best of them stand on the highest level of Buddhist art in China, while the poorest are hardly more than ordinary artisans' work. Several figures of this group might be quoted as proofs of what already has been said about the plastic formula during this transition period. Their shapes are more or less cylindrical, their heads mostly large and heavy. One may notice a general tendency to make the figures narrower towards the feet and to broaden them towards the shoulders. The thin garments fit tightly over the bodies and their softly curving folds are indicated in quite low relief or simply with incised lines. Good examples of such statues are in the Metropolitan Museum in New York. If we place such a figure beside some characteristic example of the Northern Wei art, we may observe two opposite tendencies of style. In the earlier works the mantle folds and the contours are stretched and bent outward at the feet, the shoulders are narrow, the heads small; the rhythm is rising. In the later ones the rhythm is falling instead of rising, the tempo is slow, not without heaviness; there is no bending of the contours, they are falling almost straight down; the mantle hangs over the body and it is only towards the feet, where the circumference becomes smaller, that a certain acceleration of the tempo is noticeable.

The Sui Dynasty.—The sculptures of the Sui period (581–618) form, stylistically, a direct continuation of those of the transition period during the Northern Ch'i and Chow dynasties. Most of them are still examples of the transition style, but a few may well be classified among the most perfect works of religious statuary in China. Conditions were particularly favourable for the flourishing of religious art, and the formal development had not yet passed the point where it becomes an end in itself. Sui sculpture is, on the whole, quite restrained in its formal modes of expression and its interest in nature is slight, but it marks nevertheless a distinct progress in the representation of actual forms.

PHOTOGRAPHS, COPR. OSVALD SIREN

CHINESE SCULPTURES OF THE SUI PERIOD

1. Seated Buddha accompanied by two Bodhisattvas and two monks, Cave 16 at T'ien Lung Shan; Sui period, end of 6th century

2. Colossal Buddha in a cave at T'o Shan, Shantung; end of 6th century

3. Seated Buddha accompanied by a Bodhisattva, in a niche at Yun Men Shan, Shantung

4. Upper part of a Bodhisattva, Yun Men Shan, Shantung

BY COURTESY OF (3, 4, 5) THE MUSEUM OF THE UNIVERSITY OF PENNSYLVANIA; PHOTOGRAPHS (1, 2) COPR. OSVALD SIRÉN

CHINESE SCULPTURES OF THE SUI AND T'ANG PERIODS

1. Seated Buddha in Cave 8 at T'ien Lung Shan, Shan-si; Sui period (A.D. 581–618). 2. Seated Buddha in stone, T'ang period, A.D. 639. 3. Standing Bodhisattva, a stone statue of the T'ang period (A.D. 619– 906) showing Indian influence. 4. Statue of a priest of the T'ang period. 5. Standing Bodhisattva, stone statue of the T'ang period

T'ien Lung Statues.—Some good examples of the particular style of this period are to be found in the 8th grotto at T'ien Lung Shan which is in part preserved, although the soft material has been worn by time and water and some of the statues have been smashed and decapitated. Coming to these statues from a study of the sculptures in cave 16 at the same place (mentioned above), the first thing that strikes one is that they are not at all Indian in their general appearance. The Buddhas are seated in the same postures as the earlier ones but vested in the Chinese fashion with an upper garment

BY COURTESY OF THE METROPOLITAN MUSEUM OF ART
SCULPTURE OF THE TRANSITION PERIOD OF THE NORTHERN CH'I DYNASTY

covering both shoulders and with a less hieratic bearing of the stiff bodies. The shoulders are not so broad, the waist less curving, the forms are quite undifferentiated, but the heads have increased in size and have a more human air. They are certainly more Chinese, though in a provincial sense, and they are executed by inferior artists with little feeling for rhythmic lines and decorative beauty.

Most interesting are the two pairs of Dvarapalas (guardians) outside this cave. One pair is placed at the sides of the entrance, the other at each side of a tablet near by which still contains traces of an inscription of the Sui dynasty (said to have been dated 584). The attitudes of these guardian figures are highly dramatic, not to say strained. The movement of the arms is jerky, the turning of the heads, which are looking over the shoulder, is violent. The impetuosity is, indeed, much greater in these figures than in

87

the Dvarapala statues at the earlier caves, but whether they have gained in sculptural quality as much as in dramatic force is less certain.

Typical expressions of the plastic formula of the Sui period are also to be found among the sculptures from Chihli, easily recognizable by their material which is a micaceous white marble. Common to them all is the general shape which is no longer simply pillar-like or cylindrical, but ovoid. The contours are swelling out over the hips and elbows and gradually draw closer toward the feet and over the head. Thus a general formula is created, and it is often repeated on a smaller scale in the heads. The same rhythm is taken up by the folds which in some of the figures form a succession of curves over the front endowing them with a more complete harmony and repose than may be expressed by any other shape or formula known to us.

Shantung Sculptures.—The richest and most varied provincial group of sculptures from the Sui period is to be found in Shantung. The religious fervour and interest in establishing Buddhist temples and sanctuaries seem to have been particularly great in this part of the country and, to judge from the sculptures still preserved in several of these caves, there must have existed an important tradition of religious art which was now revived by various masters of no common ability. The earliest caves are at T'o Shan and Yü Han Shan; at the latter place many of the figures are dated in the 4th, 5th and 6th year of the K'ai Huang era (584–586), but unfortunately they are largely restored with plaster and crude colouring.

The great sculptures in the second and third cave at T'o Shan belong practically to the same stylistic group as those at Yü Han Shan. None of them bears a definite date, but, to judge from their style, they must have been executed about the same time as those mentioned above, *i.e.*, about the middle of the '80s. The typical Sui formula for single figures has been enlarged on an enormous scale, not without some loss of plastic beauty and intimacy. The great Buddhas which are seated in cross-legged position on a low pedestal impress us more as a kind of architectural monolith than as plastically conceived sculptures. It is only the folds of the hem, falling over the pedestal, that have a livelier rhythm; here one may observe the very characteristic meandering wave-line which returns in most sculptures of the Sui period, and some overlapping larger curves divided by the no less significant ear-like curves.

Passing from the cave sculptures at T'o Shan to those at Yün Men Shan, which is situated across the valley, means moving into a quite different artistic centre. There are only a few large statues at Yün Men Shan and some of these are in a deplorable state of preservation, but whatever remains here is of remarkably fine artistic quality. No doubt, these sculptures are a little later than those in the caves at T'o Shan, though hardly more than ten years; the dates that are found in some of the small niches at the side of the main figures range from 596 to 599. The figures are not placed in real caves but in flat niches, and may thus be seen to more advantage than most cave sculptures in their original position; the actual play of light and shade adds something to the plastic effect.

The Yün Men Shan Buddha.—The principal group consists of a seated Buddha accompanied by a standing Bodhisattva and another figure which may have been a Dvarapala (now practically destroyed). Close to this is another still flatter niche which never contained any central statue, only a large tablet, which is now removed, and on each side of it two monumental Bodhisattvas.

The great Buddha is seated on a dais in the traditional posture with the legs crossed in front, and entirely covered by the wide mantle. The bearing of the body is, however, quite different; instead of the old stiffness there is a certain ease in the posture, a repose without any strain. He seems to lean against the wall of the niche, moving the head slightly forward as if intent on looking at something in front. The upper garment which is fastened with a string knot on the left shoulder is draped in quite broad curves between the knees. The folds are not simply ornamental or expressive of a linear rhythm, but modelled with fine gradations of light and shade, sometimes even undercut. They have become means of primary importance for creating a sculptural effect. The head is treated in a new individual manner with broad effects of light and shade. The eyes are not closed or half closed, as in most of the earlier Buddhas, but wide open, and the eyelids are undercut, which adds greatly to the impression of life. The lips are also separated by a deep shadow, as if they were opening. The whole treatment is quite exceptional and bears witness to an impressionistic style; strictly speaking, it remains an isolated phenomenon in Chinese sculpture.

The T'ang Dynasty.—It would indeed be wrong to imagine that there is an absolute break or a deep-rooted difference between the sculpture of the Sui and that of the T'ang period; quite the opposite. T'ang sculpture is stylistically an immediate successor to the art of the Sui period. When we, for convenience sake, use the dynastic names and dates also in the domain of art, it should be clearly understood that they do not signify here the same kind of opposites or renewals as in the political history of the country. Artistic evolution in China is a slow and gradual process, which only to a minor degree is conditioned by the political events.

It may also be recalled that the T'ang dynasty reigned during a longer time than most of the preceding dynasties (619–960), and the plastic arts remained by no means the same during this whole period. The production of sculpture was very intense during the first 100 years of the period, but became soon afterwards comparatively weak and insignificant. In speaking about T'ang sculpture we mean the art up to about 725, which may be considered the most mature and perfect kind of Buddhist sculpture in China. It reflects something of the same creative and expansive power that we may observe in other manifestations of T'ang culture. Its best products are characterized by a plenitude, not to say magnificence, that can hardly be found in the art of earlier epochs. The forms grow full and strong, the decoration becomes rich and exuberant, gradually approaching what we should call baroque.

An important element in this evolution was due to the growing inter-communication between China and the western Asiatic centres of artistic activity, particularly the Sassanian empire. Many new impulses were derived thence and grafted upon the old stock of Chinese art, modifying it more and more in the direction of Western ideals of style. Generally speaking, it may be said that the current that came from India was of the greatest importance for the Buddhist sculpture, while the influences from Persian art are most plainly discernible in the ornamentation of minor objects in bronze and silver.

In order to illustrate these two main currents, as well as other important elements of style in the plastic art of the T'ang period, it would be well to take into consideration other artistic products besides stone sculptures, such as objects in bronze, silver, clay and lacquer, which reflect the aesthetic ideals of the time, but this would carry us beyond the limits of this short study. Buddhist statues still form the most important province within the plastic arts of the T'ang period, though it should also be remembered that some large tomb sculptures were executed at this time, including magnificent representations of lions and horses at the tombs of the great emperors, T'ai Tsung (d. 649) and Kao Tsung (d. 683).

The Shensi Sculptures.—The early T'ang sculptures from Shensi, which then was the metropolitan province, are made in a very hard, grey limestone or in a dense yellowish marble. The fine quality of the material demands a highly developed technique in order to yield good plastic effects and ornamental details, and it may well be admitted that as far as workmanship goes many of these statues stand on the highest level of Chinese sculpture, but the artistic quality is often less remarkable. The earliest dated statue of this period known to us is of the year 639; it represents a Buddha seated in cross-legged position on a high, draped pedestal placed in front of a background slab which is bordered like a nimbus with flame ornaments. The figure is draped in a mantle which covers both shoulders, arms and feet, leaving only a small part of the chest bare. The folds are highly conventionalized in the form of thin, rounded creases and arranged in long curves over the body, the legs and the upper part of the pedestal. The decorative effect is altogether more powerful and concentrated than in earlier statues of a similar kind, and the execution is masterly. Although made in stone, the statue gives the impression of a work cast in bronze, an impression which is supported by the dark metallic hue of the hard stone.

Influence of Indian Art.—Some Bodhisattva statues, of which two may be seen in the University Museum in Philadelphia, illustrate still better an increasing influence from Indian art not only by their costumes and decorative ornaments but also by their bearing and formal character. They stand no longer in stiff upright positions with the weight of the body evenly divided on both feet; the one leg is slightly curved and moved backward, the other serves as a support for the body which consequently is curving, a movement which is continued in the neck and in the more or less marked inclination of the head. The upper part of the body is bare, except for the jewelled necklaces and the narrow scarf draped over the shoulder; the chest is well developed and the waist rather narrow. The *dhoti*, which is tied with a sash round the hips, falls in a series of curving folds over each leg, and these

91

are indicated in the same fashion as the folds of the Buddha mentioned above. It should also be noticed that these figures do not wear a crown or a diadem on their heads like the early Bodhisattvas, but a high head-dress made up of thick winding plaits, a feature which also adds to their feminine aspect.

A kind of masculine pendant to these Bodhisattvas may be found among the statues of *bikshus* or monks, executed either as individual *post mortem* portraits or as parts of altar groups (examples of such statues may be seen in the museums in Philadelphia and Boston). They are less conventionalized, less dependent on foreign models and made in closer adherence to actual life. Their heads are portrait-like, their mantles arranged in a more or less natural fashion, thus, in many instances, approaching the small clay statuettes made for the tombs during the T'ang period as well as in earlier times. Some of these portrait statues may indeed be placed on a level with the best Roman sculptures. They are character studies, not so far individualized as Renaissance portraits, but very striking types, observed in actual life. It is also worth noticing how much freer and more plastic the draping of the mantle becomes in these statues. A figure such as the headless monk in the Boston Museum might have been made by a Roman artist.

Honan Sculptures.—When we pass from the metropolitan province of Shensi into the adjoining province of Honan we may at once observe that the general character of the sculptures becomes modified. The provincial schools and stylistic differentiations seem on the whole to have become more developed at this time than at earlier epochs; it is now easier to distinguish the provincial currents.

The statues made in Honan, and particularly at the great artistic centre of Lung Men, where the decoration of the caves was continued during the 7th century, are generally more elegant than those originating from Shensi, though not always executed in such perfect technique. Unfortunately, the great majority of the early T'ang sculptures at Lung Men are partly or wholly destroyed—the heads being dispersed all over the world—so that it is now next to impossible to find there complete and good specimens of moderate size; we find them more easily in museums and private collections.

One of the finest examples is a large Bodhisattva statue, originally at

Lung Men, but now in private hands in Peking. It may be taken as a representative of a large group of standing Bodhisattvas which all show the Indian influence grafted in Chinese types and shapes, a combination which in this particular instance has led to a perfectly harmonious result. The whole figure from the head-dress down to the feet is dominated by the softly gliding movement of the double S-curve (as in some Gothic madonnas) which would appear almost too accentuated, if it were not so perfectly balanced by the position of the arms. The contemporary Bodhisattvas from Shensi, represented in a similar position, appear quite stiff and hard beside this elegant and yet so dignified figure.

The Vairochana Buddha.—The colossal statues on the open terrace, which rises above the river at Lung Men, reflect in the most monumental form the religious pathos of the fully developed T'ang art. This is true particularly of the central figure, the great Vairochana Buddha; the side figures, two Bodhisattvas and two *bikshus*, are decidedly inferior. The hands are destroyed, the lower part of the figure has suffered a great deal, but I doubt whether it ever made a stronger impression than to-day when it rises high and free in the open air over the many surrounding niches in which time and human defilers have played havoc with most of the minor figures. The upper part of this giant is well preserved and more dominating now than ever. Long ages have softened the mantle folds and roughened the surface of the grey limestone which is cracking all over, but they have not spoilt the impression of the plastic form. It may still be felt under the thin garment: a very sensitively modelled form, not a dead mass, though unified in a monumental sense. According to the inscription on the plinth the statue was made about 672–675.

The great power which is here reflected in such a harmonious and well-balanced form finds further dramatic expression in the Dvarapalas which stand at the entrance to the so-called "lion cave." The bestial heads of the figures are amazing and terrible, and even the naked form is by no means represented from a naturalistic point of view, but as a symbol of strength and vigilance. Other Dvarapalas of the same date are sometimes represented in livelier postures, bending sideways or lifting one hand to deal a killing blow to any approaching enemy. The plastic effect is decidedly of a baroque nature, a tendency which is characteristic of the mature T'ang art whenever it leaves the well-trodden path of the traditional religious imagery and ventures on more naturalistic and dramatic representations.

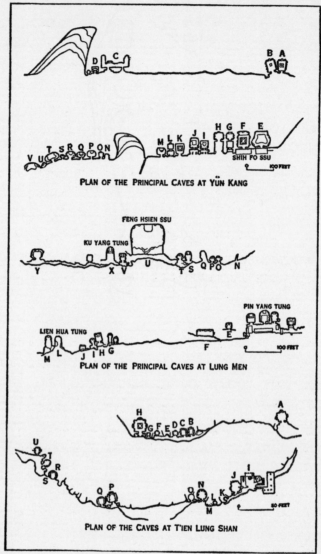

PLANS OF THE PRINCIPAL CAVES AT YÜN KANG, LUNG MEN AND T'IEN LUNG SHAN

Later T'ien Lung Shan Sculptures.—Another fairly homogeneous local group of T'ang sculpture may be observed in some of the later caves at T'ien Lung Shan where the artistic activity must have been kept up ever since the middle of the 6th century. During all these generations T'ien Lung Shan seems to have remained a special centre of Indian influence. Unfor-

94

PHOTOGRAPHS, COPR. OSVALD SIFÉN

CHINESE STATUES OF THE 7TH CENTURY A.D.

1. Vairochana Buddha, colossal statue at Lung-Men, Ho-nan, about 676
2. Standing Bodhisattva from Lung-Men, Ho-nan, T'ang period, 619–906

3. Seated Bodhisattva, T'ien Lung Shan, Shan-si, T'ang period
4. Seated Bodhisattva, T'ien Lung Shan, Shan-si, T'ang period

BY COURTESY OF (3) THE MUSEUM OF FINE ARTS, BOSTON; PHOTOGRAPHS, (2, 4, 5) COPR. OSVALD SIRÉN

CHINESE SCULPTURE: 7TH, 13TH, AND 14TH CENTURIES

1. Standing Bodhisattva, marble statue, end of T'ang period, now in a private collection in the United States

2. Kuanyin Bodhisattva, wooden statue, 13th century

3. Kuanyin Bodhisattva, wooden statue, 13th century

4. Virudhaka, one of the four Lokapâlas (guardians of the universe), relief on the Chü Yung Kuan Gate, Nank'ou, Chih-li, dated 1345

5. Girl playing the lute, marble statue, end of T'ang period

tunately, none of these sculptures is dated, and in some respects they fall outside the general stylistic current of T'ang art. Some of them show plastic motives which really did not come into vogue until some time after 700, but this may be due to the fact that they were made under foreign influence. The earliest among these sculptures are remarkably fresh and subtle while the later ones are comparatively heavy and commonplace works. The best specimens of the earlier types are to be seen in caves 6 and 14, while the later ones are found in caves 17, 19, 20 and 21.

The main group on the back wall of cave 6 consists of a Buddha seated cross-legged on a high pedestal accompanied by two side figures, which, however, are almost eaten away by time and running water, but there is a Bodhisattva on the side wall which can still be enjoyed. The figure is seated on a round lotus pedestal with the legs folded but not crossed. He leans toward the right side and turns slightly in the waist, a movement which is accentuated by the turning of the head in the same direction. The left hand is placed on the leg in front as if to give added support to the body and make the free attitude still more restful. The body is entirely bare, except for a jewelled necklace and the narrow scarf which is draped in a diagonal curve from the right shoulder. The ease of the posture in conjunction with the sensitive modelling of the youthful body endow this figure with a sensual charm which is very seldom found in Chinese statues. It would hold its place beside the most exquisite French sculptures of the 18th century and yet it impresses us just as much by its dignity and composure.

A similar artistic conception is expressed in a still ampler form in a Bodhisattva statue in cave 16. The posture of the figure is a kind of *lalitasana* (position of ease). It is seated with the one leg pendant, the other bent crosswise over the seat, but the foot is not placed on the opposite leg. The left elbow is practically touching the knee, as if to support the body which leans over toward the side, turning at the same time slightly in the waist. The movement of the head follows in the opposite direction, producing thus a contraposto effect which, although not very pronounced, serves to bring out the beauty of the ripe body and the supple limbs. It may not have quite the charm of the one noticed above, but it shows an astonishingly free treatment of the mantle, the material being a kind of *draperie mouillée*.

95

None of the other caves at T'ien Lung Shan contains statues of a corresponding importance, although there are some which reveal the strong Indian influence both in their general shapes and in the treatment of their garments. The heads, which in late years have been knocked off and spread all over the Western world, are sometimes beautiful, though less expressive than the best heads from Lung Men or earlier centres of Buddhist sculpture in China.

Changes in Style.—Similar tendencies toward a freer plastic style may also be observed in contemporary sculptures from Shensi and Chihli. Among them may be seen beautiful Bodhisattvas which not only bend in the waist but also turn on the hips, making thus quite complicated movements, which tend to bring out the beauty and significance of their corporeal form. By these freer postures their likeness to ordinary human beings becomes more striking. They sometimes remind one of the complaint of the philosopher from the end of the T'ang period who said that the artists were losing their reverent attitude toward the religious motives and were representing the Bodhisattvas in the shape of court ladies.

The difference between the religious and the secular motives seems, as a matter of fact, to become less and less important, and one meets with quite realistic *genre* figures not only in clay but also executed on a large scale in stone, very much according to the same formula as the Bodhisattvas. As a good example of this class of work may be mentioned a statue of a young lady (in the Academy of Art in Tokyo) who sits on a bank with crossed legs playing a lute, while a dog and a cat are frolicking at her feet, a statue without any religious pretext, with the same amount of free and elegant realism as we know from the tomb statuettes in clay and from some T'ang paintings. Works of this kind indicate that the sculptors no longer remained satisfied with the purely religious inspiration but turned their attention towards nature and human life. If the evolution had continued along these lines, the plastic arts in China might have become just as expressive and varied in their interpretations of purely artistic problems as Renaissance sculpture in Europe, but the creative power turned more and more from sculpture to painting.

Quite interesting as examples of the new tendencies of style are certain statues made at Ting Chou in Chihli, a centre of sculptural activity which, as

96

we have seen, was important ever since the Northern Wei period. The best of these are surprisingly free and illustrate a new interest in movement and in the full development of the human figure. Among them may be mentioned a large statue of a headless Bodhisattva in the collection of Mrs. J. D. Rockefeller Jr. in New York, which is represented in a forward stride. The figure is composed in a similar way to some early Renaissance statues represented in a walking posture, *e.g.*, St. John the Baptist—and shows the same shortcomings in the stiff limbs and the stilted rhythm, but also the same endeavour to treat the plastic form in the full round.

There are many other statues illustrating this tendency. The most original is perhaps a bare-headed monk who stands turned sideways with hands folded before the chest and head thrown back, looking almost straight upwards (in the collection of General Munthe, Peking). The movement expresses an intense religious devotion, not in the usual restrained and well-balanced form but with the flow of human feeling which leads our thoughts away from the Orient towards the most emotional religious art of Europe, such as we know it from the late Gothic and Baroque periods. The impressionistic treatment of the soft and heavy mantle points in the same direction.

The Post-T'ang Periods.—The production of religious sculpture decreases more and more towards the end of the T'ang period. Very few dated specimens are known from the 9th century, while those from the 8th are quite numerous. During the following periods of the Five Dynasties and the Northern Sung the creative energy of the nation, which in former times, particularly when religious devotion ran high, had been largely directed to the production of sculpture, turned to painting, which now definitely took the lead among the fine arts in China. The change in the relative importance of sculpture and painting is also illustrated by the fact that sculpture responded more and more to the influence of painting, an influence which became evident not only in the new impressionistic tendencies of style but also by the fact that other materials than stone and bronze came into vogue, particularly wood, clay, iron and lacquer-work, and these were usually treated with colour. Many of the new compositions introduced about this time were derived from contemporary paintings. It is true for instance of the very popular Kuanyin Bodhisattvas in the *maharajalila* (posture of royal ease) executed in stone, clay and wood, and it may also be observed in the combination of the figures with backgrounds treated like rocky landscapes or some kind of scenery with trees, buildings, animals and small human beings.

This more or less pictorial kind of sculpture spread all over northern China udring the 12th and 13th centuries, when Buddhist art enjoyed a short period of reflorescence, and wooden sculpture particularly reached a high degree of perfection. A great number of wooden statues have in later years been brought from China to various Western collections, *e.g.*, the museums in Philadelphia, Chicago and Toronto which alone contain more such statues than can be mentioned here. The majority of these represent either standing Bodhisattvas in long garments which often take on a fluttering movement toward the feet, or Kuanyins on rocky seats in the *maharajalila* posture. One of the standing figures in Toronto is said to have been dated by a tablet inserted in the figure in the year 1106, while one of the seated Kuanyins, lately belonging to the Ton Ying Company in New York, carries an inscription with the date 1168. Similar ones are to be found in the British Museum, in the museums in Boston and Chicago, in the Musée Guimet and Collection Jean Sauphar in Paris, etc.

It is during this period that Kuanyin, the Bodhisattva of Mercy, definitely changes into a feminine being usually represented in a free and elegant form, whether she be seated on a rock by the water in the *maharajalila* posture, as in so many of these wooden figures, or is standing, bending forward as if lending a listening ear to the invocations of her adorers. The womanly beauty is much more accentuated in these figures than any bodhisattvic qualities. The form has lost all its abstract serenity and become fluttering and emotional, but it is sometimes highly decorative in a new and more limited sense. Many of these figures seem to have been conceived not for a moral purpose, like the old Buddhas and Bodhisattvas, but simply to please the eye and the sentimental longings of the worshippers. Besides these wooden sculptures there are a good many made in stone, particularly series of Arhats, who are usually represented in series of 16 or 18, according to definite types and with more realistic than artistic expression. Interesting series of such Arhats executed in stone may be seen at the Yen Sha Tung and Ling Yen Ssu caves near Hangchow, as well as in the museum at Toronto. They are very uneven in quality and, on the whole, more interesting from an historical than from an artistic point of view.

CHINESE SCULPTURE

Yüan Dynasty.—After the establishment of the Yüan dynasty (1280–1367) the position of the fine arts in China, including sculpture, changed considerably. The Mongols brought no new positive inspiration, on the contrary they destroyed more than they built up, except perhaps in the art of war. Art was useful to them only in so far as it could support and glorify the temporal power of the emperor and his generals. The religious attitude of the Yüan emperors was on the whole tolerant, but officialdom was then thoroughly Confucian and the Buddhists were pushed into the background. Taoism seems now to have held its place by the side of Buddhism. The cave sculptures at Hao Tien Kuan, south of T'aiyüan-fu in Shansi, executed at the end of the 13th century, are in this respect very interesting. Some of the compositions illustrating scenes from the life of the Taoist philosopher Pi Yün Ssu, besides a great number of other Immortals, reveal an evident interest in nature as, for instance, the old man on his deathbed; he is represented lying soundly asleep on the Chinese "kang" clad in a long garment. The most successful portions in these grottos are, however, the purely decorative compositions, the low reliefs on the walls representing clouds and phoenixes, and the two guardians at the sides of one of the entrances whose fluttering draperies are arranged in ornamental curves. All these decorative designs are characterized by a buoyancy and a vigour which are hardly to be found in Chinese sculpture of the immediately preceding period. The motives are used for decoration rather than for the expression of purely plastic ideas. The pictorial tendency which characterizes the sculptures of the preceding period is still existent, although it has become coarser and of a more superficial kind. The same stylistic tendencies are also quite noticeable in a number of other sculptures of the same period, such as the four *Lokapalas* (guardians of the world) on the Chü Yung Kuan gate at Nank'ou, executed in 1345, and the Buddhist figures in a niche at Lung Tung Ssu near Tsinan-fu in Shantung, executed in 1318, not to speak of minor detached statues, dated at the beginning of the 14th century.

Ming Period.—When we enter into the Ming period (1368–1643) the dramatic power of expression seems to dry up more and more and the general artistic level is certainly not raised, although the production of Buddhist sculptures goes on with increasing abundance. Among the most popular and common creations of this time may be mentioned, for instance, series of Arhats in iron (good examples of such series are in the museums at Toronto and Gothenburg) which, however, seldom rise above the level of ordinary mass products made according to standard models. Similar motives are also treated in wood and lacquer, sometimes with good decorative effect, though with no more individual characterization. The sculpture of the Ming period is generally at its best when it takes up purely realistic motives instead of the traditional hieratic figures. It may thus become quite enjoyable in minor representations of mourners, musicians or similar *genre*-like motives, presented without any tendency to archaic restraint which otherwise is so apparent in the plastic arts of the Ming.

Summary.—Trying to sum up the general course of development of Chinese sculpture from the 10th to the 15th century in a few words, we have to remember first the comparatively low level of religious sculpture towards the end of the Sung dynasty, particularly after the capital was moved from Kaifêng to Hangchow; secondly, the re-awakening of religious imagery in the northern provinces after the Tartar dynasties had got a firm hold on this part of the country (a flourishing sculptural activity, particularly in wood, developed there in the provinces of Chihli and Shansi); and thirdly, that with the Yüan dynasty a new foreign element appears which perhaps may be called Mongolian and which expresses itself on the one hand in a somewhat dry realism and on the other hand in a whirling linear ornamentation. The religious figures have still some life and expression of their own, though no real spirituality. This development was no longer continued during the Ming period. Whatever creative power may have been left did not turn towards the production of religious sculpture. It is true that a lot of statues, or rather statuettes, in bronze, wood, porcelain and ivory were produced but no great religious works, whether in stone or other materials. The Ming sculptors have given their best in the field of decorative art such as columns, balustrades, and other architectural details, but they created no new types of plastic works, whether religious or secular. They sought their inspiration much more in the imitation of earlier models than in any fresh efforts in the field of sculpture.

SCREEN

Because of their fragile nature, no screens of great antiquity have survived, but references to them are not wanting in ancient literature. Folding screens were known in China as early as the 2nd century B.C., at which period glass or mica panellings for them are noted as of much value, their transparent nature affording both enjoyment of an outdoor view and shelter from the elements. Then, in the century preceding the Christian era, screens carved and inlaid with jade and other precious materials seem to have been produced. Already in this early period the art of painting screens was practised, for it is recorded that "Figures of Exemplary Women," illustrating the good or evil effects from right or wrong-doing were depicted on a screen. The Chinese artist Ts'ao Pu-hsing (3rd century) having dropped ink upon a screen while painting, turned it into a fly which Sun Ch'üan (A.D. 181–252) tried to brush away. Shih Hu (3rd century) made a folding screen covered with silk and painted with hermits, birds and animals, to which he added a long inscription. Chang Mo (4th century) depicted on screens the Buddhist saint, Vimalakirti, and a scene entitled "Beating Newly-woven Silk." In passing, mention may be made of a 14-fold screen in the scroll attributed to Ku K'ai-chih (4th century), owned by the British Museum, confirming the accuracy of contemporary accounts that screens consisted of numerous leaves, sometimes as many as 40. In the 5th century, Lu T'an-wei painted a lion and Fang Huai-chên the "Paragons of Filial Piety." Landscapes were not unknown in these early centuries as themes for screens, for they are referred to in old poems and other writings. Screens of tapestry, of embroidery, of crystal and of lacquer are also recorded in contemporary litera-

101

ture. Moreover, fine calligraphy inscribing moral teachings or auspicious sentiments was executed on screens from the 5th century, if not earlier. It is said that Fang Hsüang-ling (A.D. 578–648) collected precepts from all sources and inscribed them on screens which he distributed among his children as reminders of proper conduct.

The T'ang Period.—In the luxurious days of the T'ang dynasty (618–906), screens were in constant demand to adorn palaces and mansions. Those which were bedecked with gold and silver, pearl and tortoise shell, or those of fine textiles woven or dyed, bearing characteristic patterns, must have imparted great splendour to the habitations of rulers and princes. Horses sent from foreign tribes to the imperial stables furnished themes for screens, and a fabulous animal called *mo* which is supposed to eat bad dreams was deemed an appropriate subject for boudoir screens. Then, too, such noted painters as Pien Luan (who treated flowers and birds), Chang Tsao (pines and rocks), and Chou Fang (court beauties), and such accomplished calligraphers as Li Yang-ping and Chang Hsü all decorated screens. Some emperors had about them screens setting forth worthy and moral deeds performed by men of the past, in order that they themselves, as well as their subjects, might derive benefit from these constant reminders.

But for actual examples of T'ang art on screens we have to turn to Japan where, in the Imperial repository called the Shōsōin, at Nara, are still preserved relics of the art of that golden epoch. This treasure-house contains principally the personal belongings of the Emperor Shōmu, which were given to the Great Buddha of the Tōdaiji by the Empress Kōmyō, in 756. The list of donations mentions, among other objects, 100 screens, to which several more were added, at three different times, between the years 756 and 758. Among this large number of screens were examples of Chinese, Korean or Japanese origin which included paintings of landscapes, palaces, figures and flowers; others of batik and of block-resist dyeing, figuring birds, animals and flowers; and, in addition, some screens on which Chinese ideographs formed the chief decoration. Of these 100 odd screens but few remain at present, in whole or in part, among them no painted screens. Nevertheless, the pictorial accomplishments of the 8th century may still be seen in this collection in a six-fold screen, in each leaf of which is shown a figure of a woman standing under a tree. The subject was originally worked in birds' feathers

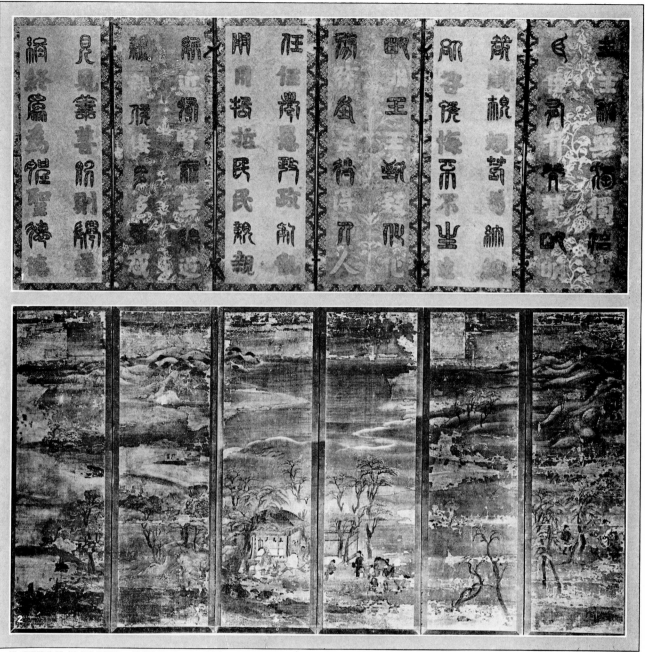

BY COURTESY OF (1) THE DIRECTOR OF THE IMPERIAL HOUSEHOLD MUSEUM, JAPAN, (2) (SHIMBI SHOIN, LTD.) FROM "THE MASTERPIECES SELECTED FROM THE FINE ARTS OF THE FAR EAST"

A CHINESE AND A JAPANESE SCREEN IN THE T'ANG STYLE

1. Chinese screen of the eighth century painted with a precept in 43 ideographs, each character written both in the "seal" and in the "running" style. The panels, which are joined with cords, are coloured alternately red and green, with designs of clouds and other conventionalized forms in white. From the Imperial Collection in the Shosoin, Nara, Japan

2. Japanese landscape screen of the 11th century, probably after a T'ang original, depicts the visitation of a noble and his servants to a hermit's house set in a landscape of trees, hills and water. The over refinement of the drawings is characteristic of the "Japanese picture" style of the Fujiwara period (900–1189). From the Buddhist monastery of Toji at Kyoto

EARLY POTTERY FROM THE PROVINCE OF KANSU, NORTH CHINA

Illustrations of 12 pottery vessels of a very early period (probably 3000 B.C.) discovered in the province of Kansu, North China, by J. G. Andersson, while excavating old sites. The pottery is generally red with black ornaments, clearly of the same family of design as the aeneolithic pottery found on many sites in the Near East

which have disappeared, leaving only the preliminary drawings. Despite the sketchy nature of the drawings of the figures, trees and rocks, one may detect the mature brush-strokes, the importance of which is so much emphasized in the art of painting in the Far East. The screen is probably Japanese, yet its conception and execution are based upon contemporary Chinese patterns. There are also two six-fold screens in this imperial collection, the chief decorative features of which are Chinese inscriptions in large characters. One contains a precept for a ruler, consisting of 48 Chinese ideographs, each written twice, once in the *chuan* ("seal") style and once in the *hsing* ("running") style. The backgrounds are of silk dyed in green and red—alternating in the six panels—bearing designs of conventionalized clouds, birds, animals, trees, plants and rocks, all in white reserve. The screen is very likely Chinese, one of many gifts sent to the Japanese court from China, although it is said that at one time there was discovered upon it a Japanese date corresponding to the year 751—a fact lacking substantiation. In the Orient, to use writing on a large scale for a decorative scheme is no less frequent than to employ a picture for the purpose. Indeed, good calligraphy (*q.v.*) is considered an art of as great importance as good painting, both being the result of brush-work and both presenting images of mental conception.

An example of the pictorial art of the T'ang as reflected in the art of Japan may be seen in a screen preserved in the Buddhist monastery of Tōji in Kyoto. It treats a landscape in polychrome: among trees surrounded by hills and water is a rustic abode within which sits a hermit who is being visited by nobles with their servants. According to an old tradition, the screen was one of the treasures brought back by Kōbō Daishi from China in 806. However, some authorities now regard the painting as a Japanese production of the 11th century, based upon a T'ang original. For, despite its Chinese design, in it are discernible certain technical peculiarities of the early Yamato-é (literally "Japanese picture") style which was developed during the Fujiwara period (900–1189) and is characterized by over-refinement of drawings. Such a landscape screen was used in the baptismal rituals of esoteric Buddhism which required a pictorial representation of a mountain scene in lieu of the natural setting in which the religious service took place in old India. No screens of a secular nature dating from the Fujiwara period are now extant, but literary sources disclose the thousands of screens painted for the use of the Japanese court and for the mansions of nobles. As in the preceding epoch, the need for screens was pressing, because of the peculiar style of the architecture of those days—wide openings on the sides of a building which were closed by wooden doors at night but which during the day needed screening arrangements. Regular and occasional State functions also required special screens appropriate to the events. That a large number of screens was produced may be gathered from the record that Yoshichika (11th century) painted 200 screens on Lord Yoshimichi's order. A story is told about Hirotaka (10th century) who delineated a scene of hell containing a demon who proved so lifelike as to convince the artist that the call to the unknown region was immediate. The subjects, some Chinese and some Japanese, mentioned in this period are varied and numerous: landscapes of the four seasons, monthly observances, trees and plants, falconry, picnics, polo-playing, the paragons of noble deeds, the descent of the Amitābha, the ten Buddhist regions, etc. In Japan, during the Kamakura period (1190–1336), in making screens they followed the preceding Fujiwara in the main, both pictorially and technically.

The Sung Period.—In China itself in the Sung period (960–1279), the practice among prominent masters of painting and inscribing screens was not abandoned. On the contrary, painters like Tuan Yüan, Yen Hsiao, Wên T'ung and Hsü Tao-ning are known to have thus expressed their art; and noted calligraphers applied their brushes after the time-honoured custom. The most significant branch of the art of the Sung period was the so-called Idealistic school of painting which was closely followed by the artists of the Yüan (1280–1367) and Ming (1365–1643) dynasties. Painters of this school attempted to express in their works certain noble thoughts and ideals. A landscape-painting, for example, was an essay which suggested the sublimity of nature and invited the beholder to identify himself with it. The inherent love of nature of the orientals, coupled with the teaching of *Ch'an* (in Japanese, *Zen*), produced artists who showed remarkable aptitude for depicting natural phenomena. *Ch'an* means "abstract meditation," the chief aim of its followers being to seek to separate the real from the unreal by divesting themselves of earthly thoughts and desires and by communing directly with nature. Inspired by this teaching, the artists developed marked individuality and their paintings were characterized by purity and suggestiveness. For their themes, the painters of the Idealistic school chose, besides landscapes, birds, animals and even withered trees and rocks, all of which ordinarily were treated in monochrome with China ink. Unfortunately there exists no example of the typical art of the Sung as applied on screens, nor are there any screens dating from the subsequent Yüan and Ming dynasties, in both of which it is recorded that painted and inscribed screens were produced. It is possible, however, that some of the paintings coming from these periods, now mounted as single hangings, were once panels of folding screens.

The Ashikaga Period.—Again turning to Japan, one can see an echo of the Chinese art of these three dynasties in paintings by Japanese artists of the Ashikaga period (1337–1573). Sōtan, Nōami, Sesshū, Masanobu and Motonobu are outstanding figures who painted in ink on screens after the Chinese idealists. A screen by Sōtan, who died in 1464, may be taken as a typical specimen of this style. The vigour of the brush, the subtle quality of the ink, the well-carried-out atmospheric perspective—all tell of the master hand which portrays the spirit of majestic nature. This screen is one of a pair which together show landscapes of the four seasons treated as one composition but nevertheless forming one composite whole. Besides the "Twelve Monthly Observances" and "Landscapes of the Four Seasons," such themes as "Flowers of the Four Seasons," "Farmers of the Four Seasons," "Lives of the 24 Paragons of Filial Piety," the "Eight Taoist Immortals," etc., frequently occur as single designs. The Idealistic school of painting was carried through the next period, the Momoyama (1574–1602), by artists of the Kano, the Unkoku and the Soga schools. In the screen by Tōhaku (1539–1610) we see a remarkable monochrome; the varied shades of China ink being so used as to suggest the presence of colours, yet with no disturbing element of pigments and no sense of monotony.

A new type of screen introduced some time in the 14th century from Korea contributed much toward revolutionizing the general scheme of composition. Heretofore, a folding screen had consisted of a group of separate panels, each with brocaded borders, tied together by means of cords passing through holes pierced at the vertical edges of the panels. In the Korean type the leaves were joined by paper hinges which were built into the body of the screen before the silk or paper for painting was pasted, a brocade border extending over the composite whole. Whereas in the former style the continuance of the design was interfered with by the frame and the brocade borders of each panel, in the latter style the tightly joined leaves made one surface for painting a picture.

Screens characteristic of the Momoyama period, the inherent love of the Japanese for simplicity notwithstanding, are more decorative in type, with backgrounds of gold leaf upon which appear bold designs in solid pigments on a massive scale. Eitoku (1545–90), who was the chief exponent of the style, is said to have supplied 100 pairs of screens for the Momoyama palace of the Taikō. He painted in two styles, ink and polychrome; the polychrome screens are very effective; for example, one of a pair in which are shown foreigners bringing tribute to the Chinese emperor, Tai-tsung, of the T'ang dynasty; the subject—"Barbarians Presenting Tribute"—being symbolic of the peace and prosperity of the country. The popular pictorial motives on screens at this time were "The Dragon and the Tiger," "Lions," "Old Pine Trees" (respectively symbolizing the conflict between spirit and matter, nobility and power, longevity and fidelity).

The Tokugawa Period.—In Japan during the Tokugawa period (1603–1868), a new movement in decorative painting was developed by Sōtatsu (1576–1643) who preserved the vigorous and broad brush-work practised by the masters in monochrome, but in place of ink used pigments on a gold ground. Even as he adopted the colouring of the old Yamato-é, so he took many themes from old sources, such as the romances of Genji and Isé, the wars of the Hogen and Heiji Eras, the wind and thunder gods. He was also a genius in the impressionistic treatment of flowers and waterscapes on screens. Following Sōtatsu's style, Kōrin (1658–1716) further enlarged upon decorativeness by introducing more brilliant colours and more daring composition. In the twofold screen depicting violent waves is apparent this artist's largeness of conception and power of technique. In the Tokugawa days, artists in all schools—the Kano, the Tosa, the Genre, the Literary, the Realistic—exerted their artistic efforts on screens. In principle, the pictorial scheme for screens by these painters of varied styles had changed little from that of the preceding Ashikaga and Momoyama periods and it is still continued to-day. A bold design is treated in dissymmetry, yet is well balanced and effective; at the same time it bears a certain moral,

(TOP) BY COURTESY OF PIERRE CARTIER. (BOTTOM) FROM A PRIVATE COLLECTION IN THE UNITED STATES

CHINESE IMPERIAL PALACE SCREENS

Above: Carved and lacquered wooden screen, dated 1673, showing the Imperial Palace ground during a ceremony at which the Emperor Kanghsi is officiating

Below: Porcelain screen of the Ch'ien-Lung period (1736–95). The central panel is painted in famille verte, and the upper and lower in famille rose

FROM THE WALTER ROSEN COLLECTION

CHINESE IMPERIAL JADE SCREEN OF THE CH'IEN–LUNG PERIOD (1736–95 A.D.)

This Chinese imperial screen is composed of a gilt teakwood frame of eight folds set with spinach-green jade panels, carved on one side with landscape designs and on the other with flowers. The photograph was taken with a light arranged behind the screen to bring out the translucent quality of the jade

historical, legendary or auspicious significance. The subjects treated were many and varied, including those which have already been referred to and also such themes as the "Eight Views of Hsiao Hsing," the "Ten Snow-Incidents," the "A-fang Pleasance," the "Four Gray-beards of the Shan Mountain," the "Seven Sages of the Bamboo Grove," the "Four Accomplishments," "Floating Fans," "Phoenixes," etc. Generally Japanese screens are six-fold, about 6 ft. in height and 12 ft. in width when stretched, and they are usually executed in pairs. Among the smaller type we may count "pillow" screens with brightly coloured pictures, which are placed about beds, and low, two-fold screens with simple decoration, or none at all, which are used in connection with the tea-ceremony (q.v.).

The Ch'ing Dynasty.—During the Ch'ing dynasty (1644–1911) in China, painting on screens was practised, as indicated by the presence of occasional examples dating from the last few centuries. But it is in screens of applied art that the period excels. It has already been said that the application of the minor arts to screens began in ancient China. The best known among such screens of recent centuries are the so-called "Coromandel screens" which are made of wooden panels finished with a coat of lacquer, through which designs—landscapes, figures, flowers, auspicious emblems, etc.—are incised and filled with various thick, opaque water-colours; a technique known from the Ming dynasty. A large portion, however, of the existing specimens are of the 17th to 19th centuries. "Coromandel" has no bearing upon their provenance, but indicates that these screens of Chinese origin were shipped to European countries from the coast of Coromandel. Other screens in the category of lacquer are those with lacquered panels (sometimes coated with white oil paint) decorated in gold lacquer; and those of red carved lacquer. Screens of carved teakwood construction set with jade and porcelain plaques, or panelled with silks, tapestries or embroideries, are occasionally seen.

Furniture.—As an article of furniture, the screen is an ornamental frame, usually of wood, but sometimes of metal, for protection from observation, draught or the heat of a fire. Screens are made of all shapes and sizes, and may consist of leather, paper or textile materials fastened to the framework; they may have several leaves or only one—thus a fourfold screen has four leaves. Fire screens are usually small, with a single leaf—indeed in the

Georgian period of English furniture they often took the form of a circular, oval, heart-shaped or oblong piece of framed embroidery fixed to a wooden pole or upright, upon which they could be raised or lowered. This variety, which was called a pole-screen, was more effective as an ornament than as a protection. The handscreen was light and portable, as the name implies. At the present time fire screens are often of glass set in metal frames. The larger type of screen, with several leaves, is of uncertain origin, but probably first came into use towards the end of the 16th century. The earlier examples were of stamped or painted Spanish leather or of some rich stuff such as tapestry; at a later date lacquer was extensively used. They were tall enough to conceal the person sitting behind them, and were frequently exceedingly handsome and stately.

POTTERY AND PORCELAIN

THE SUPREME excellence of Chinese pottery in mediaeval and later times gives an unusual zest to the enquiry into the first phases of Chinese ceramic history; and we welcome the new light recently shed on them by Prof. J. G. Andersson's discoveries in Honan and Kansu which reveal the existence of two distinct kinds of pottery in pre-dynastic times. The Andersson finds have been provisionally divided into six periods; and the earliest and, oddly enough, the most artistic of his pottery can hardly be later in time than 3000 B.C. It consists both of funerary wares and pottery for general use, made by hand (helped perhaps by a slow wheel) of finely levigated, thin and strongly baked buff and red clays, shaped in pleasing, and often quite imposing, forms and decorated with elegant painted designs in red, black, purple and white clays which have been submitted to the fire of the kiln. This painted ware, which is superior in technique to any of the pre-Han pottery of dynastic times so far known, has interesting, if superficial, resemblances to the painted pottery found at Anau, Susa and other western Asiatic sites of late neolithic date.

Alongside this painted ware Andersson found another type of pottery, a coarser, grey earthenware made without the wheel and often impressed on the exterior with markings which suggest that the wet clay had been wrapped in matting or some coarse textile. This mat-marked pottery evidently had a long life, for it was still made in Chou and Han times.

The next important discovery belongs to the Yin dynasty (1401–1122 B.C.). On the site of the Yin tombs near An-yang in Honan were found pieces of a white pottery, and of carved ivory and bone. The pottery, doubtless made of kaolinic earth, has been carved like the ivory and bone with the conventional designs and angular fret patterns which are usually associated with pre-Han bronzes. Complete vessels of this kind of carved white ware must have had a striking appearance, if indeed the fragments ever formed part of pottery vessels and were not, as has been suggested, moulds for the use of the bronze maker.

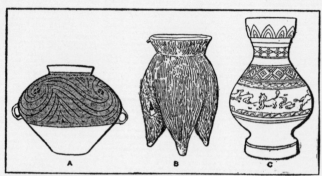

(A AND B) FROM ANDREWS, "MEMOIRS OF THE GEOLOGICAL SURVEY OF CHINA" (C) BY COURTESY OF THE BRITISH MUSEUM

EARLY CHINESE POTTERY; (A) NEOLITHIC POTTERY FROM KANSU, (B) NEOLITHIC MAT-MARKED POTTERY FROM HONAN, (C) PAINTED POTTERY OF THE 4TH CENTURY B.C.

For the rest all the pre-Han pottery which we know is funeral ware of a rough and not very interesting type, and generally following the forms of the more precious bronze vessels for which it was doubtless a substitute. It is frequently "mat-marked," and much of it is roughly coloured with unfired pigments.

The Han Dynasty (206 B.C.–A.D. 220).—The Han pottery, though our knowledge of it is still confined to the funeral wares recovered from tombs, shows a considerable advance in ceramic technique. Many of the Han vessels, such as the wine vases, are of elegant form, and they are ornamented with artistic designs in a variety of ways, by painting with unfired pigments, by stamping, by the application of reliefs which have been separately formed in moulds, and by incising. Glaze is now used, apparently for the first time, a transparent lead glaze of yellowish tone which is coloured green with copper oxide and variegated by the use of liquid clays or slips of different colours. The underlying body of the glazed ware is usually red and this showing through the transparent glaze gives a brown or reddish brown surface, when the glaze has not been coloured green by the use of copper.

BY COURTESY OF (2, 6, 7, 9) THE ART INSTITUTE OF CHICAGO, (4) THE MUSEUM OF FINE ARTS, BOSTON, (8) OTTO FUKUSHIMA; FROM (1, 3) THE GEORGE EUMORFOPOULOS COLLECTION, (5) THE WARREN E. COX COLLECTION

CHINESE MORTUARY POTTERY, HAN DYNASTY (206 B.C. TO A.D. 220)

1. Covered bowl in imitation of bronze form. 2. Ladle. 3. Hill jar decorated in relief with mythological animals, ring handles, and with usual mountain cover surrounded by waves. 4. Barnyard with goats, and man playing piccolo just in front of the little gable. 5, Example of the rare octagonal base type of wine jar with unusual strength. 6. Hill censer modelled in low relief. 7. Pavilion. Height 20¼ inches. 8. Pottery dog vigorously modelled. 9. Well-head. Height 14¾ inches

BY COURTESY OF (5, 6) YAMANAKA AND COMPANY, (4) THE ART INSTITUTE OF CHICAGO; FROM (1, 3) THE GEORGE EUMORFOPOULOS COLLECTION, (2) THE WARREN E. COX COLLECTION

PRE-T'ANG POTTERIES

1. Figure with long robe folded in front, spreading below to form a hollow base; holes for hands. Grey pottery with dressing of white slip and remains of pigment; hair painted black. Ht. 28.5''. Six dynasties (A.D. 220—618).
2. Mythological animal resembling prehistoric triceratops, possibly suggested by discoveries of fossils in the Mongolian desert. 3. Figure of a lady, with double peaked cap, holding a lotus, with bird-shaped flower. Hard grey pottery, wash of white slip, pigmentation in red and black. Ht. 30.75''. Companion figure, with crown-like head-dress. Ht. 30.75''. Northern Wei (A.D. 386—435). 4. House with sliding doors. 5 and 6. Men with Bactrian horse and camel, animals introduced into China by the Mongols

Probably this lead glaze was introduced from western Asia, where it was in use in late Roman times; for the Chinese were in touch with the Roman empire in the Han dynasty.

Many of the pottery objects recovered from Han tombs are of deep archaeological interest, for they include, besides the household and ritual vessels, models of the buildings, implements, live-stock and even human beings, which had belonged to the household of the deceased. Further it is noteworthy that the potters who supplied this funeral furniture evinced much artistic skill in the way in which they conventionalized their models. Thus the granary tower and the well-head are transformed into picturesque objects and even the model of the kitchen stove is not devoid of ornamental qualities.

Han to T'ang (A.D. 220–618).—To the interval between Han and T'ang belongs a considerable group of figures and other beings and animals are in many ways the most attractive of all the Chinese grave goods. Some of them are little later in date than the Han dynasty; but they evidently range over a long period, for whole sets of figurines of this class in the Toronto Museum are known to have been found in tombs of the Liang dynasty (A.D. 502–557). There are, besides, wine jars, vases, incense burners and toilet boxes of the 3rd and 4th centuries which are finely painted in unfired pigments with a style and execution not unworthy of the paintings on silk. The Han lead glaze continued in use, and it is by no means easy to differentiate the glazed pottery of the Han and of the immediately succeeding periods. There are, however, certain flask-shaped bottles with green and brown lead glaze over well moulded reliefs which, though certainly post-Han, are probably earlier than the T'ang dynasty. Some of them are remarkable for their Western types of ornament, such as dancing and piping figures, which would be at home in a Herculaneum frieze, surrounded by vine scrolls. Similar designs are seen on late Hellenistic pottery; and this doubtless was the source from which the Chinese potters drew their inspiration.

There is yet another kind of glazed ware which belongs to this interval,

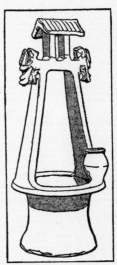

BY COURTESY OF GEORGE EU-
MORFOPOULOS, ESQ.

HAN WELL-JAR

From the George Eu-
morfopoulos Collection

and which is apparently of purely Chinese origin. It is a kaolinic stoneware of hard grey body with a high-fired glaze of greenish brown tint. Specimens of this ware analyzed by H. W. Nichols of Chicago were pronounced to be a kind of proto-porcelain. In other words they are believed to contain the elements of porcelain, though in an unperfected state. Dr. M. Nakao holds that the glaze of this ware is a wood-ash glaze evolved from the accidental gloss which often forms on pottery fired to a high temperature in a wood-fed furnace, as in the case of the Early Korean pottery. It is practically certain that this kaolinic pottery with its glaze of feldspar and wood ashes forms a

BY COURTESY OF THE BRITISH MUSEUM
PROTO-PORCELAIN VASE (3RD OR 4TH CENTURY)

FROM THE GEORGE EUMORFOPOULOS COLLECTION
FLASK OF BUFF STONEWARE WITH BROWN GLAZE; T'ANG PERIOD OR EARLIER

FROM THE GEORGE EUMORFOPOULOS COLLECTION
DISH OF THE T'ANG DYNASTY

stage in the evolution of true porcelain which we know the Chinese to have discovered by the T'ang dynasty. Indeed it is highly probable that porcelain was evolved from this material at some period in the interval between Han and T'ang. It may be added that the colour of the glaze was probably due to iron impurities in the clay, and that this glaze is the beginning of the celadon green glazes which owe their colour to iron.

The T'ang Dynasty (618–906).—In the great T'ang dynasty the Chinese empire reached its widest expansion, and China was without doubt the greatest and most civilized power in the world. It was an age of splendour for all the arts, and the potter's art was in no way behind the rest. Oddly enough Chinese ceramic literature has little to tell us of the T'ang potters. But Chinese ceramic literature is a comparatively modern growth and the secrets of T'ang pottery, only recently laid bare, were known in Europe almost as early as in China. It was in fact largely due to the excavations made by

European railway engineers during the past quarter of a century that the contents of many T'ang tombs came to light, and what we know of T'ang pottery, as in the case of the earlier wares, is practically limited to the sepulchral wares. Naturally these do not show the T'ang potters in the most favourable light, but they enable us to see the great progress which had been made in ceramic technique and to realize the artistic capabilities of T'ang craftsmen. They make it clear too that Western influences were active in China in this enlightened age, for we frequently find the traces of late Hellenistic, Sassanian and Persian art in the forms and designs of the pottery of this period.

Of the T'ang funeral pottery the figures of human beings, birds and animals are modelled in a lively and spirited fashion, especially those of horses and camels, dancing girls and musicians. They are usually of a white or pinkish white clay, soft where lightly fired but some occasionally are baked to considerable hardness. Some of them are unglazed and tricked out with red, black and blue pigments. Others are covered with a thin transparent lead glaze of faint yellowish tint, while on the more elaborate this glaze is coloured with washes, streaks or mottling of green, amber yellow or blue. The flesh parts of the glazed figures are commonly left without glaze and in this case they are painted with the pigments mentioned above. Besides the figures, vases, ewers, bowls, cups and dishes of various kinds are found in the tombs; and among them are amphora-shaped jars of strikingly Hellenistic form and ewers of Sassanian type with a bird's head below the lip, a form common again in Persian pottery of a slightly later date. The glazes used on the figures appear also on these vessels, sometimes in monochrome, more often in mottled colours, but they rarely cover the whole exterior of the vessel, stopping as a rule in a wavy line short of the base. The base of the T'ang vase is usually flat and shaved at the edge.

The decoration of T'ang pottery is chiefly effected by moulding in relief, by applying reliefs which have been stamped out separately, by carving the surface or by incising it with a pointed instrument. Painting with a brush was also used not only for the application of pigments on unglazed wares, but in rare instances for decorating in black under a green glaze.

The T'ang pottery so far discussed shows a considerable advance on its predecessors in the use of coloured lead glazes; but it is also apparent that great strides were now made with the harder, feldspathic glazes which were fired at a much higher temperature. The important excavations on the 9th century site of Samarra on the Tigris revealed quite a number of fragments of porcellanous stoneware and even true porcelain of Chinese make. From them we gather that these advanced ceramic products were not only made, but had actually become articles of overseas trade in the T'ang dynasty. They include a semi-porcelain with closely crackled, yellowish white glaze or

FROM THE GEORGE EUMORFOPOULOS COLLECTION

LEFT, PORCELAIN EWER WITH WHITE GLAZE, T'ANG PERIOD; RIGHT, WHITE PORCELAIN BOTTLE WITH UNGLAZED BASE, T'ANG PERIOD

with green and mottled glazes, or again with the sea-green glaze which we distinguish by the name of celadon; besides pure porcelain with white or ivory glaze. Other high-fired T'ang glazes are a chocolate brown, verging on black, a watery green and a brown splashed with frothy grey.

But the progress of the T'ang potter is not to be measured by improved technique alone. The beauty of the vase-forms which he threw on the wheel places him in the front rank of potters, and his incised and moulded ornaments prove him to have been a true ceramic artist.

In the half century which intervened between the T'ang and Sung dynas-

114

TOP, DELOS CHAPPELL COLLECTION; BOTTOM, WARREN E. COX COLLECTION

CHINESE EARLY POTTERY SCULPTURE

Top: Pottery horse of the T'ang dynasty (A.D. 618–906) decorated with rare blue glaze and touches of red paint on the saddle. It represents the Bactrian horse, a type introduced into China by the Mongols

Bottom: Pottery dog with puppy, pre-T'ang, an excellent example of vigorous primitive modelling, showing remnants of red and white paint on dark grey biscuit (unglazed surface)

ties ceramic history records the manufacture of two interesting wares, both of which are still a puzzle to the student. One is the celebrated Ch'ai ware which was reputed to have been "thin as paper, resonant as a musical stone and blue as the sky seen between the clouds after rain." This was an imperial ware made for a few years only in the neighbourhood of K'ai-fêng Fu in Honan; and apparently no complete specimen of it remained above ground even in the 16th century. The traditional description of it suggests a kind of porcelain, and modern opinion holds that it probably belonged to the *ying ch'ing* class of ware which will be described presently. But this is only a theory and, it must be added, a theory which is by no means universally accepted.

The other is the *pi sê* (secret colour) ware made at Yüeh Chou, the modern Shao-hsing Fu in Chekiang, for the princely house of Chien. It is generally agreed that this was a porcelain or semi-porcelain with grey-green glaze of the celadon type.

The Sung Dynasty (960–1279).—The Sung dynasty was another Augustan age of Chinese art, and ceramic writers in after years described the Sung porcelains in reverential terms as the classic wares of China. Collectors treasured them with loving care, so that not a few have survived above the ground and we are not dependent entirely on excavated funeral goods for our estimate of the Sung potter's skill. Something too is recorded of the history of the more noted Sung factories, and slender as is the information given it has enabled the modern student to attempt a reasoned, though not yet assured, classification of the principal types, namely the Ju, Kuan, Ko, Ting, Lung-ch'üan, Chün, Chien and Tz'ŭ Chou, with a few subsidiary wares in addition.

The Imperial Ju ware was made at Ju Chou, near K'ai-fêng Fu in Honan, for a brief period at the beginning of the 12th century; but we gather that it belongs to a type of ware which was made at several potteries, *e.g.*, in the districts of T'ang Têng and Yao on the north of the Yellow River—besides at Ju Chou itself. The Ju Chou ware, however, excelled the rest and doubtless the imperial works were manned by picked Ju Chou potters. The Chinese descriptions of the Imperial Ju ware, which was already extremely scarce in the 16th century, leave us in some doubt as to its exact nature, but the most plausible theory is that it was of the *ying ch'ing* type. The term *ying ch'ing*, which means misty blue or green (the colour word *ch'ing* connoting both blue and green), is applied by the Chinese to-day to a soft-looking, bubbly porcelain glaze, white in colour, but with a faint tinge of blue or greenish blue which sometimes develops a definite blue tint. This tinge of colour has been traced to the presence of a minute quantity of iron in the ware. The *ying ch'ing* porcelain is a relatively low-fired ware and the body has a somewhat granular texture. It varies much in quality, from a coarse material with impure, pearly grey glaze to an exquisite egg-shell porcelain thin and translucent and of a deliciously soft and melting quality. The best specimens are skilfully potted and of elegant shape, and the decoration, if any, is carved in low relief, incised with a fine point or pressed out in moulds. It is surmised that some of the finer *ying ch'ing* porcelain may have been made at the Imperial Ju Chou factory, while the rest comes from the numerous private factories working with more or less skill on the same lines. It must however be understood that the identification of this ware with the famous Ju porcelain is not yet proved.

Another type which is still problematical is the Kuan. The name itself leaves room for various interpretations, and the description of it in Chinese works, like most Chinese descriptions, is full of ambiguities. Kuan means imperial, and Kuan ware may be nothing more than imperial ware of whatever kind. But Chinese writers evidently intended the Kuan wares of the Sung dynasty to be distinctive types. They describe first of all a Kuan ware made in the neighbourhood of the capital, K'ai-fêng Fu, for a short time before 1127, when the Sung court was driven south of the Yangtze by the Kin Tartars. The identification of this northern Kuan is extremely uncertain, though there are reasons for thinking that it had the opalescent, blue-grey type of glaze which was developed to its full on the Chün Chou ware. The southern Kuan, made after 1127 in the precincts of the imperial palace at Hang-chou, whither the Sung court had been transferred, so closely resembled the Ko ware, that many Chinese writers do not attempt to discriminate between the Ko and Kuan.

The Ko ware is described in some detail in Chinese books. It got its name from the elder of two potter brothers Chang who lived in the Lung-ch'üan district in Chekiang in the Southern Sung period, being in fact the ware of the "elder brother" (*ko*). It is evident, however, that the term Ko

116

ware was not confined to any individual's work, but passed into general use as a generic term for a group of wares made over a long period at various places. Like the Hang Chou Kuan, the Sung Ko ware was made of a dark-coloured clay (we are told by one writer that this clay was actually brought from Hang Chou to the Lung-ch'üan district), and for this reason it has a dark brown edge on the unglazed foot-rim and a brown mouth-rim where the glaze is thin enough to allow the body material to show through it. The glaze itself was crackled, sometimes in a wide network of cracks, sometimes in a close pattern of small crackle which was likened to fish roe. The crackle

FROM THE GEORGE EUMORFOPOULOS
COLLECTION

TZ'U CHOU VASE, YÜAN
DYNASTY

A band of lotus scroll with one of foliage below, ornaments this buff grey vase which has a black finish

FROM THE GEORGE EUMORFOPOULOS
COLLECTION

HSÜAN TÊ PORCELAIN STEM-
CUP

One of the three crimson red fishes painted on the outside, is shown

BY COURTESY OF THE BRITISH MUSEUM

PORCELAIN VASE WITH
DRAGONS

was further emphasized by staining it with red or black. The colours of the Ko glaze are described as *fên ch'ing, hui sê, mi sê* which may be rendered grey green, ash colour and millet colour or yellowish, and less intelligibly as *tan pai* which was probably something of the *ying ch'ing* colour. Well accredited specimens in Western collections have a blackish body material which gives the traditional "brown mouth and iron foot," a thick opaque glaze, lustrous and fat, with crackle stained red or black, and of bluish grey, greenish grey or buff grey colours which tally well with the Chinese descriptions. We read of Ko ware made in the Yüan and even the early Ming periods; and in later times the term Ko glaze was current for all the grey and buff crackled glazes which figure so largely in the Chinese potter's output.

The crackle affected by the Chinese potter from the Sung dynasty on-

117

wards was deliberately sought by definite processes and was eventually got under perfect control, so that large or small crackle could be produced at will. It is unlikely that the earlier processes were very reliable, such as the plunging of the ware while still warm into cold water; but the Chinese eventually discovered that the mixing of a certain kind of stone (apparently pegmatite) with the glaze disturbed the relationship of body and glaze sufficiently to ensure crackle, and they learnt to prepare a crackle glaze which was applied in single, double or treble doses according to the size of the crackle desired.

Lung-ch'üan Celadon.—The Lung-ch'üan district in Chekiang, the home of the original Ko ware, had long been noted for a beautiful ware which is familiar to us under the name of celadon. It is a porcelain or semi-porcelain of greyish white body with a thick translucent glaze varying from greyish and bluish green to sea-green and grass-green. The most precious of the Lung-ch'üan celadons has a delicate bluish grey or greenish grey glaze over a finely potted porcelain body which is almost white. Such was the ware reputed to have been made by the younger Chang at the village of Liu-t'ien in the Southern Sung period; and collectors distinguish it by the Japanese name *kinuta*, after a famous vase in shape of a mallet (*kinuta*), which is preserved in a Japanese temple. Nothing could be more subtly beautiful than this soft, misty bluish grey porcelain, and nothing is more difficult to render adequately in a coloured reproduction.

It is not known how far back the industry of Lung-ch'üan dates; but the fragments of celadon found on the 9th century site of Samarra, in Mesopotamia, may well have been made there. On the other hand we are told that the kilns were transferred to the neighbouring Ch'u-chou at the beginning of the Ming period and that they flourished there till the end of that dynasty. The output must have been large, and it formed from the earliest time an important item of Chinese export trade. Fragments of celadon are found in the ruins of ancient cities all over the Near East, and we know from actual records that celadon was imported into Egypt and carried thence along the Mediterranean coasts as far as Morocco. Fragments too have been found on the coastal sites of East Africa as far south as Zanzibar. India and the East Indies had their share of the trade, and a few pieces of celadon found their way even to western Europe in the Middle Ages. This justly celebrated ware, the export celadon, was a stoutly built greyish porcelain

118

FROM THE WARREN E. COX COLLECTION

GROUP OF T'ANG GLAZED POTTERY INCLUDING TWO MORTUARY FIGURES

1. Mortuary figure representing the God of War
2. A "wood-grain" vase made of two coloured intermingled clays and covered with brown glaze
3. Pale green glazed vase showing Greek influence
4. Bulb bowl decorated with cream, yellow and brown glazes
5. Pitcher-like vase, suggested Near Eastern influences, covered with olive green glaze
6. Mortuary figure representing a court dignitary

BY COURTESY OF (2, 6) THE FREER GALLERY OF ART, (5) OTTO FUKUSHIMA; FROM (1, 3, 4, 7, 8-11) THE WARREN E. COX COLLECTION, (12, 13) THE GEORGE EUMORFOPOULOS COLLECTION

VASES OF THE SUNG DYNASTY (960–1280)

1, 4, 13. Show vigorous painted designs in brown on cream slip and glaze

2. "Temmoku" type (see Plate XL.)

3. Pure, perfect vase form covered with cream coloured slip and glaze

5. Low relief decoration with background in brown "Temmoku" glaze

6, 11. Vases decorated with painting in brown and covered with blue glaze

7, 8, 9, 10. Vases decorated with incised slip and glaze

12. Vase decorated with incised brown or "Temmoku" glaze

FROM THE GEORGE EUMORFOPOULOS COLLECTION

T'ANG VASE

Covered vase, pottery with coloured glazes. T'ang dynasty (A.D. 618–906). Height 10.15″.
The blue glaze is exceedingly rare in this period, though some exceptional specimens are found

with a beautiful sea-green glaze of considerable thickness but transparent enough to allow the carved, moulded or incised designs to show through clearly.

Besides the carved and incised designs which are of great beauty, reliefs moulded or applied were effectively used. Sometimes these reliefs—floral medallions, fishes and even figure subjects—were left uncovered by the glaze, and in this case they invariably took on a red or reddish brown colour as a result of exposure to the fire in the kiln. This browning, caused by the presence of iron in the clay, is to be seen in all parts of the ware which were unprotected by the glaze, such as the base-rims and the large unglazed ring which is often seen on the bottoms of dishes. It was thought at one time that the presence of this ring was a sign of Ming origin, but it is very doubtful if this rule holds good; and the distinction between Ming, Yüan and Sung celadons, no easy matter, must depend on an appreciation of style and finish. Much help in this delicate task of connoisseurship can be obtained from a study of the other Sung wares, especially the Ting porcelain with its carved and engraved floral designs which closely resemble those used on the celadons. In the hands of the Sung artists these designs had a freshness and spontaneity which is dulled by repetition on the Ming wares. A special type of celadon is variegated by patches of reddish brown derived from iron. This is known as "spotted celadon," the *tobi seiji* of the Japanese.

Other Celadons.—Though the industry in Chekiang is said to have died out in the 17th century, it was not to be expected that such a beautiful glaze as the sea-green celadon would be allowed to disappear. It was in fact made with slight variations in many other pottery centres. At Ching-tê Chên it was used over the white porcelain body for which that place is noted, and the Ching-tê Chên celadons have the ordinary white glaze, and sometimes a reign-mark in blue, on their bases. A celadon glaze was used on the Kwangtung stoneware; and there are many specimens with glaze of celadon type but so different in body from the typical Chekiang ware that we must perforce look to some other centre for their origin. If we consult the Chinese books we get little help in this quest. It is true that they speak of a certain T'ung ware, made near K'ai-fêng Fu in Honan, as if it were of the celadon class. But the identification of the T'ung is quite conjectural. In the absence of definite indications, we have adopted the term "northern celadon" for one large and important group. It comprises bowls, small dishes, vases, incense burners, etc., with a dry buff grey stoneware body and an olive-green celadon glaze. The decoration is carved, incised or moulded, often with much skill and taste; and it closely resembles that of the *ying ch'ing*, or Ju type of porcelain, a fact which suggests a Honan origin for the ware. This northern origin, however, is not accepted by all authorities. Dr. Nakao, for instance, holds that it is only a variety of the Chekiang celadons, in spite of the very obvious difference between it and the usual Lung-ch'üan types, and he is probably right in supposing that the art of celadon manufacture was introduced into southern Korea from Chekiang, the most accessible Chinese ceramic centre. And it must be admitted that the resemblance between the so-called northern celadon and the Korean is remarkably close.

A stoneware of celadon type but with a pale and watery glaze was made at Sawankhalok in Siam as early as the 14th century; and in more recent times good celadon wares, scarcely distinguishable from the Lung-ch'üan. have been made in several parts of Japan. And it may be added that the imported celadon wares were freely imitated in Persia and Egypt; but these imitations, made with the soft Near-Eastern pottery, are easily recognizable for what they are.

Ting Ware.—Another of the classic Sung types is the ivory-white porcelain made at Ting Chou in southern Chihli. It is a singularly pure and beautiful ware with a flour-white body, slightly translucent, and a glaze of cream or ivory tint, which, however, tends to run in tears or drops on the outside of the bowls and dishes. A peculiarity of the ware, which it shares with the *ying ch'ing*, or Ju type, is that the mouth-rims of bowls and dishes are often unglazed while the base is covered with glaze, thus reversing the usual conditions. The rough rims of such vessels are generally concealed by a band of silver or copper. The Ting ware was exquisitely decorated with carved or incised designs, largely floral and in some cases, especially in the later periods, the more mechanical method of pressing out the designs in moulds was used with good effect.

Besides the fine ivory-white Ting ware there are several varieties. One is known as *t'u* (earthy) Ting because it has a more opaque and earthy-looking body. This kind has a soft, cream-white glaze which is usually covered with faint crackle. Chinese writers also speak of Ting wares with black, red and brown or purple glazes. The two first are probably glazes of the Honan *temmoku* type; but the purple Ting has so far eluded recognition. There is also mention of a painted Ting ware, which must have resembled the painted stoneware of Tz'ŭ Chou.

The beauty of the white Ting porcelain encouraged, while its simplicity abetted, numerous imitations, some of which are admitted by Chinese writers to be practically indistinguishable from the original. There was, for instance, the Southern Ting, made by Ting Chou potters who moved south with the Sung court in 1127 and who seem to have settled in the neighbourhood of Ching-tê Chên. Then there were the famous imitations made by P'êng Chün-pao at Ho Chou in Shansi; and the Ssŭ Chou and Su Chou wares of Anhwei which were bought for Ting ware in the Sung dynasty "by persons who liked a bargain." There are the white wares of Hsüan Chou, and those made at the "white earth village" near Hsiao Hsien in northern Kiangsu. There were the cream-white wares made at Tz'ŭ Chou which were regarded as equal to Ting; and we know of a singularly pleasing stoneware with grey or light buff body covered with a wash of white slip and a beautiful waxen white glaze closely crackled and recalling the finer *t'u* Ting wares. Much of this ware has been excavated on the site of the submerged town of Küluhsien (destroyed by flood in 1108); and many of the specimens have been made additionally attractive by pinkish grey stains acquired during burial.

The Ting Chou factories themselves, though their fame died down after the Sung period, continued in operation, and Ting ware is mentioned in court records as late as the middle of the 16th century. About this time too a celebrated potter at Ching-tê Chên, Chou Tan-ch'üan, made himself a name by his wonderful imitations of Sung Ting vessels; and we gather that he had many followers who kept up the traditions of his work at Ching-tê Chên long after his death.

Chün Ware.—Yet another celebrated ware was the Chün, which was made at Chün Chou in the K'ai-fêng Fu district of Honan. It was, in fact, like the white Ting and the green celadon, one of key wares of the Sung dynasty. According to Dr. Nakao it is the type of ware which would naturally result from the firing of a kaolinic body and feldspathic glaze coloured by copper in the oxidizing flame of the typical round kiln of northern China. The finer Chün wares have a grey porcellanous body and a thick opalescent glaze full of bubbles and minute pin-holes (caused by the bursting of bubbles), and displaying a wonderful variety of colours which are due in part to the protean changes of copper oxide in an oxidizing flame, in part to a trace of iron which is present in the body material, and in part to the play of light in a highly opalescent glaze. Copper under the conditions prevailing in the Chün Chou kilns was capable of producing a range of colour from blue to blood red, and the Chün glazes display endless combinations of these colours suffusing a basically grey glaze. Thus we have in the extremes an even lavender grey and an almost uniform purplish red, and between these a variety of splashed, streaked and mottled effects of blue, grey, purple and crushed strawberry red. Again the interior of shallow dishes is often frosted over with an opaque, greenish grey; and the Chün glaze is apt to break into irregular V-shaped lines known as earthworm marks, which the Chinese connoisseurs regard as a sign of genuine Sung make. The Chün ware is strong and heavy, and the finer specimens consist mainly of flower-pots and shallow bowls which could serve as stands for the flower-pots or alternatively as bulb-bowls. This class of Chün ware has a wash of brown glaze on the base and a ring of "spur" marks formed by the pointed stilts on which the vessel rested in the kiln. It is moreover usually incised with a series number which ranges from one to ten and apparently indicates the size, No. 1 being the largest. An "outsize" is indicated by addition of the character *ta* which means *large*.

It is known that the Chün factories continued active through the Sung and Yüan dynasties and as late as the 16th century. In fact, we are not informed when their activity ended. Consequently there is much difficulty in distinguishing the Sung and later Chün wares; and the tendency is to call the finer specimens Sung and the coarser Yüan, too little regard being paid to the fact that much of the ware must be as late as Ming. All that can be said for certain is that the heyday of the Chün factories was in the Sung and that their reputation faded after the Yüan dynasty.

There is a peculiarly beautiful group of wares which belong to the Chün class, and, if fineness is a criterion, also to the Sung period. They have the grey porcellanous body of the numbered Chün wares, and an opalescent glaze which is, however, thinner and smoother than the usual Chün glaze.

FROM THE GEORGE EUMORFOPOULOS COLLECTION

CHINESE PORCELAINS OF THE SUNG DYNASTY (A.D. 960–1279)

1. Flower pot, Chün ware, 7.4″ high
2. Water pot, Chün ware of Kuan type, 3.6″
3. Incense bowl, Chün ware of Kuan type, 3.2″ high

FROM THE GEORGE EUMORFOPOULOS COLLECTION

PORCELAIN OF THE SUNG PERIOD

1. Vase, Ju type, Sung period (A.D. 960–1279) or Yüan period (1280–1368). Height 7½″
2. Ewer, Ju type, Sung or Yüan period. Diameter 5¾″
3. Bulb-bowl, Lung-ch'üan celadon, Sung period. Diameter 11¼″

Its colour is lavender grey, but it is richly suffused, or splashed, with a lovely plum purple and this purple sometimes dominates the whole surface. The glaze flows more or less evenly down to the edge of the base-rims and it usually reappears on a small patch on the base. Sometimes the purple splashes on this ware are symmetrically disposed and even deliberately designed to suggest the forms of fishes, birds, animals or fruits, showing clearly that these patches, though doubtless at first accidental, were later brought under control. To what factory does this group belong? Is it merely a variety of the Chün Chou ware or is it something else? One of the descriptions given of the Northern Kuan ware suggests that it may belong to that obscure category; and some collectors distinguish it as Chün ware of Kuan type.

It is evident that many kilns were at work on the Chün type of ware, and probably in other districts besides Chün Chou, but we have little or no information on this point. We do, however, know that the Chün wares had many imitators. Good copies were made at Ching-tê Chên, probably as early as the Ming dynasty, certainly in the Yung Chêng period of the Ch'ing dynasty (1723–35); but there is little difficulty in distinguishing these later copies which have a white porcelain body and sometimes even a reign-mark. Other imitations made elsewhere can also be detected by variations of the body material and peculiarities of the glaze. Such are the Fatshan Chün ware made at the famous stoneware factories at Shekwan near Fatshan, in Kwangtung (*q.v.*), in Ming and later times; and the Yi-hsing Chüns which were made at Yi-hsing near the Great Lake in Kiangsu, the home of the red stoneware tea-pots. The Yi-hsing imitations have a buff or red stoneware body and a thick opalescent glaze of lavender turquoise colour with or without obviously artificial splashes of purple and crimson. While easily distinguished from the real Chün wares, they are often mistaken for another type which remains to be considered. This is the "soft Chün" (also called *ma chün* by Chinese traders), an attractive ware with light buff body and a beautiful, opaque turquoise or lavender blue glaze closely crackled and suffused here and there with purple or crimson splashes. Where it was made and when are by no means certain; but the shapes of the ware suggest in some cases the Sung and in others the Ming period, and the glaze is of the northern type. A degenerate descendant of this soft Chün is still made at

123

Yü Chou which is the modern name of Chün Chou, and probably this was the original home of the ware.

Chien Wares.—Another large and widely distributed group of stoneware is commonly called, for want of a better general term, by the Japanese name *temmoku*. This name was first given to the black tea bowls for which Chien-an and afterwards Chien-yang, in Fukien, were noted in the Sung dynasty and even earlier. They are made of a blackish stoneware with a thick treacly glaze of purplish black shot with brown lines like hare's fur or mottled with brown like the breast feathers of a partridge. Their glaze stops in a thick irregular welt short of the base outside and forms in a deep pool on the bottom inside. The "hare's-fur or partridge" cups were commonly preferred for use in the tea-testing competitions, as their thick structure made the cup cool to handle and their dark glaze showed up the least trace of the green tea dust. In Japan they have always been fashionable in the tea ceremonies. The Chien glaze owes its colour to iron, which under varying conditions produces a reddish brown as well as a black colour. Indeed the brown and black seem to be always struggling for the mastery in the Chien glaze. Sometimes the brown completely dominates the black: sometimes it only emerges in streaks and spots, and sometimes again these spots are crystalline and have a silvery sheen.

The black ferruginous glaze is by no means confined to the Fukien factories. It was, and still is, made in many parts of China, chiefly in the north; and one of the northern wares which has this black and brown glaze over a whitish stoneware body is known to collectors as Honan *temmoku*. The northern black glazes are often of a peculiarly rich and luscious quality, and sometimes they are boldly flecked with lustrous brown and even painted with sketchy designs of flowers and birds in the same brown. On rare specimens the glaze is strewn more or less regularly with silvery crystals, the "oil spots" so greatly prized by the Japanese; while on others it comes out a uniform reddish brown, the *kaki temmoku* of the Japanese. Another ware which is commonly grouped with the *temmoku* is that believed to have been found on the site of the old Sung potteries at Yung-ho Chên near Ch'i-an Fu, in Kiangsi. In this case the body is a buff stoneware and the glaze is a rather thin blackish brown which flows evenly to the base and is often mottled with golden brown in tortoise-shell fashion or streaked and dappled with frothy

124

grey. A further feature is painted ornament—prunus blossoms and sprays, birds, butterflies, inscribed medallions and symmetrical designs—in dull golden brown in the black or dappled glaze.

Tz'ŭ Chou.—The last important group of Sung wares takes its name from the great pottery centre Tz'ŭ Chou, once in Honan and now in the south-west corner of Chihli. The Tz'ŭ Chou ware is a grey or buff-grey stoneware, which is usually coated with white slip and covered with creamy glaze. The plain cream white Tz'ŭ Chou stoneware has been mentioned among the Ting types, but the ware is more usually decorated with painted or incised designs. The painted designs, floral or otherwise, are laid on with a bold brush in black or brown slip, sometimes supplemented by an ochreous red under the cream glaze. Painting in enamels—green, yellow and red—over the glaze was also used, occasionally in the Sung period and frequently in later times. The incised, or *graffiato*, Tz'ŭ Chou ware has many varieties. Simple incised designs are comparatively scarce, the more usual practice being to coat the vessel with white or brown slip which was then scraped away so as to leave the design slightly relieved in white or brown against a buff-grey body. A coating of transparent cream glaze over this produced cream white design on a mouse grey ground, if the slip was white. Where brown was used the slip usually contained the glazing material and the design appeared in brown or black glaze against an unglazed ground. Both of these *graffiato* types have great decorative value. The black and brown painted Tz'ŭ Chou is the commonest type and its merits vary with the quality of the drawing.

The Tz'ŭ Chou potteries have a history which can be traced from the 6th century to the present day, and there will always be room for debate as to the age of particular specimens. Further, most of the Tz'ŭ Chou types were made at other potteries scattered over northern China, and doubtless much that we call Tz'ŭ Chou really belongs to other potteries which worked on similar lines. This will explain variations in the body material of wares of the Tz'ŭ Chou type, and why a red body, quite unlike the original buff grey, is found on some of the most beautiful members of the group, such as the vases with black painted and *graffiato* designs under transparent green glaze or with black painted designs under a lovely peacock blue. The potters who made these choice objects must have been among the foremost of

125

their craft, but, though they used the Tz'ŭ Chou methods, their wares differ fundamentally from what we know as Tz'ŭ Chou.

Chinese ceramic records name several other Sung potteries in various parts of China, but they are hardly more than names to us and we know little or nothing of their productions. Practically all the Sung wares which we know, however, are comprised in the types already described. The forms, except where they were moulded after those of old bronzes, are simple and elegant, such as come naturally from the hands of a gifted "thrower" on the potter's wheel. The character of the classic Sung wares may be summed up in two words, simplicity and refinement.

For the purpose of this brief sketch the Yüan dynasty (1280–1368) may be regarded as a continuation of the Sung. The Mongol conquerors had nothing to bring into the stock in trade of the Chinese potter except a taste for certain Western forms and designs acquired in the other extreme of their transcontinental empire. Further we are told that they were hard taskmasters and that the ceramic industry, in common with many others, especially the more artistic crafts, lost ground under their unsympathetic rule.

FROM THE GEORGE EUMORFOP-
OULOS COLLECTION

MING EWER (1368–
1644); INCISED DECORA-
TION AND TURQUOISE
GLAZE

The Ming Dynasty (1368–1644).—In 1368 the Yüan was replaced by the native dynasty of the Ming, which ruled China till 1644; and, when the country had recovered from the inter-dynastic struggles, the ceramic art took a new lease of life, though under somewhat changed conditions. The Sung monochrome wares, the celadons, Chün wares, etc., went out of favour and the old factories sank into obscurity, while the fame and importance of the great porcelain town of Ching-tê Chên, near the Po-yang lake in Kiangsi, overshadowed all the rest. The first Ming emperors had their capital in Nanking and the proximity of Ching-tê Chên to the seat of government doubtless helped its development. At any rate from this time onwards the fine white porcelain of Ching-tê Chên was in general demand and the imperial factory there was rebuilt and reorganized to keep the court supplied with it; and Chinese ceramic writers thenceforward speak of Ching-tê Chên and little else.

126

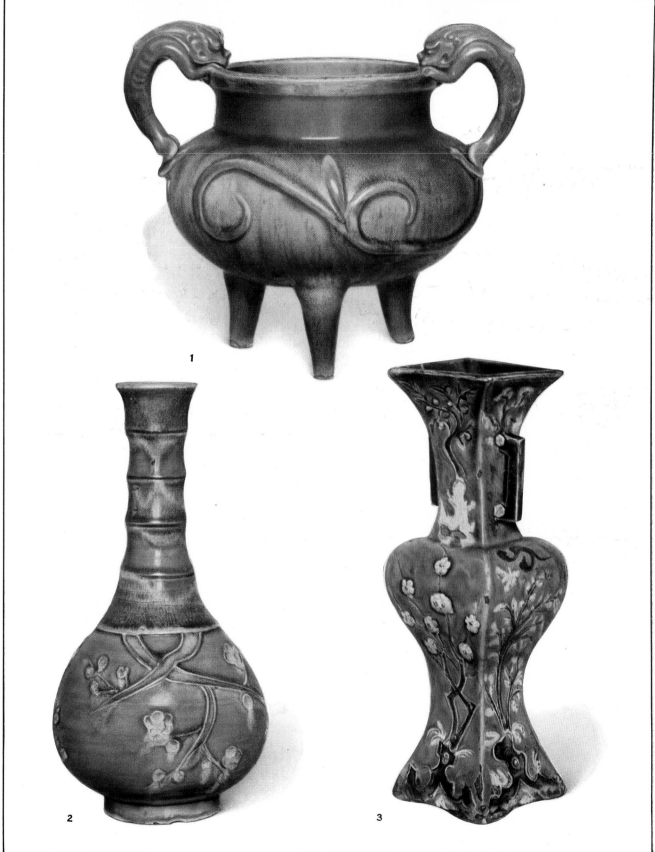

FROM THE GEORGE EUMORFOPOULOS COLLECTION

MING THREE–COLOUR ENAMEL WARE

1. Incense bowl with low relief decoration. Height 7″

2. Bottle-shaped vase with usual ridges on outlines of design to

keep colours from running in firing. Height 10.75″

3. Vase from bronze form. Height 13.7″

FROM THE WARREN E. COX COLLECTION

TZ'Ŭ CHOW VASE. SUNG DYNASTY (960–1280)

The remarkable painting of the lotus—each petal of which is executed with a single vigorous brush stroke—and with strong quality of the incised characters, meaning "snow," "moon," "wind," "flower," make this an outstanding specimen of its type

BY COURTESY OF (11) THE TRUSTEES OF THE BRITISH MUSEUM; FROM (1-10, 12) THE WARREN E. COX COLLECTION

HONAN TEMMOKU POTTERY, SUNG PERIOD (960–1280) HAVING GREYISH WHITE, LIGHT BUFF AND BROWN BODIES

1. Brushholder with brown "oil spot" glaze applied so as to leave an open pattern. 2. Gallipot with incised light brown glaze. 3. Gallipot with grooves from the turning and speckled "tea dust" glaze. 4. Gallipot with even lustrous black glaze. 5. Gallipot jar in dark "tea dust" with silvery design. 6. Jar with beautiful tortoise shell doubly applied glaze and silvery pattern. 7. Graceful bottle with dark lustrous brown glaze and silvery pat-tern of bird. 8. Jar with thick glaze running black, dark blue and brown. 9. Jar with thick black glaze leaving lower part exposed. Each handle con-sists of two loops. 10. Pear shaped vase with lustrous black glaze over glaze running thin to a deep blue near base and splashed with iron rust brown patches. 11. Tea bowl with thick "hare's fur" glaze. 12. Exceptional jar of the deepest plum shade glaze, almost black, on dark brown body

POTTERY AND PORCELAIN

The neighbourhood of Ching-tê Chên had long been noted for its excellent ceramic wares. It was ordered to supply goods to the court as early as the 6th century, and it received its present name in the Ching Tê period of the Sung dynasty (1004–07). All that the industry required in the way of material was lavishly supplied by the neighbouring hills, *kaolin* (china clay) for the body of the porcelain and *petuntse* (china stone) to mix with it and to form the glaze, wood ashes to soften the glaze, and cobaltiferous ore of manganese to make the blue for the underglaze painting and the blue glazes. The staple product of Ching-tê Chên is the fine white porcelain which has made China a household word throughout the world; and as this ware lent itself peculiarly well to painted decoration, the vogue for painted porcelain rapidly replaced the old Sung taste for monochromes. They fall into three chief groups, namely blue and white, enamelled wares and three-colour glazed wares, all of which are essentially pictorial in their decoration.

Blue and White.—The beautiful cobalt blue is one of the few ceramic colours which will stand the high temperature required to melt the porcelain glaze, and which consequently can be used under the glaze. Thus the blue colour, painted on the body of the ware and covered with a transparent sheet of glaze, gives a perfectly protected picture which will last as long as the porcelain itself. The idea of painting porcelain in this fashion was not new in the Ming dynasty. It was known to the Sung potters, but it was only in the Ming dynasty that blue and white became fashionable. Nor is the idea necessarily of Chinese origin, for blue painting was certainly known to the Near-Eastern potters as early as the 9th century, and we have as yet no indication of its use in China at so early a date. In the Ming dynasty, however, the Ching-tê Chên potters made it specially their own, and their blue and white was not only supplied in large quantities to the imperial court but was exported all over the eastern hemisphere.

During certain reigns—Hsüan Tê (1426–35), Chêng Tê (1506–21) and Chia Ching (1522–66)—the native supplies of cobalt blue were supplemented by a superior blue imported from the Near East and known as Mohammedan blue. This imported material was scarce and costly and was at first reserved for the imperial factory, and even so it was usually diluted with the common native cobalt. Later on supplies of it found their way into the hands of the private manufacturers. According to Chinese accounts it varied much in

127

tone, but the kind best known to us is the Mohammedan blue of the Chia Ching period which is a dark violet blue of great strength and intensity. In general the Ming blue is painted in one of two ways, either in finely pencilled line drawing or in strongly outlined designs filled in with flat washes. The better class of Ming porcelain, made for imperial and native use, was potted thin and finely shaped; and this is now rare and only to be acquired from Chinese collections. But there is a commoner class which was more strongly and roughly fashioned to meet the exigencies of the export trade, and this has been found in considerable quantities in India, the East Indies, Persia, Egypt and even in Europe. But all the Ming blue and white, whether made for home or foreign consumption, is distinguished by a freshness and freedom of design which make the commonest specimen a desirable possession.

BY COURTESY OF THE BRITISH MUSEUM
TURKISH POTTERY JUG

BY COURTESY OF THE BRITISH MUSEUM
LAMP FROM THE MOSQUE OF OMAR

Another colour used, like the cobalt blue, under the glaze, is a red derived from copper. It was a difficult colour to control but it was used with success in several Ming reigns, notably the Hsüan Tê and Ch'êng Hua, both as monochrome and in designs painted in the same way as the blue and white.

Ming Enamelled Wares.—Pictorial designs having become fashionable, means were found to paint them on the glaze as well as under it. The chief advantage in on-glaze painting lies in the wider range of colours available.

128

POTTERY AND PORCELAIN

The over-glaze colours, commonly distinguished as enamels, are made of coloured glass ground to powder and liquefied so as to be usable on a brush. They are "fixed" in a small stove, or muffle, at a low temperature which is sufficient to melt the enamel powder and make it adhere to the glaze without actually melting the latter. The colours used are leaf green and turquoise green derived from copper, a brownish yellow derived from iron, and aubergine purple derived from manganese, besides which a dry black pigment was obtained from manganese and a thin tomato red (half-way between a pigment and an enamel) from iron. The Ming red is apt to become iridescent and lustrous; both it and the black are used for painting outlines, and the latter was sometimes washed on and covered with transparent green to form a composite black. Gilding was also used. With this palette the Ming potters produced richly coloured porcelain, decorated with pictorial designs and formal brocade patterns. In some cases the enamels were combined with underglaze blue and this colour scheme, though known in the 15th century, was so popular in the Wan Li period (1573–1619) that it has come to be known as the *wan li wu ts'ai* or Wan Li polychrome. Another type, known as the "red and green family," is characterized by the absence of blue and the predominance of red and green, and again there are effective combinations of two colours such as red and yellow, blue and yellow, blue and green, red and green, red and gold and more rarely green and gold.

Besides being painted on the glaze the enamel colours were sometimes painted on the biscuit, *i.e.*, the fired but unglazed porcelain body; but this technique was commoner in the succeeding dynasty and will be discussed later.

"Three-colour" Ming Wares.—There are few kinds of ceramic ware, Chinese or otherwise, that make such a brave show as the Ming three-colour (*san ts'ai*) porcelain. Though nominally combinations of three, the glazes which make up the colour scheme of this group are dark violet blue, turquoise, aubergine purple, yellow and a neutral white; and they are used in washes over designs set in single-colour ground which is usually dark blue or turquoise. To prevent the colours from overrunning each other the designs are outlined by incised lines or by threads of clay, or they are carved in open work. The glazes themselves, though harder than the enamels discussed in the last section, do not require the full heat of the porcelain kiln to

129

melt them, and consequently the ware has to be "biscuited" (subjected to a preliminary firing) and then, when the glazes have been applied, fired again in the cooler parts of the kiln. They are, in fact, what the French call them, glazes *du demi-grand feu*.

The decoration of the three-colour ware is bold; it includes large floral subjects, lotus and cranes, peonies and peacocks, and a few set figure subjects such as the Eight Immortals paying court to the God of Longevity, Wang Chih watching the game of chess, etc. The details are often built up in slight relief, certain parts such as faces and hands of human figures being left unglazed. The glazes are thick and inclined to be opaque. Much of the three-colour ware dates from the 15th century. In the 16th century the glazes tend to become sleeker, smoother and more transparent, and incised decoration is used.

The three-colour decoration was not confined to porcelain. Excellent specimens of it are seen on both stoneware and earthenware bodies. Indeed some of the most beautiful three-colour vases have a buff stoneware body and bold floral designs in minutely crackled glazes which include a peacock blue of peculiarly attractive tone. Where this group of fine pottery was made is not known; but it is found in widely separated parts of China and may have been made in several factories.

Other Ming Wares.—Though monochrome porcelains no longer held the premier position, they were still made in considerable quantity and some of them received special notice from Chinese writers. The sacrificial red (*chi hung*) of the Hsüan Tê and Ch'êng Hua periods, a brilliant underglaze red derived from copper, was most noted; and next came the *chi ch'ing*, an intense blue glaze of the Hsüan Tê period; and a lovely blue glaze of slightly mottled texture is found on some of the Chia Ching porcelains. There were, besides, celadon green, lustrous black and brown glazes; and all the *demi-grand feu* glazes of the three-colour porcelains were used individually as monochromes, the turquoise blue being especially effective. Very beautiful, too, are the pure white porcelains (white was the colour required in certain forms of ritual and also by the court during periods of mourning); and special mention is made of the exquisite white "egg-shell" bowls of the reign of Yung Lo (1403–24) and of the white altar cups of the Hsüan Tê and Chia Ching periods. If any decoration was added to these white wares it was

130

CENTRE VASE—WARREN E. COX COLLECTION; OTHERS—THE METROPOLITAN MUSEUM OF ART, NEW YORK

CHINESE POTTERY AND PORCELAIN, MING DYNASTY (1368–1644)

Upper left: Black rectangular vase bearing Wan Li mark (1573–1619) decorated with enamels. *Upper right:* three-colour vase and bowl with aubergine ground; 16th–17th century. *Centre:* Large deep peach-bloom glazed vase decorated with enamels and bearing Hsüan Tê mark (1426–35). *Lower left:* Three-colour jar and cover with turquoise ground; 15th century. *Lower right:* Five-colour jar and cover; 16th century

faintly carved, incised or traced in white slip under the glaze, a subtle form of ornament known as *an hua* or secret decoration. Another and more conspicuous form of slip decoration is traced in white on blue or green glazes in a manner resembling the modern *pâte sur pâte*. Reliefs in white biscuit and remarkably fine open work distinguish some of the later Ming porcelains, the open work being of such superhuman delicacy that it was called *kuei kung* or devil's work. A quantity of stoneware and earthenware was made all over China in the Ming period. The best known are the tile work and architectural pottery which are often finely modelled: they are usually glazed with green, yellow, aubergine purple, turquoise or blue. On parts of the famous Nanking pagoda, built in the beginning of the 15th century, white porcelain was also employed for the same purpose. Many vases and vessels of everyday use were also made as by-products of the tile works which existed in all large centres of population to supply local needs; but it is hard to distinguish the common pottery of the Ming from that of the earlier and later periods, except where there is a close analogy with some known type of Ming porcelain to help us.

In the early years of the 16th century direct contact was established between Europe and China; and Chinese porcelain, together with silk and tea, soon became an important item of European trade. From this time onwards we note the influence of European taste affecting the Chinese porcelain to a steadily increasing extent.

The Ch'ing Dynasty (1644–1912).—The Ch'ing dynasty of the Manchus replaced the Ming in 1644; but it was not till about 1680 that its rule was firmly established over a pacified country. A succession of three able and enlightened emperors—K'ang Hsi (1662–1722), Yung Chêng (1723–35) and Ch'ien Lung (1736–95)—gave China a long period of good rule and the ideal conditions for the development of the arts, which indeed enjoyed at this time an unusual amount of imperial patronage. The imperial porcelain factory at Ching-tê Chên was managed by a series of exceptionally capable directors. Ts'ang Ying-hsüan, appointed in 1682, remained in charge till the end of the K'ang Hsi period. Nien Hsi-yao was appointed by the Emperor Yung Chêng and in 1728 he was given as an assistant the celebrated T'ang Ying, who succeeded him in 1736 and held the post with great distinction till 1749. T'ang Ying left behind him several treatises on the manu-

131

facture under his control, and in addition to these we have the letters of
the Jesuit father d'Entrecolles which were written from Ching-tê Chên in
1712 and 1722, giving us an intimate picture of the life and industry of the
great porcelain centre with its 3,000 furnaces.

The period from 1680 to 1749 must be regarded as the most fertile in
the annals of Chinese ceramics. The porcelains of this time are distinguished
by fine finish and perfect command of material and technique. They
do not, however, differ basically from those of the Ming potters, who had
little to learn in the essentials of their craft; and on the whole they suffer by
comparison with the Ming in the matter of originality and freshness. The
Ch'ing wares indeed are often a trifle stale and mechanical. Still they have
enjoyed a long period of popularity in Europe, and their relative weakness
has only recently become apparent; for we have only recently made ac-
quaintance with the better types of Ming porcelain.

Ch'ing Blue and White.—Old Nanking is a household phrase in Europe
for Chinese blue and white. None the less it is a misnomer, for while much
of that ware was transhipped from Nanking, none of it was actually made
there. Old Nanking is in fact the blue and white porcelain of Ching-tê
Chên and chiefly that made in the K'ang Hsi period and imported into
Europe by the Dutch and other East India merchants. It was justly famous, for never was more care expended on the preparation of the ware and
the refining of the blue. The best K'ang Hsi blue is pure sapphire, without
the tinge of violet or grey so often observable in the Ming blue; and it is
usually laid on in graded washes which give it its splendid, vibrating depths.
As to the painted designs they are mainly Ming themes, when they are not
of the formal arabesque type; but some of them are of outstanding beauty,
such as the design of ascending and descending branches of flowering prunus
reserved in white in a ground of marbled blue which is netted over with lines
suggesting cracked ice. The prunus blossom falling on the breaking ice is
a symbol of returning spring; and this motive is a favourite one for the decoration of the jars in which gifts of fragrant tea and sweetmeats were sent
at the new year—a festival which falls in China three to seven weeks later
than in our calendar. The vogue of blue and white seems to have died down
at the end of the K'ang Hsi period, for after that time the ware in general
sank into mediocrity, though exceptions must be made of two types. One

is the close imitations of Ming blue and white made in the Yung Chêng period; and the other is the so-called "soft paste" blue and white, a ware prepared with "soapy rock" (*hua shih*), a kind of pegmatite, and exquisitely painted with the finest brushwork and the purest blue under a soft-looking crackled glaze. Another name given to this porcelain is "steatitic," in the belief that the *hua shih* was soap-stone or steatite. It was an expensive ware and chiefly used for small objects such as snuff bottles and the furniture of the writing table, in which the Chinese *literati* take special delight.

Famille Verte.—This is the name given to the K'ang Hsi porcelain decorated in transparent enamels. These enamels are in the main the same as those used in the Ming period, but there are a few differences. The iron red is a coral rather than a tomato red, the yellow is clearer than the brownish Ming yellow, there are additional shades of green, and the Ming turquoise green is replaced by a beautiful violet blue enamel. The enamels are either painted over the glaze or washed over black-outlined designs painted direct on the unglazed porcelain or biscuit. The latter process was not unknown in the Ming period, but most of the existing specimens, though often miscalled Ming, belong to the Ch'ing dynasty. Some of the finest Ch'ing porcelains are enamelled on the biscuit, such as the sumptuous vases with grounds of green-black (*famille noire*), figures and groups.

Not unlike the porcelain enamelled on the biscuit is that decorated with washes of coloured glazes, chiefly green, yellow and aubergine. This is the Ch'ing version of the Ming three-colour ware; but the Ch'ing glazes are sleek and transparent. Sometimes they are laid on in patches making a motley decoration which is known in the trade as "egg and spinach" glaze.

Ch'ing Monochromes.—The Ch'ing monochromes comprise the Ming types, close imitations of the old Sung glazes and many novelties. Among the best known is the *lang yao* red which follows the Ming *chi hung* but has a character of its own, varying from bright cherry red and deep ox-blood (*sang de boeuf*) colour to a dappled glaze of crushed strawberry tint. This red is called after a potter family of the name of Lang; and, though imitated in subsequent reigns, it was never so well controlled or so fine in colour as on the K'ang Hsi porcelain. Another success of the K'ang Hsi period was the "peach bloom" glaze, pinkish red in colour but flecked with russet spots and broken by passages of green. Between the peach red and *lang yao* are many shades of maroon and liver colour. Other K'ang Hsi glazes are the mirror-black, the powder-blue and the pale lavender or *clair de lune*; and Chinese writers mention turquoise, eel-skin yellow and snake-skin green as specialities of the period.

We need not dwell on the many other monochromes—whites, celadons, lustrous browns, aubergine purples, violet blues and so forth; but there is a group of composite glazes which requires notice. They are formed by washes of enamel over a stone-coloured crackled glaze; and they include "apple-green", camellia leaf green, sage green and mustard yellow. Coral red was also used in monochrome, but this and many enamels of the *famille rose* types belong chiefly to the Ch'ien Lung period, as also do the splashed or *flambé reds* which came at first by accident but which T'ang Ying succeeded in getting under perfect control.

Famille Rose.—In the third decade of the 18th century a revolution took place in the enamelled porcelains. A new palette of colours was introduced, opaque enamels among which rose pinks (derived from gold) are most conspicuous. The Chinese called these new colours *juan ts'ai* (soft colours) or *yang ts'ai* (foreign colours), and we have adopted for them the French name *famille rose*. The *famille rose* displaced the *famille verte*, and it brought with it a new and more effeminate type of decoration with delicate designs executed with a miniature-like refinement. The colours are seen at their best on the Yung Chêng porcelain with a few sprays of flowers thrown artistically across the white surface. The more elaborate ruby-back dishes and table services with crowded figure-subjects and complicated borders are less satisfactory; but these were painted in the Canton enamelling establishments and were destined for the European trade. At Canton, too, were decorated large quantities of Ching-tê Chên porcelain with coats of arms and other European designs directly ordered by the foreign merchants.

The *famille verte* enamels, though eclipsed by the *famille rose*, were not entirely suppressed; and they emerged again in a mixed palette of transparent and opaque colours. These mixed enamels were effectively used by a school of painters who worked in the style of one Ku Yüeh-hsüan, a maker and decorator of glass in the early years of Ch'ien Lung's reign. Good specimens are rare, for they are prized by Chinese collectors. Other specialities of the Ch'ien Lung period are "lace-work" porcelain with designs deeply

BY COURTESY OF (3) THE ART INSTITUTE OF CHICAGO; FROM (1, 2, 6, 7) THE GEORGE EUMORFOPOULOS COLLECTION, (4, 5) THE WARREN E. COX COLLECTION

POTTERY AND PORCELAIN OF THE SUNG DYNASTY (A.D. 960–1280)

1. Ko ware, pale *café au lait*
2. Northern Celadon with characteristic incised design, olive green
3 and 5. Ting ware, pure white
4. Tu Ting ware with lightly incised design
6. Kuan ware, pale bluish grey
7. Ting ware, pure white

BY COURTESY OF (1, 6, 7) THE TRUSTEES OF THE BRITISH MUSEUM; FROM (2-5) THE GEORGE EUMORFOPOULOS COLLECTION

CHINESE PORCELAINS

1. Yung Chêng eggshell porcelain

2. *Famille verte* dish, K'ang Hsi period

3. K'ang Hsi group with coloured glazes

4. Powderblue bowl

5. Chia Ching jar, blue and white

6, 7. K'ang Hsi vases, blue and white

FROM THE GEORGE EUMORFOPOULOS COLLECTION

CHINESE VASE

Lang Yao *sang-de-boeuf* vase of the K'ang Hsi period (1662–1722). Height 17½ inches

incised and forming semi-transparencies; and "rice-grain" porcelain in which the designs are actually cut out of the side of the vessel though allowed to fill up with glaze. A third type, known as *graviata*, has a covering of opaque *famille rose* enamel which is diapered with incised scroll-work.

The monochromes of the Yung Chêng and Ch'ien Lung periods include those of the K'ang Hsi with numerous additions, some of which have already been mentioned. Great ingenuity was exercised by the Ch'ien Lung potters in the imitation of natural substances in glaze; the effects of tea dust, iron-rust and bronze are cleverly produced, and enamelled metal, shells, birds' eggs, grained wood, jade, ivory, etc., are copied so closely as to deceive the eye. But these *tours de force* are symptoms of an art which had passed its maturity; and after the 18th century the porcelain has little interest, being mainly of an imitative kind. Exceptions may be made of the Peking medallion bowls, the finer snuff bottles of the Tao Kuang period (1821–50) and some of the imperial porcelains which maintained a high standard of technique. The devastation of Ching-tê Chên during the T'ai-p'ing rebellion in 1853 was a crowning disaster to the ceramic industry of China.

Provincial Porcelains and Pottery.—The bulk of the Ch'ing dynasty porcelains which have reached Europe is of Ching-tê Chên make; but there were many provincial factories which supplied local needs and which also catered for the sea-borne trade to India and the East Indies. These provincial wares are generally of a coarse type; but a shining exception is the white porcelain made at Tê-hua in the province of Fukien. This is the *blanc de Chine* of the old French catalogues, which was freely exported from Amoy in the 17th and 18th centuries, and which served as a model for most of the early European porcelains. It is a beautiful, translucent ware with a soft-looking, melting glaze of milk or cream white, sometimes warmed with a pinkish tinge; and it was chiefly used for ornamental objects such as vases, libation cups, incense burners, figures and groups, less often for table wares. It is decorated, if at all, with slight, applied reliefs, moulded or incised designs, rarely with painted enamels. The Tê-hua factories are known to have existed in the last half of the Ming dynasty, and they are still active to-day; and as the character of the ware has changed very little, the dating of specimens will always be difficult.

Immense quantities of earthenware and stoneware have been and are

135

still made in every part of China. We know little of the individual potteries, but there are two centres which must be mentioned. Yi-hsing, on the west side of the Great Lake in Kiangsu, has been noted since the 16th century for a fine stoneware, chiefly red but also buff, grey and of other colours formed by clever blending of the local clays. The red tea ware of Yi-hsing came to Europe with China tea as early as the 17th century. It was classed at that time with the American *buccaro* ware; and it was copied closely by Dutch, English and German potters, notably by Böttger at Dresden and by Dwight and Elers in England. The Yi-hsing tea-pots were cleverly fashioned, often in fanciful shapes, and decorated with reliefs, moulded and incised designs and in some cases with glazes and even enamels.

The second centre lies in the province of Kwangtung, the principal potteries being at Shekwan near Fatshan, a few miles west of Canton. The Shekwan ware is a stoneware verging on porcelain; and the standard type has a thick flocculent glaze of brown mottled with blue and grey and sometimes with vivid red. Glazes of the Sung Chün type and celadon green, as already mentioned, besides *flambé* red were also used; and some of the Shekwan stoneware dates back to the Ming period, though the bulk of it is of comparatively recent date.

The reader is reminded that true Chinese decoration is never meaningless. Its meaning may be directly expressed in semi-religious emblems such as the Eight Buddhist Symbols, the attributes of the Eight Immortals, the Eight Precious Things, etc.; or indirectly by motives which suggest good wishes, such as the peach, crane, tortoise and pine (long life), the bat (happiness), the pomegranate (fertility). Again combinations of flowers, animals, etc., can be read rebus-fashion into auspicious phrases; for the Chinese language abounds in homophones and the Chinese delight in puns. They also delight in themes of religious and historical import; and the understanding of their decorative designs involves a deep study of their religion, history and folk-lore.

Numerous marks and seals are used on Chinese pottery and porcelain; but for these again the reader must consult special books. The most important and the most frequent of the marks are the reign-names (*nien hao*) of the emperors; but there are also potters' names, phrases of good omen, symbols and the names of halls and workshops, which it would be futile to enumerate without giving the actual marks and their readings.

JEWELLERY

Nature and use.—There can be few branches of craftsmanship in which the characteristics of a race are more clearly expressed than in its jewellery. Not only is the refinement born of centuries of civilization to be set against the untutored love of mere glitter, but many other factors have to be considered. Some of these become obvious at once when a comparison of the jewellery of the Far East with that of western Europe or America is attempted. Even the circumstance that in such a comparison Japan would have to be left almost entirely out of the question is relevant. Living in a mountainous country with scanty natural resources, and parted from their neighbours by the ocean, the Japanese hardly know the meaning of jewellery.

The character of the personal ornaments depends to a large extent upon the minerals and metals which a country provides, upon its climate, and upon the amount and nature of the clothing worn. Consideration must also be given to religious beliefs and national customs, giving to this or that article of jewellery a special significance, and limiting its use to persons of a particular age, condition or station. Personal ornaments may serve as indispensable articles of dress, rather than as mere embellishments, and their nature is thus to a large extent determined by the purpose they serve. The influence of religion and ritual observance is too obvious to need emphasizing. In the East, the custom of accumulating savings in the form of jewellery is a factor not to be overlooked. A young bride's dowry may consist entirely of personal ornaments in gold or silver, or of a head-dress strung with coins or precious stones. But others too find in jewellery a convenient means of holding their wealth, enabling them to have it continually with them, both for safeguarding and for use when occasion requires.

Jewellery in China is characterized by a delicacy and manipulative elaboration for which the Chinese craftsman shows great aptitude. Silver is by far the most usually employed of the precious metals, though ornaments are occasionally of solid gold. Silver jewellery is generally gilt to safeguard it from tarnishing. Rubies, amethysts and other precious and semi-precious stones are used—not cut in facets, but polished and set *en cabochon*. Gems and pearls are frequently drilled through and attached by means of a fine wire. Flexible strings of jewels, often interspersed with plaques of carved jade or enamel, are worn as personal ornaments and employed in a variety of other ways. This practice gives a distinctive character to Chinese jewellery.

Personal jewellery in China often takes the form, or bears the images, of the animals, real or fabulous, and the numerous ritual and symbolical objects of Chinese art and culture. A dragon or phoenix may form a bracelet or decorate a head-dress or a hairpin. The "precious ornaments," or eight Buddhist emblems of happy augury, are strung with rows of pearls or used separately. It should be noticed that the first of the "precious ornaments" is a round jewel wreathed with a fillet, and that innumerable works of art represent the dragon pursuing or grasping the flaming jewel of omnipotence. Emblems often indicate the rank and office of the wearer, from the emperor downwards. Special ornaments were worn by the Manchu or Chinese ladies, and various limitations were imposed by sumptuary laws.

Gold and silver plaques were manipulated in several ways. They might be pressed into moulds, hammered in relief, cut into openwork patterns or engraved. The dexterity of the Chinese craftsman has carried the art of filigree (*q.v.*) in the precious metals to a degree of intricacy and minuteness unsurpassed elsewhere. It is used for the most elaborate head-dresses and for all kinds of personal ornaments. Jewellery in gold and silver is often enamelled—gold generally in light blue obtained from copper, and silver in dark blue from a cobaltiferous ore; both colours are also used together.

The gold filigree bracelet is in the form of two dragons. The head-dress was worn by a Manchu lady of high rank. It has a wire foundation covered with silk and mounted with panels of silver-gilt filigree in the form of bats (for happiness) and peaches (for longevity). It is overlaid with kingfisher plumes and enriched with amber, jadeite, amethysts, coral and pearls. The cap of state, from the Summer Palace, Peking, is also of silver-gilt filigree with kingfisher plumes and enrichment of pearls and coral. The ornament includes figures of Taoist immortals, birds and butterflies. The bride's head-dress is of the same materials, showing a temple pavilion, dragons and phoenixes. The chatelaine has a row of silver-gilt toilet articles. There are various forms of hairpins, hair-ornaments, cap-ornaments, earrings and buttons in silver and silver-gilt, with jewels, enamels and kingfisher plumes.

The Indian practice of inlaying precious stones in finger-rings and plaques of jade was copied in China, where jade and jadeite rank among the most valued of precious stones. Figure-subjects are sometimes carried out in gems and semi-precious stones, encrusted on plaques of white jade. Small personal ornaments of many kinds have been carved in jade.

ENAMEL

Enamels do not appear to have reached China until long after they were to be found throughout Europe. The Chinese make no claim to their invention; but, on the contrary the native term, "*Fu-lin* ware" (hence *Fa-lan*), directly suggests an origin in the eastern Roman provinces, that name having been applied to the Byzantine Empire by Chinese historians as early as the 7th century. The derivation of the word has been the subject of controversy and is uncertain; but all authorities are agreed as to the western origin of the art; which was, in all probability, introduced into China by Arab traders, or by travelling craftsmen working their way eastwards as opportunity arose of plying their craft profitably. Glass, which in China was also of alien origin, was imported from the Roman Empire certainly as early as the 3rd century A.D.; but it was not until the reign of T'ai Wu (424–452) of the Northern Wei dynasty that craftsmen from an Indo-Scythian kingdom on the northwest border of India came to the Wei capital in Shansi and succeeded in making excellent opaque glass of various colours from local minerals.

Although the Chinese were thus informed as to the production of an essential material for the making of enamels and were already most highly skilled in the working of bronzes and other metals, it is remarkable that there appears to have been no development of the art of enamelling at least until the 13th century, when the Mongolian conquests introduced into the Far East so many arts hitherto unknown. A record exists, in the *Ko ku yao lun*, a book on antiquities published in 1387, of the production on a large and varied scale of enamelled ware which "resembles the cloisonné work of

140

Fo-lang." This is herein termed also *Kuei kuo yao*, ware of the devils' country. It also states that natives of Yunnan have established factories for this ware in Peking and that the enamels made at the provincial capital, Yunnan-fu, are "fine, lustrous and beautifully finished." It appears therefore that the *Ta shih yao* or Arabian (so-called) enamel ware was well established in China at this period; and that Byzantine work of similar character was also so well known as to invite comparison with the native product and that, as pointed out by M. Paléologue, "the workmanship (of the Chinese enamels) presents occasionally, in fact, striking resemblances with certain enamels of the Byzantine School: the mixture of different enamels inside the wall of the same cell, the employment of gold encrustations in the treatment of the figures and hands, etc."

From the technical point of view, Chinese enamels fall into three categories—cloisonné, champlevé and painted. In none does the technique vary appreciably from that employed in western countries.

Cloisonné.—In cloisonné, the outlines of practically every detail of the design are defined with narrow bands or ribbons of metal—copper, silver or gold—soldered edgewise to the base, in such a way as to cover the whole surface to be decorated, with shallow cells sometimes called *cloisons*, but this term is more correctly employed to designate the bands themselves. These are then filled with the appropriate enamel colours, ground to a fine powder, moistened and tightly packed into their respective cells. "The piece," says Dr. S. W. Bushell, "is usually fired in the open courtyard, protected only by a primitive cover of iron network, the charcoal fire being regulated by a number of men standing round with large fans in their hands." This process has to be repeated several times, on account of the shrinkage, under heat, of the enamel, and the pitting which also takes place. When the whole surface is thus satisfactorily covered in this manner it is ground down to an even texture with pumice stone and polished with charcoal; the metal surfaces of the cloisons, now clearly visible being gilded, as well as those parts of the object which have not been adorned with enamel; for instance, the neck, rims and foot of a vase as well as any decoration in relief which projects beyond the enamelled surface.

The earliest examples of cloisonné enamel that can be authentically associated with the Far East are mirrors in the *Shōsō in* ("lonely building"), at Nara in Japan. The backs of these have cloisonné work, somewhat crude in character. There is no doubt that these and other objects in the collection were deposited in the *Shōsō in* in the year 756 by Kōmyō-Kōgō, widow of the Emperor Shomo-Tennō (724–749), with other treasures collected during his life. We have here, therefore, authentic examples of the art that must date back at least to the T'ang dynasty, and may, as is certainly the case with some other objects in the collection, be of Chinese workmanship. It is generally agreed that they are neither Japanese nor Byzantine. So far as is known at present, the sequence of Chinese enamels with which we are acquainted begins, however, only in the Yuan period; and the earliest recorded marks belong to the reign of the last emperor of that dynasty (1341–1367). The great period of the production is certainly that of the Ming dynasty which followed and existed until 1643.

The mark most commonly found within this epoch is that of the Ching T'ai reign (1450–1456); so Dr. Bushell suggests that there must have been a great revival of the art at this time, as even in his day the term *Ching T'ai Lan* was "commonly used in Peking as a general synonym for cloisonné enamels." He points out the significance of the fact that this reign covers the time of the last siege and capture of Constantinople by the Turks (1453) when some of the craftsmen then dispersed may have even penetrated to China. However this may be, the Ming enamels, bold in design, with fine depth and purity of colour, were never surpassed in later epochs. The two shades of blue, a dark lapis-lazuli tone and a pale sky-blue with a very slight tinge of green, are particularly excellent. The red is of dark coral tint and the yellow full-bodied and pure. Greens derived from copper are sparingly used and Dr. Bushell states that *rouges d'or* (reds made of gold) do not come into the colour scheme at all. The black and white are the least successful; the former shallow and dull, the latter clouded and muddy. At the same time, an imperfection of technique is noted, a close examination revealing minute pitting in the enamels, due to inadequate packing of the material, and some want of polish in the surface. These technical defects, however, do not appreciably detract from the artistic value of the Ming enamels and, indeed, serve as a clue to their identification.

To the patronage of the Emperor K'ang Hsi (1662–1722) was due a great revival of art industries. In 1680 he established a whole series of

BY COURTESY OF THE METROPOLITAN MUSEUM OF ART, NEW YORK

CHINESE PORCELAINS OF THE K'ANG HSI (1622–1722) AND CH'IEN LUNG (1736–95) PERIODS

Top Row: Peach-bloom chrysanthemum vase marked Ta Ch'ang K'ang Hsi Nein Chih, and rouge cup. *Clair-de-lune* Amphora. Mirror black Amphora, later period. Blue and White Hawthorn Ginger Jar. Apple Green Galley pot. Celadon Chrysanthemum Vase. Coral red enamel vase of the later period. Second Row: Temple Jars of the so-called *Famille Verte* type painted with enamels, the two at the left being called *Famille Jaune*, and *Famille Noire* because of their back-ground colouration. Bottom Row: Powder blue Temple Jar with reserved medallions in enamel decoration. *Famille Noire* Temple Jar. *Famille Rose* Temple Jar of later period with enamel decorations

BY COURTESY OF THE DIRECTOR OF THE VICTORIA AND ALBERT MUSEUM

CHINESE (MANCHU) HEAD-DRESSES AND JEWELLERY

1. Bracelet of gold filigree work in the form of two dragons
2. Head-dress of silk and silver-gilt worn by a Manchu lady of high rank
3. Silver-gilt filigree cap, probably a wedding head-dress, worked in a design of human figures and insects; ornamented with kingfisher plumes, pearls and coral

4. Bride's head-dress of silver-gilt filigree with applied ornament in form of a temple, dragons and phoenixes. Height, 12 in.
5. Chatelaine of gilt metal chains and pendants holding seven silver-gilt implements for the toilet. Length 15¼ in.

BY COURTESY OF (1) S. AND G. GUMP COMPANY, (3, 4, 5, 6, 8) THE METROPOLITAN MUSEUM OF ART, NEW YORK, (7) THE DEPARTMENT OF FINE ARTS, BROOKLYN MUSEUM

PAINTED, CLOISONNÉ AND CHAMPLEVÉ CHINESE ENAMELS OF THE XVIII. AND XIX. CENTURIES

1. Imperial teapot of Peking enamel painted, Ch'ien Lung period (1736–95)

2. Round screen of Peking enamel, with a landscape design

3. Incense burner of cloisonné on copper, in three parts, bowl, ring and cover. It is decorated with floral designs and openwork on turquoise blue ground; height, 16 inches. 19th century

4. Incense burner in cloisonné with stand and cover of same material and design. Turquoise blue ground; 24½ x 12½ inches. Ch'ien Lung period

5. Large dish of Peking enamel decorated with Taoist sages walking. Ch'ien Lung period

6. Cloisonné snuff bottle of turquoise blue and white enamel ground, with coral stopper; height, 2-3/7 inches. Ch'ien Lung period

7. Seated figures and tripod censer of cloisonné. The figures, 37 inches in height, are on garden seats, also in cloisonné, and represent an empress (left) and a princess, probably of the Ch'ien Lung period. The robes of the former are executed with designs on chocolate colour ground and those of the latter on a ground of blue and imperial yellow. Faces and hands are gilt. The censer is enamelled in both cloisonné and champlevé on turquoise blue ground. The handles are of archaic sceptre-shape and the cover is surmounted by a gilt bronze finial; height 36 inches. Era of Tao-kuang (1821–50)

8. Gourd-shaped cloisonné snuff bottle, with metal and enamel stopper, on wood stand; height, 2⅞ inches. Ch'ien Lung period

imperial factories for this purpose, of which that devoted to the manufacture of enamels was No. 6 on the official list. Here he had made sets of incense vessels of cloisonné enamel for presentation to the numerous Buddhist temples in the neighbourhood of Peking, founded under his auspices and other objects for the honorific gifts which were characteristic of his enlightened reign. The enamels of his time were marked by an improvement in technical quality as compared with those of the Ming period, while the finer qualities of the latter are still, to a considerable extent, in evidence. In many cases the forms of ancient bronze vessels were revived for these purposes, with the addition of enrichments in enamel. The style of this reign persisted during that of K'ang Hsi's successor, Yung Chêng (1723–1735); while the long period on the throne occupied by Ch'ien Lung (1736–1795) was marked, as in the case of many other industrial arts, by a further perfection of technique, but with the loss of much of the vigour of design and breadth of execution that distinguished the products of earlier periods. Modern enamels, chiefly imitations of older work, are more hurriedly made and not so well finished. The quality of the gilding especially is far below that of the older productions.

Champlevé.—In *champlevé enamels*, cloisons are not used, the hollows to be filled with colour being cut out of the metal with graving tools. Otherwise the process is similar to that last described. It is probably the oldest method of enamelling known, and there is no evidence as to the date of its introduction into China, though some of the most ancient examples extant belong to this class. The general trend of design and execution, historically, is much the same as that of cloisonné. Examples in which both methods are employed are not infrequent.

Painted Enamels.—The *painted enamels* of China, generally known from the principal seat of their manufacture as *Canton enamels*, are practically identical in technique with the Limoges and other painted enamels of Europe. Specimens of these are known to have been taken to China by the missionaries of the late 17th and 18th centuries, and not only to have exercised direct influence on the Chinese ware, but also, in some cases, to have been copied. Representations of European subjects, copies of engravings and armorial decorations, are also found there. Painted enamels are termed by the Chinese *Yang t'zu* (literally "foreign porcelain"), the palette of colours

143

used being the same as with enamelled porcelain though in the case of enamels it is termed *Yang ts'ai* (foreign colours). A ground of opaque enamel, generally white, is laid on the copper; and on this the colours are superimposed and fired. Owing to the soft nature of the ground, these sink in and are incorporated with it, producing a loss of brilliance, which, as admitted by the Chinese, renders them inferior to enamelled porcelain with which they may well be compared. The earliest dated example of Canton enamel consists of a set of objects inscribed *Yung chêng yu chih* (1723–1735) made to imperial order. Although imitations have continued to be made, nothing of real quality in this style was produced after the termination of the reign of Ch'ien Lung in 1795. The method has always been looked upon by the Chinese as in alien taste; a writer of 1782 (quoted by Bushell) remarks, "They are only fit for use as ornaments of ladies' apartments—not at all for the chaste furniture of the library of a simple scholar." Enamels of this kind were also made, with characteristic decoration, for the Siamese market.

Translucent (as opposed to opaque) enamels were occasionally made by Chinese artisans. Important pieces are rare, but sometimes of fine quality, a deep blue, obtained from a native cobaltiferous ore of manganese, and a pale turquoise blue from copper being especially successful. This method more often appears in conjunction with gold and silver in Chinese jewellery; in which, also, imitations, in enamel, of real gems are frequently employed.

Japanese Enamels.—The examples of enamel in the imperial treasury at Nara, Japan, have already been referred to; and it may now be repeated that they cannot be attributed to Japanese craftsmanship. No examples of authentic enamels of Japanese origin that can be dated earlier than the end of the 16th century seem to exist. The western influence which promoted the art in China does not appear to have penetrated to Japan; the first Japanese appearance of the art seems to have been in the form of the decoration of sword furniture by the founders of the Hirata family who worked at Kyōto under the patronage of the Tokugawa Shōgun, Iyeyasu about the year 1611. They made use, on a small scale, both of the cloisonné and champlevé methods. A dull green was one of the first colours obtained. The range of colours was afterwards extended with a white of good quality. There was no further development of importance until the 19th century,

144

when Kaji Tsunikichi (born A.D. 1802) of Nagoya established in that city an important and successful manufacture of cloisonné which obtained a considerable vogue especially among foreigners. On this basis further developments have taken place of considerable interest.

Modern Japanese artists have modified the cloisonné process with remarkable ingenuity and have produced work of great interest, in which the cloisons are sometimes completely veiled, the resultant effect being that of enamelled porcelain with realistic designs of flowers, etc., and a wide and almost unrestricted range of colour. Namikawa of Tōkyō has been one of the most successful of these. A Kyōto artist of the same name has worked with credit in true *cloisonné*. J. Ando of Nagoya has obtained novel effects by the use of translucent enamel on a silver basis. These developments have carried the art of enamel very far from the old traditions, but, while the skill and ingenuity of technique they evince may be appreciated, it cannot be said that in decorative value they compare with the older Chinese tradition. During the 19th century, the Japanese produced many imitations of the latter; which, for a time, gave rise to quite a false appreciation of their place in the history of the art.

JADE AND OTHER HARD STONE CARVINGS

JADE

THERE ARE three minerals that are called jade: (1) Nephrite, known since earliest times; (2) Jadeite, described in 1868 by A. Damour, the famous French mineralogist, as new. The stone was of pure white with a faint purple tint. Jadeite is also often the finest jade; it is almost emerald green; (3) Chloromelanite, a dark green, almost black material. Analyses of these three minerals are given below. Although the most intensive investigations have been carried on concerning the origin and uses of Jade from the earliest times, it was not until 1868 that Damour found that nephrite contained lime and magnesia, whereas jadeite and chloromelanite contained alumina and soda.

Structure.—The structure of jadeite is either granular or fibrous, the former being more characteristic. It may be studied to the best advantage in such thin, translucent, highly polished objects as bowls, cups or plates. On holding such a specimen against a light each crystal composing it often stands out quite sharply, owing to the fact that the light strikes the surface and cleavages of each crystal at a different angle, thus giving to each a slightly different appearance. The individual grains are sometimes prismatic in shape, and sometimes equidimensional, with diameters up to 3 mm. in exceptional cases.

The structure of nephrite is characteristically fibrous, and of such a fine grain that the individual fibres are but rarely visible except under the microscope. The fibres in this aggregate are arranged in various ways: parallel

146

BY COURTESY OF (1, 2, 7) THE METROPOLITAN MUSEUM OF ART, NEW YORK, (3, 4, 5, 6, 8) THE DEPARTMENT OF FINE ARTS, BROOKLYN MUSEUM

THE CLOISONNÉ PROCESS AND CHINESE CLOISONNÉ ENAMELS OF THE XV.–XVIII. CENTURIES

1 and 2. Stages in the process of cloisonné enamelling, showing first, the metal plate on which the design is executed by soldering thin metal bands or *cloisons* to the base to form shallow cells (second step). These cells are filled with powdered enamel colours, and the piece is then fired and polished. 3. Beaker-shaped imperial vase with gilt bronze dragon and phoenix handles. Turquoise blue ground sustaining flowers and vines; height 41½ inches. Reign of Ch'ing Tai (1450–56), Ming dynasty. 4. Trumpet-shaped vase decorated with eyes and cloud forms on turquoise blue ground; height, 14½ inches. Ming dynasty. 5. Beaker-shaped vase with floriated ornament, scrolls and palmettes; height, 21½ inches. K'ang-hsi period (1662–1722). 6. Twin vases enamelled in green and joined by bronze ornaments, signifying the unity of the universe; height, 25½ inches. Era of Yung-Cheng (1723–35). 7. Jui sceptre (repaired); length, 15¾ inches. K'ang-hsi period. 8. Dove-shaped altar wine vessel on wheels, patterned after a type of ancient vessel used at rituals. Besides the conventional ornamentation, the decoration consists of scrolls and various designs, such as monsters' heads, copied from very old bronzes; height, 22 inches. K'ang-hsi period

BY COURTESY OF (1, 2, 3, 4, 6, 10) THE FIELD MUSEUM OF NATURAL HISTORY, CHICAGO, (5, 8) THE MUSEUM OF THE UNIVERSITY OF PENNSYLVANIA, (7) THE AMERICAN MUSEUM OF NATURAL HISTORY, (9) THE SMITHSONIAN INSTITUTION

JADE, LAPIS LAZULI AND OTHER STONES

Chinese: 1. *Pi* disc or symbol of heaven with associated symbols of dragons. 2. Jade images and symbols of the deity Earth. Chou period, 1122–255 B.C. 3. Jade celt, 22 cm. long. 4. Symbol of Deity of Earth, ornament for scabbard, and archer's thumb-ring. Han period, 206 B.C.–A.D. 220. 5. Lapis lazuli vase, ht. 28 in, Ch'ien Lung period, 1736–96. 6. Green jade monster, Han period. 8. Ornamental green jade table screen. Ch'ien Lung period. 9. Crystal ball, 12.83 in. diam., wt. 106.75 lb.; the most perfect one of large size known. Made in China in 1924. In the U.S. National Museum. 10. Resonant white and greenish jade. Ch'ien Lung period. *Mexican:* 7. Votive ceremonial axe from Oaxaca; green jade

to one another over considerable areas; in tufted or fan-shaped groups; or curved, twisted, interlocked and felted in most intricate fashion. The coarser visible structure is due to groups of these fine fibres, and is dependent on their internal arrangement. A sinewy or horn-like appearance is extremely common, being visible on both rough and polished surfaces. It seems to be due to the groupings of the fibres into tufted or fan-shaped bundles, sometimes of considerable size, and separated from each other by indistinct parting surfaces which are often curved into irregular forms.

Composition.—The following table shows characteristic chemical analyses for nephrite, jadeite and chloromelanite.

	NEPHRITE	JADEITE	CHLOROMELANITE
	%	%	%
Silica (SiO$_2$)	58.00	58.24	56.12
Titanium dioxide (TiO$_2$) .	..	..	0.19
Alumina (Al$_2$O$_3$) . . .	1.30	24.47	14.96
Ferric oxide (Fe$_2$O$_3$) . .	..	1.01	3.34
Ferrous oxide (FeO$_3$) . .	2.07	..	6.54
Manganese oxide (MnO) .	..	..	0.47
Lime (CaO)	13.24	0.69	5.17
Magnesia (MgO) . . .	24.18	0.45	2.79
Soda (Na$_2$O)	1.28	14.70	10.99
Potash (K$_2$O)	..	1.55	trace
	100.07	101.11	100.57

Colour.—Absolutely pure jadeite should be white, without a tinge of colour. So also an ideal nephrite, containing only lime and magnesia, should be colourless. The colours which actually exist are due to the admixture of other bases in the composition. In general, the green colour of jadeite is due to chromium—the colouring matter of the emerald, but jadeite is never transparent as is the emerald, but is at its best translucent—and that of nephrite to iron. Occasionally, however, anomalies are found, and the analytical data fail to account for the colour or lack of it of an occasional particular specimen.

Lustre.—The lustre of both jadeite and nephrite on fresh fracture is dull and wax-like, with very few reflecting surfaces. Polished jadeite has ordinarily a somewhat vitreous lustre, while polished nephrite ordinarily has an oily lustre. This oily appearance is highly characteristic of many of the green nephrites.

Sonority.—The resonant character of jade has been known to the Chinese since ancient times, and when united with the proper translucency and colour, was regarded as a sure sign of the genuineness of the material. "Sounding-stones" and stones for polishing them are mentioned in the earliest historical records of China (23 centuries B.C.).

The musical jade is often cut in the form of a fish and suspended by a thong, and when struck the full tones can be heard.

Occurrence.—Although jade objects in considerable numbers have been found over rather wide-spread areas, there are only a few localities identified where it is known to occur in place. In addition to these there are several others where jade has been found, having been transported there from its place of origin by the action of rivers or glaciers. And finally, there are other localities in which worked jade is found, sometimes in considerable profusion; in many of these cases the source of the material is pure conjecture, while in others the character of the material is such as to give some indication as to its point of origin. The greatest source of material, and the one that has been studied the most, is in the Kachin country of Upper Burma, near the junction of the Chadwin and Uru rivers, at about 25° to 27° N. lat. and 95° to 97° E. longitude. These quarries were discovered in the 13th century, but it was not until 1784 that trade was established with China, and a regular supply of stone was carried to Yunnan. Since the beginning of the 19th century Mogaung has been the centre of the jade trade in Burma.

Jade occurs in small amounts in several places in Central India, particularly in the State of Rewa. Although conclusive evidence is lacking, the indications seem to show that the Indian jade is all nephrite. One of the oldest and most important of the jade-producing districts is in the K'un Lun mountains, south of Khotan, in southeastern Turkistan, described by the Seklogewitt brothers. Here are found both nephrite and jadeite, the former, however, greatly predominating. It was from this district that much of the early Chinese material was obtained.

The occurrence of nephrite in Siberia has been known since early in the 19th century, but it was not until 1896–97 that any definite information was

148

obtained. At that time a Russian Government expedition under Von Jaczewski discovered several occurrences of nephrite in place in the Sajan mountains of central Siberia, between the Belaja and Kitou rivers on the north and south, and the Onot and Urick rivers on the east and west.

Although boulders and worked objects of jade had been known in Europe for many years, it was not until 1884 that it was discovered in place by Traube at Jordansmühl, and a few years later at Reichenstein, in Silesia. This material is nephrite. These discoveries were supplemented in 1899 by that of Dr. George F. Kunz, who found at Jordansmühl one of the largest pieces of nephrite that has ever been quarried. This specimen, weighing 4,812 lbs., is now in the American Museum of Natural History in New York City. Although several nephrite boulders have been found in glacial deposits in other localities, no other occurrences of nephrite in place are known in Europe. No occurrence of jadeite *in situ* is known in Europe but it is mined extensively in Mogaung, Burma.

In North America nephrite has been found in place in Alaska, about 150 m. above the mouth of the Kowak River, at 67° 5' N. lat. and 158° 15' W. longitude. Boulders of nephrite have also been found along the lower Fraser and the upper Lewes rivers in British Columbia. While material has not been found in place in either of these localities, all indications lead to the conclusion that the boulders had originated in the immediate locality.

Nephrite has long been used by the natives of New Zealand in tools, ornaments and magnificent ceremonial implements of various kinds. The material occurs in boulders chiefly on the west coast of South Island, although other localities of lesser importance are known. Nephrite is found in place on the west coast of the island of Uen, off the southeastern point of New Caledonia.

Although a fondness for jade is almost a national characteristic in China, there are no known occurrences in China. Most of the material used by the Chinese has come from either Chinese Turkistan or Burma. It is also possible that some Siberian or New Zealand material has been used.

Of the many thousand pieces of carved jade from China and India, with the possible exception of the small buttons, there are scarcely two pieces alike. The artist studied the piece of rough material to discover what could

149

best be made of it and then made the design to fit the piece. The result is that most of the pieces are artistic and the lapidary work unique. They stand in an art by themselves. +

In Europe worked objects of both nephrite and jadeite have been found over wide areas. Nephrite has been found particularly in the vicinity of the ancient lake villages of Switzerland. Jadeite objects were more widely distributed in Germany, France, Belgium, Switzerland and Italy. In Mexico and Central America large numbers of jadeite objects have been found. While these are the chief localities, there are also numerous others in which either jadeite or nephrite objects, or both, have been found, without clear evidence as to the source of the material.

There have been two historic debates concerning the occurrences of jade, both of which extended over many years. The first was concerned with the question as to whether jade was to be found in place in Europe, or whether the material used by the prehistoric peoples of central Europe was all brought from the outside, either by glacial action or by commerce. This question was definitely settled by the discoveries of Traube and Kunz, described above. The second concerned a similar question with regard to Mexican and Central American material. No jade has as yet been discovered in place in these countries, and many have thought that its presence and use there was an indication of ancient contacts between these peoples and the Orient. While this theory has been actively promulgated by many adherents, no definite proofs have as yet been forthcoming on either side.

Uses.—It is remarkable that men even from the earliest times, whether the prehistoric lake-dwellers of Europe, the ancient inhabitants of the valley of Mexico, the aborigines of northwest America, the natives of New Zealand, or the people of China, found small blocks or boulders of jade, of a wide variety and range of colour, but which they had the acumen to determine were of a hard, tough material suitable for axes and other utilitarian purposes, as well as for artistic uses. We know that there was prehistoric jade in the graves in China, and more would have been found had there not been a sentiment against opening up the buried remains in that country. Later on jade was selected as a material possessing many of the most charming qualities of beauty, lustre and toughness, so that many thousands of pieces of jade, from the purest white and the palest green to a dark green, have been carved in the designs of many countries, pieces that in many cases have required years to make. As an example of the endless patience used in the execution of such pieces, there is a necklace of 100 links with a pendant, all of one unbroken piece, in the American Museum of Natural History. And in the F. O. Mathieson bequest to the Metropolitan Museum of Art are four covered vases which open in the centre for fruits, the cover and lower part all of one unbroken piece.

The greatest rulers of the East have treated this stone with a reverence attributed to no other material. The poems of emperors have been recorded on tablets of jade and the great fish bowl in the Bishop collection, weighing 120 lbs., has the poem of an emperor on its inner base. There spect and reverence placed in this stone is well deserved, and if the Chinese had all the articles that were originally in China, they would form a collection not rivalled by that of any other nation or by that of any other material.

Great masses of a wonderful material stained brown by contact with bodies, or stained brown to look as if they had been buried with bodies, is known as tomb jade. Some of it is believed to date back 20 centuries. The Chinese have obtained some of the most magnificent jade and frequently have spent as much as a year searching for a single piece. Some splendid examples of these may be seen in the Heber R. Bishop collection in the Metropolitan Museum of Art; the Johnson collection in Philadelphia, gifts in memory of Dr. George Byron Gordon. Other specimens are in the Boston Museum of Fine Arts, the British Museum, the Louvre and in Berlin, and many other places throughout the world.

Jade of different colours was used in China for the six precious tablets employed in the worship of heaven and earth and the four cardinal points. For the worship of heaven there was a dark-green round tablet, and for the earth an octagonal yellow tablet; the east was worshipped with a green pivoted tablet, the west with a white "tiger tablet," the north with a black semi-circular tablet, and the south with a tablet of red jade. The yellow girdles worn by the Chinese emperors of the Manchu dynasty were variously ornamented with precious stones, according to the different ceremonial observances at which the emperor presided. For the services in the temple of heaven, lapis lazuli was used; for the altar of earth, yellow jade; for a sacrifice at the altar of the sun, red coral; and for ceremonies before the altar of the moon, white jade.

Jade amulets of many different forms were popular with the Chinese, as were also rings, ear-rings and beads, but in general, jade was much more used for decorative pieces than for articles of personal adornment. While in other localities jade has been used extensively for axes, adzes, knives and other purely utilitarian objects, for which its hardness and toughness make it peculiarly applicable, the reverence with which the stone was held in China seems to have precluded its use in such fashion, and the purely utilitarian is almost entirely absent in the Chinese uses; here the ornamental features greatly predominate, and where the utilitarian features do come in, it is usually in a vase, cup, plate or bowl, or some similar object, in which beauty may be combined with utility. It is possible that the pre-Chinese used jade for axes and celts but the later Chinese ornamented and recarved these.

The jade objects found in Mexico and Central America are frequently of a rich, almost emerald-green colour, and there have been thousands of pieces found, from the smallest fragments to the great adze weighing 16 lbs., which is now in the American Museum of Natural History. Much of the Mexican material has been used in religious ceremonies, but utilitarian and ornamental material is also found. The outstanding find of jade objects in Mexico was at the sacred well of Chitzinitza in Yucatan, into which had been cast as votive offerings hundreds of pieces of jadeite. This valuable discovery was made by Dr. E. H. Thompson of the Peabody Museum, who spent a lifetime in this region.

In New Zealand, where the most primitive methods held, jade was in high esteem among the Maori chiefs, who had their *patou-patous* (small axes which they held under the arm) perforated at the upper end and ornamented with jade. *Hei tikis*—crudely carved small human figures—were made of jade with narrow slant eyes of abalone shell, usually facing to the right, but occasionally to the left. These were worn as amulets and frequently handed down from one generation to another, as the material is almost indestructible.

Commercial Value.—Jade of medium colour cut into the form of bead necklaces sell as low as $50, but exceptional quality commands correspondingly high prices. An emerald green *feitsui* necklace, 30 in. long, of 125 beads, weighing 304 carats (approximately 2 oz. Troy), with a centre bead ½ in. in diameter, and end beads ⅛ in. in diameter, commanded a price of $80,000; larger necklaces have brought more than $100,000. Exceptional pieces have been made into brooches at prices from $1,000 to $5,000. Ring stones cut cabochon on top sell at from $100 to $2,000 each. The thumb rings worn by the Chinese nobility frequently commanded over £1,000, and, it is claimed, even up to £2,000 for the ring which is a relic of the time when the archer drew his bow with a thumb ring of wood, horn, agate or jade. An exceptionally fine ring of this character was worn by the former ambassador to the United States, Wu Ting Fang; this ring had been originally worn on a larger hand, and had a lining of fine gold to fit it to the finger of the new wearer of the ring.

Minerals and Imitations Mistaken for Jade.—Under this heading we have three types of material to consider: those which through a close similarity to jade in colour, toughness and lustre may be mistaken for the true material; those which have been stained, coloured, or otherwise treated in order to enhance this similarity; and those that are purely and entirely artificial imitations. The natural minerals that resemble jade most closely are those having a similar chemical composition, *i.e.*, complex silicates, but various forms of pure quartz and a few other minerals also fall into this group. The determination of the hardness and specific gravity of the specimen is usually sufficient to differentiate between the true and false jade. Jadeite has a hardness of approximately 7.0 and a specific gravity of 3.2 to 3.4; nephrite has a hardness of 6.5 and a specific gravity of 2.9; very few other minerals show this particular combination of hardness and gravity.

Saussurite is probably the most important of these materials easily mistaken for true jade. It is a compact, tough, heavy mineral with a hardness and gravity almost identical with jadeite, and this makes the differentiation difficult. Next in point of resemblance is fibrolite, or sillimanite. Like saussurite it has the hardness and gravity of jadeite, but it is readily identified chemically, being a practically pure silicate of aluminium. The Alaskan natives have frequently used pectolite for jade. This has a gravity close to nephrite, but is much softer. Wollastonite, occasionally confused with jade, can be detected by its softness as compared with jade. A number of different varieties of feldspar sometimes resemble jade. These are also lower in

153

gravity than jade, and most of them are lower in hardness. Chief among these are amazon-stone, eupholide, saccharite and labradorite.

Jadeite is classed chemically as a pyroxene, and in the same family of rocks are several other minerals quite similar to it, particularly omphacite and eclogite. These have the gravity of jadeite, but are softer. Diopsite has the hardness of nephrite and the gravity of jadeite, but can be distinguished by the difference in cleavage. Nephrite is an amphibole rock, and in this group we find also actinolite closely resembling it, but differing in the texture of the fibrous structure.

Outstanding among the green minerals is the emerald, a green variety of beryl, and it is possible for an opaque emerald to be mistaken for jade, though it may be readily differentiated by its higher hardness, lower gravity, and the presence of beryllium in its composition.

One of the minerals that most frequently resembles jade, especially in the East, is a variety of serpentine known as bowenite. This has both hardness and gravity higher than the average serpentine, but still lower than nephrite. It has a texture similar to that of jadeite, and where the colour was lacking, it has been stained in imitation. Antigorite and williamsite are translucent varieties of serpentine of a rich, green colour. Although the latter is much harder than the former, both are far softer than jade. Williamsite has an intense rich green colour.

A material recently placed on the market as South African jade is really a compact, translucent, green garnet. It is higher than jade in both gravity and hardness. Numerous forms of pure quartz may, by their colour and opacity, be mistaken for jade, particularly prase, plasma, chrysoprase, jasper, aventurine and moss agate. All these have a lower gravity than jade, and a hardness equalled only by the hardest jadeite. The minerals most difficult to differentiate from jade are prehnite, epidote, vesuvianite and agalmatolite. Prehnite has the hardness of nephrite and a gravity close to the lower limit for nephrite; its colour is good, but it lacks lustre, and is more brittle than true jade. Epidote has the hardness of jade, and a gravity in the upper limits of the range for jadeite, from which it may be distinguished by its strong cleavage, a more vitreous lustre, and the presence of considerable iron in its composition. Vesuvianite has about the same hardness and gravity as epidote, and like it has a more vitreous lustre than jade; it is

154

also more brittle, and has an uneven fracture. Another form of vesuvianite is named californite by the author. Agalmatolite is one of the minerals most frequently sold to the uninitiated in China, under misrepresentation as jade. It is readily detected, however, by its extreme softness, and less readily by its lower gravity. It has a compact, fine and homogeneous structure that makes it ideal for carving, but its colour is such that it is usually stained green in imitation of nephrite. It is stained in many other colours.

Under some conditions turquoise (a phosphate), malachite (a copper carbonate), and mossotite (a lime carbonate), may be mistaken for jade, but identification is simple in all cases by hardness, gravity and chemical composition.

China probably takes the lead over all other countries in the number of substances that have been mistaken, or substituted, for jade. This is due partly, particularly in earlier times, to lack of exact mineralogical information and technical methods of identification, and partly to the natural tendency toward substitution for, or imitation of, a highly prized and equally highly priced material. Prominent among these fabrications is the so-called pink jade, which, if truly pink, and not the pinkish-lavender characteristic of some Burmese jade, has always turned out on careful examination to be quartz, aniline dye absorbed into fine cracks and fissures in the material. This may be detected by rubbing the piece with cotton moistened in alcohol.

Another important type of fabricated material is made from a heavy lead glass, carefully tinted and most ingeniously polished to give the characteristic jade-like lustre by first giving a high polish and then deadening this to the desired degree by a fine hard powder. One form of this is made in imitation of the white and green "imperial jade" of China, and may be found in bracelets, ear-rings and other trinkets, in almost every Chinese shop. Another type is all green, in imitation of the Burmese jadeite, and another, known under the name of *pâte de riz*, is white with a faint bluish-green or bluish-grey tint. This same method of preparation of the surface has also been used on varieties of green quartz to simulate the lustre of jade.

Descriptive Literature.—Of all the Chinese works on jade the most interesting and most remarkable is the *Ku yü t'ou pu*, or *Illustrated Description of Ancient Jade*, a catalogue divided into 100 books and embellished with nearly 700 figures. It was published in 1176, and lists the magnificent collection of jade objects belonging to the first emperor of the Southern Sung dynasty. One of the treasures here described was a four-sided plaque of pure white jade, over 2 ft. in height and breadth. The design was a figure seated on a mat, with a flower vase on its left and an alms-bowl on its right, in the midst of rocks enveloped in clouds.

The most complete and modern descriptive work on jade is the catalogue of the H. R. Bishop collection of jade in the Metropolitan Museum of Art. This is the most remarkable collection of jade in existence, and the two great volumes of the catalogue and accompanying descriptive matter fully match the collection itself in magnificence. The catalogue was illustrated by some of the greatest artists of the time. The volumes were not sold, but were distributed to libraries and museums here and abroad, to a few royal personages, and to several of Mr. Bishop's relatives. The author of this article devoted 12 years of his leisure to the mineralogical studies and the guidance of the scientific study of the many experts whom he called upon to aid in this great work.

OTHER HARD STONES

AMONG the other hard stones that have been cut, engraved and polished along lines similar to jade are the various forms of quartz (rock crystal, agate, carnelian, chalcedony and jasper) and the softer but highly valued materials, such as malachite, fluorite, rhodonite and lapis lazuli. All of these materials lend themselves well to this type of treatment, and in fact, as has already been mentioned, many of them have in some form or other frequently been mistaken, or substituted, for jade.

Of all the hard stones, probably rock crystal and agate have been most used, and in a wide variety of forms. Crystal has been particularly popular in vases and other ornamental forms, and as crystal balls. The outstanding example of the latter form is a ball 30 in. in diameter, made from Burmese crystal, and finished in Japan.

Jasper (q.v.) found in Russia is not excelled by that of any other country. It has a grey, almost putty colour, and a texture of wonderful homogeneity. Of this material tables and other pieces are made which are unequalled by any other lapidary work in existence. Aventurine, a quartz containing brilliant scales of other coloured minerals, is found in the Ural Mountains, and has been used in vases up to 6 ft. in height. Rhodonite (*q.v.*) is a member of the pyroxene group, the same family to which jadeite belongs; it is usually a beautiful rose or red colour, but is sometimes a light brown. The name rhodonite, from the Greek word *rhodon*, rose, suggests its colour. The mineral has been used as a gem, and for various types of ornamental objects; the sarcophagus of the Tsar Alexander II. was constructed from rhodonite found near Ekaterinburg (now Sverdlovsk). It is also found associated with manganese deposits in other parts of the world, its composition being manganese silicate. It has a hardness between 5 and 6, and a specific gravity of 3.5 to 3.6. It is slightly translucent, has little lustre, but takes a fairly good polish. Rhodonite was especially the imperial stone of Russia, and is there found in great masses.

One of the tsarinas of Russia wished an egg cut of pure rose rhodonite, without a streak of black in it, and one ton of this material was cut without finding a single piece large enough to cut the egg which did not have a streak of some kind in it.

It is strange that two great colours have been generally known and appreciated throughout the ages, one a royal blue and the other a royal green —lapis lazuli and malachite. Both of these being opaque, very wonderful pieces can be made from them, as they can be cut into thin sections, from $\frac{1}{8}$ to $\frac{1}{4}$ in. in thickness, and then strengthened by cementing them to a suitable backing, either slate or some material that does not contract or bend.

Lapis lazuli (*q.v.*) is one of the oldest of the gem materials, having been used for 6,000 years, and the supply has been continuous. During this entire period the chief sources of supply have been Persia and Afghanistan. It is sent to the markets in masses of from 1 to 5 lbs. One mass of 160 lbs. reached the United States several years ago, and another of 30 lbs. was found in the Oxus River district of Afghanistan. One of the results of the visit to Europe of King Amanullah in 1928 was a grant to a German firm of a monopoly for the exportation of Afghan lapis lazuli.

Obsidian (*q.v.*), or volcanic glass, is found in great quantities in the Valley of Mexico. Some wonderful chipping, grinding and polishing have been done on this material. One of the best examples is the Father Fisher knife in the Blake collection in the National Museum in Washington—a knife

19 in. in length. Another fine example is a mask, almost the size of a human face. Ornaments for the ear and for the lips were frequently made with the thinness of paper and polished exquisitely and carved in the centre. Mirrors 1 in. thick were made of this material, some of which may be seen in the American Museum of Natural History that are 15 by 12 inches.

Emeralds (*q.v.*) were looted and mined in great quantities by the Spanish when they invaded Peru; these stones were also brought from the mines of the United States of Colombia. Five cases are believed to have been lost at sea. Large assignments were shipped to Spain and then sold in Paris. The more perfect stones were kept by the Spanish and French and the rest were shipped to India, Persia and Turkey, where the natives engraved them to hide the flaws. For many centuries they were known, and still are, as Indian emeralds. It is quite possible that these sustained the expense of the great traveller, Tavernier, who took many of these to India where he traded them for rubies from the Burmese mines and then sold the rubies in Europe. Louis XIV. is said also to have financed him. Some of these—very large ones—were found when the British captured King Thebaw's palace at Rangoon and they are now in the Indian Museum at London. Several hexagonal sections of the crystal were used, over three inches. There is hardly an Indian, Persian or Turkish ruler who does not possess some of these emeralds even to the present day, and frequently an en cabochon un-engraved emerald is worn in one ear and an en cabochon ruby in the other ear. These emeralds must have been sent to Turkey and Russia eastward by the thousands and it is very possible that Tavernier is responsible for the placing of many of them, and the great quantity that he had made his great trip possible. Among the Russian crown jewels and in some of the jewels of the Ourejene, Kremlin, and the treasury of the bishops are many fine emeralds, one of which the writer saw which was more than an inch across and excellent in colour.

IRON IN ART

Iron BEGAN to take its place in the brilliant Bronze Age culture of China about 500 B.C. By the end of the 2nd century of the present era bronze weapons had been almost completely supplanted, while iron had been generally substituted for bronze in common use in utensils and vessels of various kinds, tools, chariot-fittings and even small pieces of sculpture. These were commonly cast in sand-moulds, were patterned after bronze prototypes and were typical in style and decoration of the Han period.

The Iron Age in Japan is supposed to have begun in the 2nd century B.C., though the chief early remains are weapons from the dolmens of the 2nd to the 8th centuries A.D. The Japanese iron founder attained a considerable skill at an early date and acquired a social position which was never attained by the bronze caster, or by the iron workers in China where the bronze age tradition was much stronger.

From the 9th century iron increasingly took the place of bronze in China as a material for sculpture, especially in the north and under the Sung dynasty. The few extant examples from the 11th century and later show work done on a larger scale and in coarser technique than the bronzes, though the modelling is usually more naturalistic.

Several iron pagodas, ranging in size from miniature models to towers 30 or more metres in height, and dating from the 10th to the 14th century, give further evidence of the dexterity of the Chinese iron caster. These imitate in detail both the structural and decorative effects of the more common tile-roofed brick pagodas. Iron for temple furniture has long been

159

in use, and a large number of the braziers, censers, caldrons and bells found to-day in the temples are of iron.

In China in the 17th century the iron picture was developed, the craftsmen seeking to reproduce in permanent form through the medium of wrought iron the effects of the popular ink-sketches of the master painters. When completed, these pictorial compositions were mounted in windows, in lanterns or in frames as pictures. When in the latter form a paper or silk background often bore the signature and seal of the maker, heightening the resemblance to a painting. The craft flourished in Anwhei province and is still practised, though with less patience and fineness than formerly.

Embellishment of Armour.—It is apparent that iron has been used in China chiefly as a substitute or imitative medium, worked often with great skill but with little artistic invention. In Japan, however, the iron worker developed a distinctive and original means of expression and high artistic attainment in furniture for the sword. With the rise of feudalism and the establishment of the samurai class after the wars of the 12th century, the equipment of the warriors became an object for the efforts of the artist. At first these efforts were devoted to the embellishment of defensive armour, but from the 15th century the sword became the centre of attention. The blade is not properly part of our subject, but in the mountings, especially the guards (*tsuba*), we find exquisite artistry expressed chiefly in iron. A remarkably soft and pure variety of the metal especially free from sulphur was employed. It was worked by casting, hammering and chiselling; and innumerable surface effects were obtained by tooling, inlaying, incrustation, combination with other metals and patination by various, usually secret, processes. Simple conventional patterns, crests and pictorial designs were the bases for the decoration. As these were often furnished by painters or designers the criterion of connoisseurship in Japan is the unsurpassed technical quality of the handling of the iron itself. With the promulgation of the edict of 1876, prohibiting the wearing of swords, this art came to an end, but the skill of the Japanese iron worker may still be noted in numerous small decorative objects.

IVORY CARVING

Ivory has always been an important medium of expression for Chinese carvers, and many exquisite examples of their work have come down to us, though their names are rarely known. Chinese ivory carvers have generally had a greater appreciation of the intrinsic value of the material for their work than the carvers of Japan. An abundant supply and close intimacy with this material have doubtless helped to foster this appreciation among Chinese carvers, whereas the paucity of the supply and something in the Japanese character which was happier when carving wood, together with differences in certain phases of their culture, have prevented the higher development of ivory carving in Japan, though some excellent works have been produced. The former existence of elephants on Chinese soil is authenticated by linguistic, pictographic, historical, as well as archaeological evidence. The *Tso Chwan* (548 B.C.) records that the elephant has tusks which lead to its destruction owing to their use as gifts, and there are also a number of other references showing that ivory was taken as tax and brought as tribute to China and was greatly valued in early times. It came next to jade and was used as a mark of luxury for various purposes. Even articles such as pins for scratching the head, and the tips of bows, were made of elephant ivory in early Chinese antiquity. A 3rd century B.C. Minister of State, Mong Ch'ang-Kün, famous for his extravagance, possessed an ivory bed, which he presented to the prince of Ch'u. Ivory was used for personal ornament from time immemorial, and as early as the Ch'u dynasty (1122–247 B.C.) chopsticks were made of it and it was used to decorate the principal parts of some of the emperors' chariots. Later it became fashionable as a

161

decoration on the palanquins of important officials. Narrow memorandum tablets or *hu* of ivory, originally used at court by princes and high officials, later a mere symbol of rank and an indispensable accessory to ceremonial dress, were articles of great importance. Examples of ornamental ivory carving with angular, spiral, geometrical and floral designs, dating back to the Ch'u period, have come down to us.

In time the demand for ivory outgrew the native supply and large quantities of tusks had to be imported from Siam, Burma and India, which were described as long and large, and from Annan, which were small and short, as well as a variety yielding a red powder when cut by a saw which was pronounced to be of excellent quality. As early as the 12th century the Chinese knew that African ivory was the best. From the early 14th century at least the ivory from a slain elephant was esteemed the best; that taken not too long after natural death came next, while tusks discovered long after the elephant's death were least esteemed because the ivory was dull and opaque, and irregularly speckled.

Uses.—The Chinese cultured classes had always appreciated articles made of ivory, and ivory carving received imperial attention. In 1263 a bureau for carving in ivory and rhinoceros horn was established with some 150 craftsmen and an official in charge, and couches, tables and chairs, various implements, and ornaments for girdles inlaid with ivory and horn were made for the imperial household. In 1680 the emperor K'ang Hsi established *Tsao pan chu*, or imperial ateliers covering 27 branches of industry, including one for ivory carving, within the palace at Peking, and practical craftsmen from all over the empire were here brought together to produce fine work. They were in existence for over 100 years, turning out large numbers of excellent works bearing the stamp of the artistic fervour of the age. Authentic pieces from this imperial ivory carving atelier may be hard to identify, but many which exist in museums and private collections may reasonably be credited to it by reason of their superior workmanship which often reveals a marvellous quality of technical skill and harmonious beauty.

Great ingenuity is often displayed in the delicate workmanship of such an article as a fan, which may be made of finely cut plaited ivory threads, overlaid with carved flowers and birds, held by firmer pieces, likewise of

162

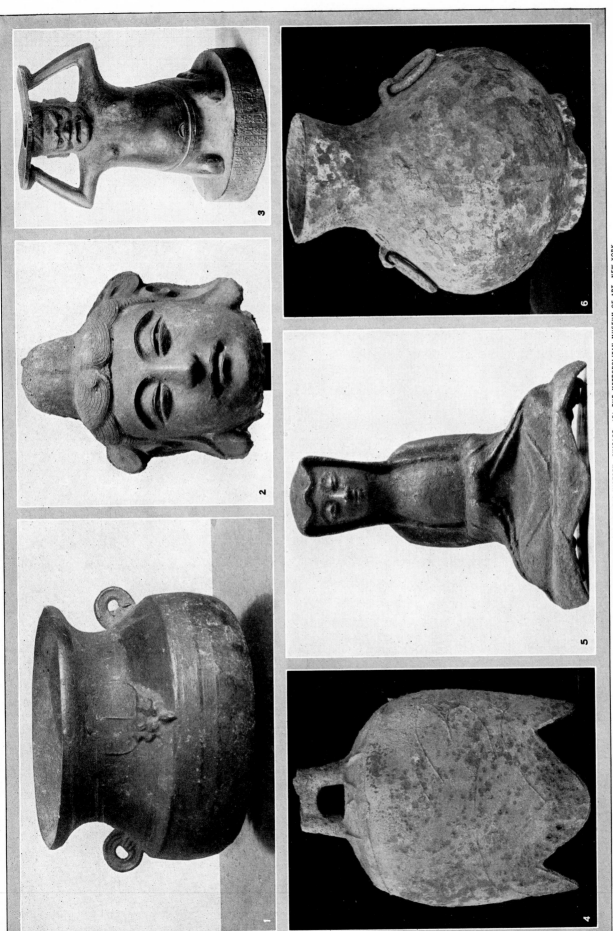

CHINESE CAST IRON WORK

BY COURTESY OF (1) WARREN E. COX. (2) THE MUSEUM OF FINE ARTS, BOSTON, (3, 4, 6) THE FIELD MUSEUM OF NATURAL HISTORY, CHICAGO, (5) THE METROPOLITAN MUSEUM OF ART, NEW YORK

1. Cast iron vessel of the Han dynasty (206 B.C.–A.D. 220)
2. Cast iron head of a Bodhisattva Sung dynasty (960–1280)
3. Cast iron figure, Ming dynasty (1368–1644); dated, equivalent to A.D. 1618
4. Cast iron bell, Sung dynasty (960–1280)
5. Cast iron statuette, Ming dynasty (1368–1644)
6. Cast iron vase, Han dynasty (206 B.C.–A.D. 220)

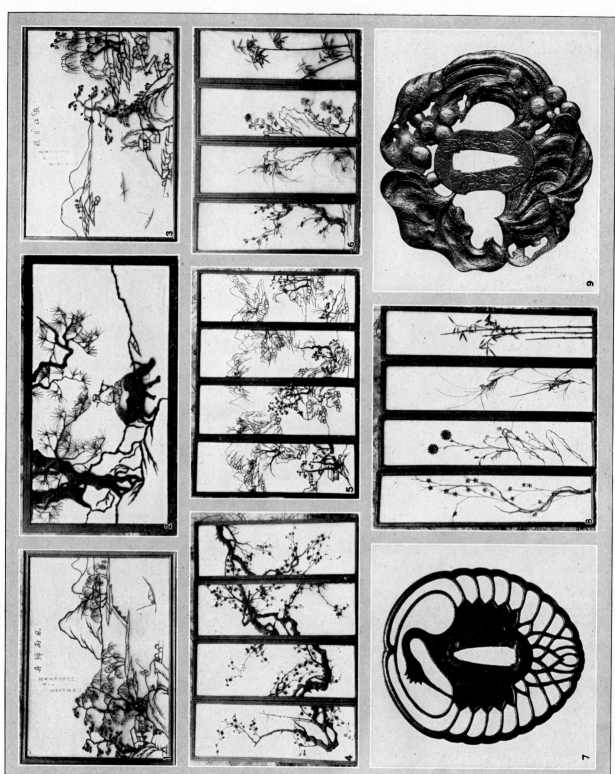

BY COURTESY OF (1-6, 8) JOHN REILLY, JR., (7, 9) THE MUSEUM OF FINE ARTS, BOSTON

GROUP OF CHINESE IRON PICTURES WITH PAPER OR SILK BACKGROUNDS AND JAPANESE SWORD GUARDS

1 and 3. Chinese wrought iron landscapes signed by T'ang P'eng (dated   5. Iron landscape panels
       equivalent to A.D. 1705)   6. and 8. Two groups of four iron panels each, depicting the four seasons
2. Wrought iron landscapes, with figures, 18th century   7. Japanese iron sword guard, 17th–18th century

carved ivory, having exquisitely carved and incised designs, which form the rim and the handle. Even more wonderful in their technical achievement as ivory carvings are the concentric spheres made in Canton as early as the 14th century and known as "devil's work balls," which are still being produced there. Endless patience and toil are needed to produce such concentric balls, carved one within the other, each having the most delicate patterns in pierced work. Models of palaces with carved roofs and intricate screens, peopled by tiny figures, and surrounded by trees and walls, all of ivory, were also a speciality of Canton; but most of them are known for their technical rather than their aesthetic triumphs as ivory carvings. Chinese ivory carving, however, is by no means wholly represented by these minutely and elaborately carved works, though for more than a century China has catered to foreign taste in producing this line of work. Excellent pieces of high artistic value are often found among carved religious and philosophic figures, especially those of *Kwan-yin*, Goddess of Mercy, with her graceful form and flowing robes, and of the Arhats, with their beatific expressions. Fine artistic work is also to be found in some of the brush-holders (*pi tung*), which are often covered with a landscape in relief enlivened by figures; and in the arm-rests likewise designed for the scholar's table, and in snuff bottles which are often dyed and then carved so as to bring out the unstained ivory beneath—a technique known in Japan under the name of *bachiru*, where examples of it are to be seen among the 8th century relics now preserved in the imperial treasure-house, Shōsōin. Works of no common talent are also frequently found among girdle pendants, covers for cricket-gourds, and ivory plaques in relief used as insets on carved wood or lacquered screens and cabinets. Other articles for which the Chinese have used ivory as a favourite material as ornament, in various degrees of elaborateness, are the handle and sheath of the writing brush, trays, cages for crickets and birds, implements for opium smoking, toilet articles such as combs, small boxes, and pieces for various games. The Chinese, in the course of their history, have utilized the ivory of the elephant, the mammoth, the walrus and the narwhal, the last three having been used as substitutes for the first. Ivory carving in one form or another is still an important industry in Canton, Peking, Shanghai, Amoy and Suchow, large numbers of carvings being produced for the foreign market.

LACQUER

LACQUER is a general term for coloured and frequently opaque varnishes applied to certain metallic objects and to wood. The term is derived from the resin lac, which substance is the basis of lacquers properly so-called. Technically, among Western nations, lacquering is restricted to the coating of polished metals or metallic surfaces, such as brass, pewter and tin, with prepared varnishes which will give them a golden, bronze-like or other lustre as desired. Throughout the East Indies lacquering of wooden surfaces is practised, articles of household furniture, as well as boxes, trays and toys, being decorated with bright-coloured lacquer. This process of applying the lacquer to decorative articles of wood is also known as *Japanning*.

The lacquer of the Far East, China, Japan and Korea must not be confused with other substances to which the term is generally applied; for instance, the lac of Burma, which is the gummy deposit of an insect, *Coccus Lacca*, and the various solutions of gums or resin in turpentine of which European imitations of Eastern lacquer have been and are concocted.

TECHNIQUE

LACQUER, properly so-called and as used in China and Japan, is a natural product, the sap of a tree, *Rhus Vernicifera*; subject to the removal of impurities and excess water, it can be used in its natural state, though it was frequently adulterated. The tree, which is indigenous to China, and has certainly been cultivated in Japan at least since the 6th century A.D., is tapped at about the age of ten years, lateral incisions being made in the bark and the running sap collected during the months of June to September.

164

Branches of a diameter of one inch or more are also tapped, the bark having first been removed. Smaller branches are cut off, soaked in water for ten days, and the sap collected, producing a lacquer (*seshime*) of particular quality, used for special purposes. These processes kill the tree, but the wood, when of sufficient size, is of some use for carpentry. From the roots five or six shoots spring up, which become available for the production of lacquer after about six years, and the operation can be thus continued for a considerable length of time before the growth is exhausted. The Chinese and Japanese methods are practically identical in this respect, but the cultivation of the tree does not seem to have been so systematic in China as in Japan. The sap, when extracted, is white or greyish in colour and about the consistency of treacle. On exposure to the air it turns yellow-brown and then black. It is strained through hempen cloth to remove physical impurities, after being pounded and stirred in shallow wooden tubs, to give it uniform liquidity. It is then slightly heated over a slow fire or in hot sunshine and stirred again to evaporate excess moisture, and stored in air-tight vessels. The characteristic constituent of lacquer is termed by chemists *urushiol* (from the Japanese name of lacquer, *urushi*) and its formula has been stated as $C_{14}H_{18}O_2$. Japanese lacquer is said by Prof. K. Mijama to contain from 64.00 to 77.6% of *urushiol* as compared with an average of 55.84 for Chinese; the difference being due, probably, to inferior methods of cultivation and extraction, and perhaps in some cases to climatic differences. Lacquer is a slightly irritant poison, but workers in the industry soon become inoculated. A series of implements used in the preparation of lacquer with an illustration of the system employed in the actual gathering of the sap is exhibited in Museum No. 1 of the Royal Botanic Gardens, Kew, England.

Lacquer-ware.—The basis of lacquer-ware, both in Japan and in China, is almost always wood, although it was also occasionally applied to porcelain and brass and white metal alloys. In some instances, objects were carved out of solid lacquer. The wood used, generally a sort of pine having a soft and even grain, was worked to an astonishing thinness. The processes that follow are the result of extraordinary qualities of lacquer itself, which, on exposure to air, takes on an extreme but not brittle hardness, and is capable of receiving a brilliant polish of such a nature as to rival even the surface of highly glazed porcelain. Moreover, it has the peculiar characteristic of attaining its maximum hardness in the presence of moisture. The Japanese, therefore, place the object, to secure this result, in a damp box or chamber after each application of lacquer to the basic material (wood, etc.). The Chinese are said (in an account of the industry dating from A.D. 1621–28) to use a "cave" in the ground for this purpose, and to place the objects therein at night in order to take advantage of the cool night air. It may, indeed, be said that lacquer dries in a moist atmosphere. The joiner's work having been completed, and all knots or projections having been most carefully smoothed away, cracks and joints are luted with a mixture of rice paste and *seshime* lacquer, till an absolutely even surface is obtained. It is then given a thin coat of *seshime* lacquer to fill up the pores of the wood and to provide a basis for succeeding operations: in the case of fine lacquer, possibly as many as 20 or 30 or even more; of each of which the following may be taken as typical. On the basis, as above described, is laid a coat of lacquer composition, allowed to harden, and ground smooth with whetstone. Next comes a further coat of finer composition, in which is mixed some burnt clay, which is again ground, and laid aside to harden for at least 12 hours. On this is fixed a coat of hempen cloth (or, rarely in Japan, but more often in China, paper) by means of an adhesive paste of wheat or rice flour and lacquer, which needs 24 hours at least to dry. The cloth is smoothed with a knife, and then receives several successive coats of lacquer composition, each demanding the delay necessary for hardening. On this is laid very hard lacquer, requiring a much longer drying interval, afterwards being ground to a fine surface. Succeeding coats of lacquer of varying quality are now laid on, dried and polished; and this *preliminary* work, occupying in the case of artistic lacquer-work at least 18 days, produces the surface on which the artist in lacquer *begins* his task of decoration. A large number of processes were at his command, especially in Japan. but the design was first generally made on paper with their lacquer and transferred to the object while still wet, or drawn on it direct with a thin paste of white lead or colour. In carrying it out he made use of gold or silver dust applied through a quill or bamboo tube, or through a sieve to secure equal distribution. Larger fragments of the precious metals (*hiraine* or *kirikane*) were applied separately by hand, with the aid of a small, pointed tool. In one

166

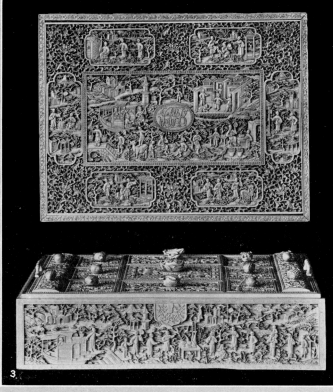

BY COURTESY OF THE DIRECTOR OF THE VICTORIA AND ALBERT MUSEUM

FIVE CHINESE IVORIES

1. Ivory pendant, with many concentric balls one inside the other

2. Ivory brush holder (*pi-tung*). Brushstands are carved out of the central portion of the tusk

3. Ivory box and lid

4. Ivory figure with a child

5. Ivory arm-rest for writers; under side

BY COURTESY OF (1) SPINK AND SON, LTD., (2, 3, 4, 5) THE DIRECTOR OF THE VICTORIA AND ALBERT MUSEUM

CHINESE LACQUER WORK OF THE 16TH, 17TH AND 18TH CENTURIES

1. Formal-garden seat of carved lacquered wood, Khang H'si period (1622–1723). 2. Screen of black lacquered coromandel wood with designs incised and painted in gold and colours. 18th century. 3. Vase of cinnabar lacquer, coloured by the brilliant red mercury or cinnabar ore or oxide, carved. Attributed to reign of Ch'ien Lung (1736–1795). 4. Ewer with panel decorations inlaid with shell, coloured ivory and carved red lacquer, 16th century. 5. Throne, in flat lacquer of various colours on black. Early 17th century

typical instance the writer has counted approximately 500 squares of thin gold foil thus inserted, within one square inch. These decorative processes each entailed prolonged hardening periods and meticulous polishing. Relief was obtained by modelling with a putty consisting of a mixture of lacquer with fine charcoal, white lead, lamp-black, etc., camphor being added to make it work easily. Lacquer was sometimes engraved, both in China and Japan.

The carved lacquer of China (*tias ch'i*) which, although imitated in Japan was never equalled in that country (as the Chinese have never reached the perfection of the Japanese gold lacquer-ware), needs particular notice. In this, the lacquer was built up in the method above described, but to a considerable thickness; and, when several colours were used, in successive layers of each colour, arranged in the order in which they were to predominate and of uniform thickness. When the whole mass was complete and homogeneous, it was cut back from the surface, so as to expose each colour as required by the design. The carving was done with a V-shaped tool kept very sharp, and when the lacquer was cold and hard. The cutting was done with amazing precision—no correction of faults was possible, for each layer had to be exactly and accurately reached, and the final result precisely foreseen and allowed for from the beginning of the work. The red lacquer (*tan sha*), so well known and justly appreciated, was coloured with cinnabar (red sulphuret of mercury). Other colours which are employed include a deep and a lighter olive-green, buff, brown, black and aubergine.

In Japanese lacquer, the following are the chief processes used:— *Nashiji* (pear-skin), small flakes of gold or silver sunk to various depths in the lacquer. *Fundame*, fine gold or silver powder worked to a flat, dull surface. *Hirame*, small, irregularly shaped pieces of sheet gold or silver placed on the surface. *Togidashi*, the design built up to the surface in gold, silver and colours with many coats of lacquer and then polished down to show them. *Takamakiye*, decoration in bold relief. *Hiramakiye*, decoration in low relief. *Rōiro*, polished black. *Chinkinbori*, engraved lacquer. *Kirikane*, square dice of sheet gold or silver, inserted separately on the surface. *Raden*, inlaid shell and metal. From the earliest times of which we have record, shell was used in the adornment of lacquer in China as well as in Japan, being inlaid on the surface in patterns, as well as in small squares

167

like *kirikane* and dust. For this purpose various shells were used, mother-of-pearl for larger work and that of nautilus, pear-shell, sea-ear (*Haliotis*, Jap. *Awabi*) and *Turbo Cornutus* (Jap. *Sazaye*). For a very charming form, called by the French *Lac Burgantée*, the shell of the sea-ear, of iridescent blue and green, was employed in combination with gold and silver and delicately engraved, as early as the Ming period (A.D. 1368–1644) and also in Japan. Chinese lacquer was also inlaid with hard stones such as jade, aralachite, etc., as well as coral, soapstone, ivory, porcelain and other decorative substances.

HISTORY OF LACQUER

THE use of lacquer in China goes back traditionally to legendary times. A late Ming manuscript, the Hsui-shih-lu, states that it was first employed for writing on bamboo slips, then for utensils of food made of black lacquer, and subsequently for vessels for ceremonial use of black with red interiors. During the Chou dynasty (1122–255 B.C.) it served for the decoration of carriages, harness, bows and arrows, etc., and was the subject of official regulations, being accepted also in payment of taxes. At this time, gold and colours are said to have come into use. About the 2nd century B.C. buildings were decorated with lacquer and musical instruments are similarly described. Under the Han dynasty (206 B.C.–A.D. 25) further development took place and pot-covers of paper, covered with lacquer, were found in 1910 by Ryūzo Torii near Port Arthur which are definitely attributed to this period. Of the lacquer of the T'ang dynasty we have more reliable information, for the collections still preserved in the Hōryw-ji temple in Japan, founded A.D. 607, and those collected by the Japanese emperor, Shōmu (A.D. 724–749) and deposited after his death, by his widow, in the Imperial Treasury (Shōsō-in) at Nara, contain many objects to which must be given a Chinese origin; in particular, musical instruments with inlay of cut-out figures of gold and silver, inserted on the surface, covered with lacquer, which was then rubbed down till the metal ornaments were again brought to view. Under the Sung dynasty (A.D. 960–1279), the industry further developed and the use of gold and silver lacquer in the utensils made for the palace is particularly recorded. The late Dr. S. W. Bushell considered that all branches of lacquer work now carried on in China can be traced as far back at least as the Sung dynasty and that the chief seat of manufacture at that period was Chia-hsing-Fu, between Hangchow and Soochow—the latter city being also an important centre of the industry. A lacquer box of the early Sung period, probably once of rhinoceros horn colour, black and red, with gold dust and silver wire, was recently exhibited in London and is one of the very few known examples of the period so far discovered. Towards the close of the period (c. A.D. 1220) it is stated that lacquer-wares were exported from Fu-kien to Java, India, Persia, Japan, Mecca and other places. Chinese writers record the existence of carved red lacquer during the time of the Yuan dynasty (A.D. 1280–1367) as well as of pierced ware and that inlaid with shell. Of the state of the industry under the Ming dynasty (A.D. 1368–1644) we have contemporary Chinese descriptions; for instance, the *Koku yao lun*, published during the reign of the first Ming emperor, and the *Ch'ing pi ts'ang* of A.D. 1595, both quoted freely by Dr. Bushell. The *Hsui shih lu*, of which a Japanese translation was published in the *Kokka* (No. 113), dates from A.D. 1621–28 and from these a good account of the progress of the art can be realized. From these records we glean that there were, in the early years of the dynasty, special factories of carved red lacquer at Ta-li Fu in Yunnan, which also produced spurious imitations. Nanking was noted for work of the same kind of high quality and for gold lacquer with pictures, as also were Peking and Ning-kuo Fu in Kiangnan. Inlay of mother-of-pearl is also mentioned. The excellence of the carved lacquer made during the reigns of Yung Lo (A.D. 1403–24) and Hsiian-Tê (A.D. 1426–35) is also recorded; and also that encrusted with shell, inlaid with sheet gold and silver, and flecked with powdered gold. Examples of carved lacquer are extant which can reasonably be attributed to this period. They are bold in design and free from the superabundance of small detail which characterized later productions; the colour also is generally deeper and richer than that of the 18th century pieces. The Victoria and Albert Museum, London, has several good examples of the period. Towards the end of the Ming dynasty, a factory was established at Peking, but fell into disuse during the troubles accompanying the fall of the Ming emperor. The first and, perhaps, the greatest of the Manchu emperors, K'ang Hsi (A.D. 1662–1723), revived it in A.D. 1680, when he established, in the precincts of the palace at Peking, a series of 27 workshops for artistic handicrafts.

Carved lacquer was, however, also made at Canton, Tongking, Soochow and Foochow; and the Jesuit father, Louis le Comte, who arrived in China in 1687, gives a good account of the flourishing state of the industry at that time. In this connection it is worth noting that the period of K'ang Hsi is that which saw the first considerable importation of lacquer-ware (and other objects of industrial art) into Europe. The consequent development of imitation lacquer applied to furniture, etc., which, during the reigns of William and Mary and Anne, had so extended a vogue, was one of the conspicuous features of the *Chinoiserie* craze of that time. A curiosity of the vagaries of fashion is that objects then made in counterfeit of Chinese art are now more highly prized than the originals. A screen is still in existence made by command of K'ang Hsi for presentation to the emperor Leopold I., whose badge, the double-headed eagle, is incorporated in the design. Carved lacquer of this period hardly attains to the rich colour of that of the Ming period, nor to the breadth and simplicity of design of the latter—though these qualities are far from negligible. In technique the K'ang Hsi ware shows an advance and is generally free from the small cracks too often found to have developed in the Ming products. The perfection of this quality, apart from other considerations, is found in the lacquer-ware of Ch'ien Lung (A.D. 1736–96), a devoted admirer of this branch of industrial art, who employed it on a large scale for the furniture and fittings of his palaces, for ceremonial and commemorative gifts and other purposes. The workmanship of objects made under his auspices is brilliant in the extreme, and ranks with the finest products of a nation whose mere craftsmanship has been almost unrivalled. But the colour is hard compared with earlier work, and the design tends rather to a somewhat stereotyped formalism. Still, one can hardly call the 18th century a period of decadence in the industrial arts of China—the superb execution of its productions, a characteristic which will always, and justly, command admiration, redeems it from adverse criticism. The downward course began in the 19th century, with loss of originality and a falling-off, due to adulteration, in the quality of the material. What was left of the imperial factories was burnt in 1869, and though carved red lacquer was made after that date, the industry had already ceased to have artistic importance.

Lacquer in Gold and Colours.—Lacquer artists in China, curiously enough, never developed the use of gold lacquer to anything like the extent or to the high standard of merit attained by the Japanese, though, rarely, specimens can be found of fine quality. For the most part, gold was used as a simple, flat decoration, especially on a ground of black as in the screens and boxes, frequently of considerable decorative value, made at Canton and other ports in touch with foreign trade and largely exported by European merchants, especially at the beginning of the 19th century. On the other hand, the Chinese used to advantage a wider range of colour than was generally employed in Japan; and brilliant hues of green, red, brown, cream, purple and other tints are found on objects dating from the later years of the Ming period onwards. Screens, too, were often thus decorated most effectively, and sometimes enriched with applied hard stones, shell or porcelain. The most effective form of this typically Far Eastern article of furniture is provided by the so-called Coromandel work, in which the design is first cut out in *intaglio* and then completed with varied colour or gold. Such screens, which are sometimes of considerable size—as much as 20 ft. in width and 8 ft. in height, and with 12 leaves—were largely imported into western Europe at the end of the 17th and early years of the 18th century, by East India merchants whose headquarters (French and English) were either on the Coromandel Coast or (Dutch) at Bantam in Java—the latter place also providing a name often used by old writers. These imported screens were remorselessly cut up to make cabinets and other articles of furniture, in which form their remains are by no means rare at the present day.

Lac Burgantée.—One of the most delicate and charming manifestations of the Chinese lacquerer's art is that called by the French, *Lac Burgantée*, of which the technique has already been described. The effects of colour produced by the use of iridescent shell, sometimes engraved, and occasionally in combination with gold and silver, are exquisite. This work is generally on a small scale, and though temple utensils and other articles of fair size are to be found, as well as miniature table screens and vases, a favourite production took the form of little wine-cups, originally in sets of five and lined with silver. This branch of art dates certainly from the Ming dynasty and has hardly yet received the attention that its qualities merit.

Subjects of Decoration.—Chinese ornament as applied to lacquer-ware

171

(as to other of the industrial arts) is almost entirely symbolical and the subject-pieces generally derived from legends of the Buddhist, Taoist and Confucian personages. The more usual of the former are the "Eight Buddhist Emblems of Happy Augury," the "Eight Musical Instruments," and the "Eight Precious Things" (Taoist). The "Hundred Antiques" appear on Coromandel screens and other large works. Among figure subjects may be mentioned representations of Shou Lao, a deification of Lao Tze, the founder of the Taoist philosophy, the "Eight Taoist Immortals," the "Sages of the Bamboo Grove" and those of the wine-cup. Children at games are much favoured, and landscapes with pavilions, trees, mountains, lakes and formal gardens. Among animals the mythical dragon—if with five claws, peculiar to the emperor—and phoenix or *feng-huang* associated with the empress. The long-tailed tortoise, unicorn (*Ch'i-lin*), lion, crane, bat, butterfly and fish are frequently seen, all being symbolical of long life, good fortune, happiness, etc. The peach, pine, bamboo, peony, lotus, chrysanthemum and prunus are the chief motives selected from the vegetable kingdom. Of abstract pattern the meander or key-pattern and swastika are the chief. The forms of vessels resemble, as a rule, those either of porcelain or bronzes.

BRONZE AND BRASS ORNAMENTAL WORK

THE BRONZE products of China have been from the earliest times of so high a degree of excellence, both artistic and technical, that they may truly be classed among the fine arts.   So early as any reliance can be placed upon records the Chinese appear to have been enthusiastic amateurs and collectors of bronzes, and up to the present day it is this very enthusiasm which has seemed to prevent a scientific attitude among Chinese antiquarians when the question of the dating of old bronzes is concerned.   Many volumes have been written in Chinese and European languages, but the authoritative work has not as yet appeared.   There are so many factors besides artistic merit which enter into the consideration of a bronze that facts have been collected and various theories advanced without arriving at any definite knowledge.

The bronzes in the Chinese collections may be divided roughly into two classes: (1) those whose surface has been worked over and (2) those which remain in the same condition as when they were first excavated.   Those bronzes which have been for many years in famous Chinese collections have in most cases been worked over and vastly improved in appearance. Bronzes, as first excavated, should prove the most reliable documents, but scientific excavation is as yet hardly established in China, and it is difficult to ascertain the true facts concerning the finding of any piece which may come upon the market.   Even though a perfectly reliable eyewitness may testify to having been present at the excavation of a bronze, the chances are that he is not a trained archaeologist, and is unable to interpret correctly the conditions under which the bronze has been found. So far, we know of only one important excavation of bronzes which may be dated with any approximation of certainty. Remarkably fine specimens of bronzes exist in the collections of China, Korea, Japan, Europe and America, and the history of some of the pieces in the Chinese collections is known for several hundred years, for illustrated catalogues of bronzes were compiled during the Sung dynasty (A.D. 960–1279), and have come down to us together with later and more copious works, some in many volumes. They include: a famous work called the Ting Lu, written in the 6th century by Yu Li, and another in 20 volumes called the San Li Tu written in the 10th century by Nieh Tsung-yi. Both of these, however, have relied too much on imagination to be considered reliable. The most important early catalogue is in 30 volumes and dates from the Sung dynasty; its title is Hsiian Ho Po Ku T'ou Lu, and it was written in the 12th century by Wang Pu; it has been often reprinted. The most famous of all the catalogues is one in 42 volumes, compiled for the Emperor Ch'ien Lung and printed in 1751. It illustrates his splendid collection of bronzes in the Peking palace and is called Hsi Ch'ing Ku Chien. There are many others of which a number are devoted to a discussion of inscriptions on bronzes.

Treatises on bronzes were written during the Chou dynasty (1122–255 B.C.) and from one of these we get our first information about their manufacture. Indeed, so great is the respect for ancient bronzes in China that in the year 116 B.C., when an old bronze *ting* was found in the bank of a river in Shensi, the name of the reign was changed in honour of the event. The reverential attitude of the Chinese towards antiquity, the permanent nature of the metal alloy, and the fact that the earliest important bronzes are all of a ceremonial or sacrificial nature have combined to place them high in the esteem of Chinese connoisseurs from the earliest times.

A Chinese collector will not hesitate to date an old bronze a full dynasty earlier than would a cautious European or American collector. Thus we are told that in many Chinese collections a considerable proportion of the bronzes were made in the Shang dynasty (1766–1122 B.C.) when such an attribution would seem to be based merely upon a pious hope. Since with some degree of certainty bronzes have been established as dating from the 5th century B.C., and are of accomplished workmanship, they are doubtless of more recent date than many others with which collectors are familiar,

BY COURTESY OF (1, 2, 4) THE ART INSTITUTE OF CHICAGO, (3) BARON SUMITOMO, (8) THE METROPOLITAN MUSEUM OF ART, NEW YORK; FROM (7, 9) THE DAVID WEILL COLLECTION, (6) THE GEORGE EUMORFOPOULOS COLLECTION; PHOTOGRAPH, (5) COLLECTION ARCHIVES PHOTOGRAPHIQUES

CHINESE BRONZES OF THE CHOU AND HAN DYNASTIES

1. Ceremonial jar (Hu) of bronze inlaid with copper, Han dynasty, 206 B.C. From the Art Institute of Chicago

2. Ceremonial vessel (Yi), Chou dynasty, 1122–249 B.C. From the Art Institute of Chicago

3. Ceremonial vase (Tsun), Chou dynasty. From the Sumitomo Collection, Japan

4. Ceremonial tripod (Ting), Chou dynasty. From the Art Institute of Chicago

5. Elephant, Han dynasty or earlier. From the Louvre, Paris

6. Ceremonial wine jar (Yu), Chou dynasty. In the Eumorfopoulos Collection

7. Double lock, Chou dynasty or later. From the David Wey Collection, Paris

8. Bronze altar table with ceremonial vessels. Chou dynasty. From the Metropolitan Museum of Art, New York

9. Double-headed animal, Han dynasty. From the David Wey Collection

but there are few trained archaeologists outside China who will venture to state that any known bronze is definitely of the Shang dynasty. Within the next few years it may be possible, from dated excavations yet to be made, to determine the types of manufacture sufficiently to attribute bronzes to the early or the late Chou dynasty (1122–255 B.C.). That is, however, at present beyond the bounds of our knowledge. From Han times (206 B.C.–A.D. 220) we are on a somewhat firmer footing, and the recent excavations of Kozlov, in Mongolia, have shed a great deal of light upon Han civilization enabling us to place in the Han dynasty, with some assurance, bronzes that would otherwise have received a much later dating. Dated bronzes of the Six dynasties (A.D. 265–589) and the T'ang dynasty (618–907) exist, but during the Sung dynasty (A.D. 960–1279) the taste for reproducing old bronzes arose, and the manufacture was carried on side by side with contemporary designs, so a state of confusion has resulted. It is highly probable that many of the so-called ancient bronzes are comparatively modern copies of the Sung period. In such pieces anachronisms are noticeable in the type and use of decorative motives rather than in the appearance of the objects as a whole. We know a good deal about the porcelain of the Ming dynasty (1368–1644), many pieces of which are dated, and a fairly good way of determining Ming bronzes is to compare them with Ming porcelains, which were often based upon bronze forms; some of them were undoubtedly copied from early bronzes, but anachronisms are bound to creep in. Except for deliberate forgeries, of which quantities exist, there is little danger of confusing a modern bronze with an ancient one, for little of the exquisite technique of the early bronze founders has survived. This is due rather to cheapness of production and careless slipshod methods, than to any loss of knowledge of the processes.

Bronze Composition and Manufacture.—Bronze was used at a very early date for both ceremonial and utilitarian purposes and doubtless the ceremonial use was the later development. It must first have been cast in single stone moulds, then in piece moulds, and finally by the lost wax process, to which complicated method we owe the earliest bronzes now known to us. The simple piece moulds were used for coins, spear-heads, halberds, swords, and such objects, where the forms were simple and flat. Large basins were also cast by this method and Voretzsch believes that it is often possible to tell from examining the surface of a bronze how many pieces had previously been cast in the same mould. The ceremonial vessels varied greatly in form, some being very complicated, with elaborately modelled handles and surface decoration in several different planes. While the earliest of these are cast by the lost wax process, and are technically superb, it is interesting to note that from the Han dynasty onwards we find an increasing number of bronzes whose component parts were separately cast and afterwards assembled by welding. So proficient were the workers in the craft of bronze founding, that bronzes of the good periods seem to have come from the mould so cleanly and sharply defined that very little work was necessary to finish them with chisel and file. The fact that a bronze was cast in one piece does not necessarily indicate that it is old, but a bronze cast in several parts and welded together could hardly antedate the Christian Era, and would probably be of much later date.

There have been several series of experiments conducted to determine the composition of early bronzes. One of the most complete has recently been published by Prof. M. Chikashigé, a Japanese, who analysed chemically and physically a number of mirrors. It has been stated in a work pertaining to the Chou dynasty, but possibly of later date, the K'ao Kung Chi, that the proportions of copper and tin were definitely established for the making of bronzes for specific purposes. It is certain, however, that neither these metals nor any others were available to the Chinese in a form at all pure, so in all the alloys there are other metals present such as lead, zinc, antimony, iron and silver. Some of the early bronzes have a beautiful golden colour under the patina, and there are dealers who have not hesitated to state that this was due to the presence of large quantities of gold in the alloy. Chemical analyses show no gold.

The proportions used in the Chou dynasty, according to the K'ao Kung Chi, are as follows:

5 parts copper, 1 part tin for bells, gongs, kettles, ceremonial vessels and measures of capacity.
4 " " 1 " " " axes and hatchets.
3 " " 1 " " " halberd-heads and tridents.
2 " " 1 " " " two-edged swords, spades, hoes and similar agricultural implements.
3 " " 2 parts " " arrowpoints and knives used as styluses for writing.
1 part " 1 part " " mirrors.

The varying proportions of metals in the alloy would of course affect the colour, and we have, in consequence, a range from a coppery red colour through lighter reds and golden yellow to the nearly pure silver colour of the mirrors. The surface of most ancient bronzes, when cleaned from deposits and patina, has a dull silvery colour due to mercury. This is said by some to be the result of the accidental presence of mercury in the alloy, which has worked to the surface during long years of burial. It is more probable, however, that the mercury was used deliberately to coat the surface of the bronze and thereby produce a silver-coloured plating in cases where the alloy itself was not white. The colours produced by age and careful manipulation, now so highly valued, were of no interest to the Chinese of early ages who preferred the bronzes to be of a steely colour.

Forms and Uses.—The uses of the bronze ceremonial vessels are largely conjectural. Our information is gained from works based upon the researches of the archaeologists of the Sung dynasty, who undoubtedly had material not available to us, but whose deductions and theories would hardly be called scientific. It is believed that the sacrificial forms were based upon idealizations of vessels in common use; that some held liquids such as wine and water, and others, cereals and prepared meats. Some of them may have been used only for commemorative purposes. A man raised to high rank would cause a bronze vessel to be made in honour of the occasion, and would inscribe it, sometimes to his ancestors, to whom he believed his preferment was due, sometimes to himself. It is not known whether or not such vessels were used in family sacrifices or religious ceremonies. Since Shang bronzes are still problematic it may be well to consider briefly the forms of ceremonial bronzes most widely used during the Chou dynasty.

All Chou bronzes can be characterized as dignified and massive in proportion. Whether they be large or small there is always an appearance of strength and solidity; and although not essentially clumsy, there is as yet little charm of contour such as would have been so essential to the Greeks. The few exceptions are in the profiles of some of the simpler *tsun*, and these are as sensitive in line as any works of art that have ever been made. So keenly was the line felt in such instances that the slenderness or sturdiness of the *tsun* was perfectly expressed in the quality of the profile, regardless of bulk. There is crudity perhaps in the conception of some of the decorative

177

motives, but it is the crudeness of conception of the Romanesque period, without any traces of its awkwardness of execution.

Chief among early bronze forms is the *ting*. Originally a tripod cooking pot, it assumed a great variety of shapes, some clumsy and topheavy, and others refined, but always sturdy. There is at present in the Buckingham collection in the Art Institute of Chicago, an unusually fine example of an early but refined type. It was formerly in the Tuan Fang collection. The patina is a beautiful tea-dust green, and has evidently been hand-polished for generations.

The *hsien* is generally a three-legged vessel the bottom section of which is covered by a perforated and sometimes hinged lid; it was a steamer often made in two parts, occasionally separable, and is really an archaic version of a cooking utensil well known in Chinese kitchens. It is always clumsy in form, as compared with other bronze forms, which may be another indication of its early origin.

The *yu* is a covered bucket-like utensil with a swinging bale. It has a bulbous body, always elliptical in section, and the cover fits closely down over the neck. In some cases the swinging handle is so arranged that it moves through a limited distance, allowing only sufficient room for the easy removal of the lid. The function of the *yu* was the storage and transportation of sacrificial wine, or possibly of wine for less solemn occasions.

The *tsun* which, in its simplest form, is a cylinder-like beaker with concave sides, goes through a variety of changes in form without change of name. Some of the most beautiful of all the ancient bronzes are *tsun*. These beakers were used to contain liquids.

The *yi* is a wide cup, generally with two handles, though some handsome variants are known with four. The handles are sturdy, with animal heads at the top and a rectangular pendant at the bottom. This form must originally have had significance, but its origin is lost. A few specimens have been found mounted upon a square hollow base, cast all in one piece, from under the top of which depends a loop. Some Chinese archaeologists claim that a bell originally hung from this loop, which rang when the *yi* was lifted. Although the bell is of very ancient origin in China it was without a clapper for some centuries after the *yi* in question were made, so it seems hardly possible that a voiceless bell should have hung there. Bells were struck with

FROM THE WARREN E. COX COLLECTION

CHINESE BRONZE INCENSE BURNER

Chinese bronze incense burner of the Sung dynasty (A.D. 960–1280) in the form of a water buffalo upon which is riding Lao-tse, the philosopher who founded the Taoist religion. The water buffalo, being one of the most dangerous and difficult beasts to tame, is chosen as a symbol of the power of the gentle thought of the philosopher. The casting of this piece is paper-thin

a wooden mallet on the outer surface, and a person who held a heavy *yi* aloft in both hands could certainly not have struck a bell hanging beneath. The use of the loop remains therefore still problematical, and would not have been mentioned here were it not that it furnishes an excellent example of the fantastic speculations which have passed current in China as archaeology. The *yi* was used for offerings of grain.

Another form called *yi*, but differently written, is sometimes the most fantastic of all the sacrificial vessels. These *yi* are often animal forms conventionalized into containers for sacrificial wine, and generally of a deliberately ugly or menacing aspect. The animals are usually not recognizable as members of any known species, but are extremely convincing, nevertheless.

A form called the *hu* became very popular during the Han dynasty. It is a round-bellied jar with a spreading cylindrical neck, and a cylindrical foot. It has two ring handles suspended from flat tiger masks on the shoulders, and was used as a container for wine or water. Three of the finest of these examples are in the Buckingham collection. One bears engraved upon the neck four characters reading "Number seven eastern palace." Another of these jars approximately the same size and shape has the entire surface covered with an engraved pattern consisting of geometrical ornament and dragon-headed interlacing scroll patterns. Both these jars are of reddish bronze with a heavy gold plating, but the decorated jar has the pattern relieved in silver colour evidently obtained by painting the gold surface with mercury. The masks which support the handles of this jar are very crisply chiselled, and there can be little doubt that it is an imperial piece. The third of these jars is inlaid with a metal now much decomposed, but probably copper. A pattern of sprightly animals, facing each other in pairs, and in different registers, alternating with spirals gives vigorous decoration over the entire surface. The form of the jar is extremely simple, but it is saved from monotony and raised to a high degree of beauty by the unusual vitality of the decorating shapes.

Bells and mirrors deserve special mention. Fine bronze bells of the early periods have long been highly esteemed by Chinese collectors, particularly when they bear inscriptions, and an inscribed bell was always considered superior to an uninscribed one of greater artistic merit. The forms of early bells are all more or less alike, and they may be generally considered

179

as representing one class, although there is a great variety in proportion and in the surface decoration. Most of the bells have projecting bosses, sometimes called nipples, arranged in regular pattern on the surface, and these have given rise to some amazing speculations among Chinese amateurs. Perhaps the most amusing is that they are the survival of tuning pegs, such as are used at present in harps and pianos. It is claimed that strings or wires were stretched between them and that the bells were tuned to various musical pitches. A simpler solution of the problem would be that they represent rivets which in early times fastened plates of metal together in bell forms before bronze could be easily cast. The bells are all flat in section, like pointed ellipses, and this form could easily develop from metal plates.

Mirrors were probably introduced from the West, as highly artistic metal mirrors were in use in Greece some time before they seem to have appeared in China and crude earlier Scythian examples are known. With one or two possible exceptions the earliest Chinese mirrors we know date from the Han dynasty. The earliest examples are circular and very simple. The reflecting surface is as a rule slightly convex, and the back is decorated with concentric bands of geometrical patterns. Ritualistic mirrors sometimes had concave reflecting surfaces. Sometimes there are birds or beasts in raised outline, and sometimes characters and signs of the zodiac in the field inside the bands. A boss in the exact centre, pierced from side to side, allowed the passage of a cord which was twisted into a tassel and used as a handle for the mirror. Some of the finest mirrors date from the T'ang dynasty. The backs are covered in high relief with intertwining patterns of vines, leaves, birds and running animals, and are reminiscent of Persian taste as well as the repoussé silver work done in Asia Minor from Hellenistic times. Caravans were passing continually between China and the West, and, from the time of the Han dynasty, outside influences become a distinct factor in the development of all the crafts of China.

Much has been said about the style of the Ch'in dynasty, a period of less than 50 years between the Chou and the Han, filled with uproar and confusion. There is little doubt that many practices of the Chou dynasty came to a rather abrupt end, but styles do not end with one dynasty nor begin with another, and it is doubtful if such a thing actually exists as a Ch'in style. The use of bronze became more widespread among the people during the Han dynasty, and from that time its uses multiply. There are splendid representations of animals, generally on a very small scale, singly, and in fantastic groupings. These occur from Han to T'ang.

During the Six dynasties it became the custom to cast votive figures in gilt bronze, and the monasteries seem to have made a practice of keeping large numbers of these on hand, ready for dedication by the pious. It is from the inscriptions engraved on the bases at the time of such dedications that we have gained much of our information on sculptural characteristics and religious practices of the Wei and T'ang dynasties.

From the end of the Chou period there is a tendency to simplify bronze forms and rely upon engraved or inlaid patterns in place of the early decorations in relief. During the Sung dynasty the keen delight in archaeological research prompted the manufacture of exact counterparts of early forms, as well as all sorts of archaistic approximations. Very few Ming bronzes have much to recommend them as works of art. They are generally the products of the virtuosity of mediocre craftsmen, produced at a time when lavish decoration had taken the place of purity of form.

Inscriptions.—In the identification of ancient bronzes the Chinese lay great stress upon inscriptions. There is still some doubt as to the meaning of certain of the ancient characters, but most of the inscriptions can be read. They vary in length from one character to several hundred, and often give accounts of historical events and the names of personages, but without dates, and without sufficient detail to make attributions to definite times or places anything more than conjectural. One of the longest on record is in the South Kensington Museum, London. The shorter inscriptions read: "To the venerable father," "I have dedicated this bronze to my father Ting," "Serviceable for sons and grandsons," etc. There are also single marks, more or less pictographic, some of which represent animals, birds or men. The meaning of others is not at all clear.

As bronzes with inscriptions bring higher prices, many dealers have felt it their duty to see that all bronzes in their possession bore the right, or wrong type of inscription. Many bronzes, perfectly genuine, excellent specimens artistically, have had inscriptions added at a later date, in characters sometimes meaningless. In the ancient bronzes the inscriptions were cast in the surface like the ornament, and it is practically impossible to imitate a cast inscription by means of engraved characters, so a microscope, and even the eye alone, will detect the added inscription. This is not, however, a practice of recent origin, and some very fine bronzes of the Chou dynasty bear inscriptions in Shang or Chou characters which were added to them several hundred years later.

Decoration.—The religion of the Shang and Chou dynasties was animistic, and the decorations on the early bronzes have been interpreted as representations of the forces of nature, sometimes in demoniac form. Almost all decorations consist of two parts, an arrangement of forms of animistic or zoömorphic origin in rather high relief, strongly modelled, and a pattern of thin lines, closely spaced, in sharp relief, either outlining the stronger forms, or in an all-over pattern of spirals, completely filling the ground. These lines are extraordinarily crisp in execution, and unvarying in thickness throughout the pattern, and were carved in the surface of the original model, from which they were cast in the bronze. Later bronzes often have patterns of this type applied by means of stamps to the mould, with the result that the character is entirely different, the crispness of execution being totally lacking, and the relief much shallower. These line motives are of the well-known and widespread key or fret design and are generally known as the "thunder" pattern. Very delicate single lines in relief often form bands around *tsun*, *yu*, and other vessels. They are extremely regular, but careful inspection will detect slight variations in direction, showing that they were not mechanically done. The Chinese call them "bowstrings." Other linear motives are found of intersecting lozenge or diamond patterns on the handles of vessels.

Of the non-geometrical decorative forms of the Chou dynasty the T'ao-t'ieh, or ogre's head is the favourite. Often it is represented only by a pair of eyes—hemispherical bosses with an incised centre. Sometimes the upper part of a face is indicated, but the lower jaw is never shown, so it appears, even in its most complete form, as a sort of mask. It is abstract, but nevertheless there is something intense about it which has an awe-inspiring effect even upon the uninitiated. In late Chou bronzes, zoömorphic forms are sometimes arranged in opposition so as to form parts of a T'ao-t'ieh. In spite of many and ingenious theories it is still uncertain what the T'ao-t'ieh represents, but his representation is always easily identified.

HSIEN

TING

YU

HU

TSUN

YI

FROM ALBERT J. KOOP'S "EARLY CHINESE BRONZES"; (LEFT TO RIGHT, TOP ROW) PLATES XX, II; (MIDDLE ROW) PLATES XI, LIII; (LOWER ROW) PLATES IV, X-A.

EARLY CHINESE BRONZES

183

Animal heads are often used as ornamental bosses in the centre of a band of decoration, and as handle ends on the swinging bales of the *yu*. Some of the heads are horned and some are not. Some have spreading mouselike ears. They are variously identified, but none of them seem closely patterned after nature. They are abstractions based upon animals rather than animal portraits.

In considering the decorative zoömorphic motives on Chou bronzes and those of similar design it might be safe to say that a recognizable animal always argues a comparatively late date. We can see bird-like, and animal-like forms, and even very close likenesses of the cicada, which lends itself easily to geometrical conventionalization, but as soon as elephants or other recognizable animals appear we realize that the piece is later in date or even archaistic.

Very noticeable as decorative forms are the projecting flanges on the corners of square bronzes, or dividing the surface of the round bronzes into vertical panels. It is one of the favourite motives of the Chou dynasty. As will be noticed in the illustrations they are usually cut and perforated into decorative forms. In some cases they are so fantastic as to detract from the beauty of the piece.

One sees no reason to doubt that their origin was the projecting "fins" which are always left in castings from piece moulds, and that long after the piece moulds had ceased to be used for fine bronzes, the decorative descendants of their "fins" were cast, as ornamental motives.

In the Han dynasty, and later, there is a great deal of inlaying in gold lines of the most elaborate patterns. Evidently a new flood of folk-lore from outside sources was pouring over China at that time, and all sorts of animals and warlocks chase each other through mountains and clouds. There was then a breaking away from the heavy and sombre traditions of the Chou dynasty and a tremendous expression of energy. Many of these inlaid gold bronzes have recently come to light and have been ably discussed by Rostovtzeff in his book "Inlaid Bronzes of the Han Dynasty." The animals or spirits, or whatever the forms represent, were in most cases animals not seen or known—heard of perhaps in wild tales of barbarian tribes, or copied from foreign animal motives imperfectly understood; imagined, or evolved as personifications of the forces of nature.

184

During the Han dynasty the tale of the Kun-lung mountains with their peachtree on which grew the peaches of longevity was popular, and the "hill" type of incense burner came into being. Though prevalent in Han pottery, in bronze it is hardly met before the Six dynasties, and then, although the conical cover moulded to resemble mountain peaks hardly changed its shape, the cylindrical base most common in pottery was replaced by forms of greater fancy and grace. Coiling dragons of strength and vigour often supported the censer in their jaws.

Dragons were not very common as bronze decorations before the Han dynasty. It has been proved that they were a comparatively late importation from the west, but from T'ang times onwards they are the commonest of all decorative motives. Taoist figures become popular in Sung and Ming times, such as Lao Tzu riding upon an ox, and in the following centuries bronze has been the medium for comparatively trivial ideas. The majesty of the early days is gone forever. A conspicuous exception, however, is the set of large bronze astronomical instruments cast in 1279 for the observatory on the walls of Peking. The Ming emperors sought dignity on an enormous scale, and huge bronze vessels and dragons were cast for use in the palace and the palace grounds, but few of them were successful and most were extremely awkward and ungainly.

The walls of early bronze vessels, except for the basin-like ones, are generally thick, and the walls of later bronzes are always comparatively thin. The early bronzes show a tenseness of conception, the later ones a suavity of line and simplicity of mass that tends to become insipid. All the handles and other freestanding parts of early bronzes seem so perfectly suited to their function and the needs of the design that they appear inevitable. The handles on Ming and Ching bronze jars are frequently monstrosities, violating all design canons. The decoration on early bronzes seems always produced with the particular piece in mind, but in the later bronzes it is simply a matter of stock patterns applied with dies and stamps.

Patina.—Inasmuch as an interesting patina will to-day bring a high price for a bronze of little or no artistic merit some discussion of patinas may be useful here. True patination is produced by chemical changes brought about by the action on the bronze of chemicals in the soil in which it is buried, hastened more or less by the amount of moisture present.

Some bronzes have been found in water, which produces a distinctive effect, and some are thought never to have been buried. Europeans and Americans prefer a green patina, and the Chinese consider that a velvety black is the best. Good patinas are very appealing in colour and texture, particularly if they have received careful grinding and polishing for generations, so it is not surprising to find bronzes in many museums which have absolutely no merit beyond the accidental one of colour. When a bronze is excavated its surface is naturally covered with dirt and incrustations more or less thick, underneath which is the patina caused by the disintegration of the metal surface and its combination with elements which surround it. If the patina is thick and its colour good it may be carefully ground down and polished away until the resultant bronze is actually the handiwork of a more recent craftsman who has carved out of the heavy patinated surface the original form of the bronze. The favourite Chinese method is to polish with the bare hand, relying on the oils of the skin for the sole lubrication. Generations of such polishing by hosts of patient servants has given to many famous bronzes their charm of colour. At the present time many bronzes are coming on the market just as they have been excavated, and there is an evident attempt to preserve all dirt which can be made to cling to the surface. Many European collectors wax and polish the surfaces of their bronzes, but the practice is not followed in America.

Unscrupulous dealers have not hesitated to apply artificial patinas to genuine old bronzes to increase their saleability, and this is done in a variety of ways. The simplest method is to paint them. Watercolour paints will wash off in water, and turpentine or naphtha will act as a solvent to oil colours, so these methods of falsification are easily detected. Sodium silicate, which is very slow to dissolve, is often used and in Japan exceedingly clever work is done with coloured lacquers. Waxes are used also. There is, unfortunately, no way to be absolutely certain that a bronze is genuine, but there are many ways of finding out when they are not genuine. A true patina is not easily damaged. Boiling a few hours in water, and washing with paint and varnish solvents will easily remove the more recent traces of antiquity. The lacquer does not come off so easily, but where lacquer, or a silicate, has been applied, the surface beneath is generally roughened so that if a small bit of the surface is exposed, the artificial roughening can be

186

seen. The true patina has actually eaten into the surface and cannot in most cases be easily removed. Where the process of patination has gone far the entire bronze shell is sometimes changed in composition, and if genuine fragments of ancient bronzes are examined it will be seen that the patina penetrates deep below the surface, sometimes leaving only a slight core of the original bronze which, too, has changed in composition, if not in colour, and has become extremely brittle. On the other hand under different conditions the strength, the toughness and even the appearance of old bronzes have been little affected. Some very careful forgeries have been made by applying fragments of true malachite to the surface of the bronze with lacquer. Some types of bronze patina are actually like malachite in structure, appearance, and chemical composition, but forgeries of this type may be detected under the magnifying glass by observing the stratifications of the colour layers which will not harmonize with each other.

BIBLIOGRAPHIES

TEXTILES AND EMBROIDERIES

Victoria and Albert Museum, *Catalogues;* "Chinese Art" (*Burtengten Magazine Monograph,* 1925); A. Von le Coq, *Chotscho* (1912); Sir A. Stein, *Scrindia* (1921).

AESTHETIC DEVELOPMENT OF CHINA

E. Dillon, *Porcelain* (1904); R. L. Binyon, *Painting in the Far East* (1908. 3rd ed., 1923); E. F. Fenollosa, *Epochs of Chinese and Japanese Art* (1912); M. Anesaki, *Buddhist Art* (1916). For China, see E. J. Eitel, *Handbook of Chinese Buddhism* (1870. 2nd ed., rev., 1888); B. Laufer, *Jade. A Study in Chinese Archaeology and Religion* in Field Columbian Museum Publications. Anthropological Series, vol. 10 (Chicago 1913); S. W. Bushell, *Chinese Art* (1904–06, new ed., 1921); A. L. B. Ashton, *An Introduction to the Study of Chinese Sculpture* (1924); B. Laufer, *Chinese Grave-Sculptures of the Han Period* (Leipzig 1911); O. Sirén, *Chinese Sculpture from the 5th to the 14th Century* (1925); A. J. Koop, *Early Chinese Bronzes* (1924, *see* also Bushell, *Loc. Cit.*); T. J. Arne, *Painted Stone Age Pottery from the Province of Honan, China,* Geol. Survey of China (Peking 1925); W. G. Gulland, *Chinese Porcelain* (1898); W. C. Monkhouse, *A History and Description of Chinese Porcelain* (1901); S. W. Bushell, *Description of Chinese Pottery and Porcelain* (1910); R. L. Hobson and A. L. Hetherington, *The Art of the Chinese Potter from the Han Dynasty to the End of the Ming* (1923), and *The Later Ceramic Wares of China* (1925). E. F. Strange, *Chinese Lacquer* (1926); *The Burlington Magazine Monographs* (1925); *Ars Asiatica* (ed. v. Golonbew, 1914); *Artibus Asiae* (Dresden, 1925); *The Chinese Journal* (Shanghai, 1923). *See* also CHINESE ARCHITECTURE; CHINESE PAINTING; CHINESE SCULPTURE; BRONZE AND BRASS ORNAMENTAL WORK: *Chinese. See* further JAPANESE PAINTING AND PRINTS; KOREA: *Aesthetic Development;* POTTERIES AND PORCELAINS; *Near and Far East.*

ARCHITECTURE

The only original Chinese work on architecture is the *Ying Tsao Fa Shi* (1103; 2nd ed., 1145; reissued by the Shanghai Commercial Press). Good accounts of the work were given by P. Demieville in *Bulletin de l'École Française d'Extrème-Orient,* tome xxv. (1925), and Percival W. Yetts in the *Burlington Magazine* (March, 1927), the latter containing a discussion of earlier European books dealing with Chinese architecture.

BIBLIOGRAPHIES

Of greater importance are, however, the works published by various Japanese authorities on their own early buildings since these are closely connected with those of China. See *Japanese Temples and Their Treasures* (last ed. 1915); also articles in the *Kokka* and other Japanese reviews, especially C. Ito and J. Tsuchija's report about the imperial palaces in Peking, in the *Bulletin of the School of Engineering of the Tōkyō Imper. University* (1905), a kind of text for the portfolio publications; *Photographs of Palace Buildings of Peking* and *Decoration of the Palace Buildings of Peking* (1906). *See* also Boerschmann, *Baukunst und religiöse Kultur der Chinesen* (1911–14) and *Chinesche Architektur* (1925); Osvald Sirén, *The Walls and Gates of Peking* (1924), and *The Imperial Palaces of Peking* (Paris, 1926); Tokiwa and Sekino, *Buddhist Monuments in China* (Tōkyō, 1926–27), of which only one part has been issued in English.

The drawings of this article are executed partly on the basis of sketches by Prof. Sekino and partly after photographs by the author.

PAINTING

S. Omura, *Chinese Painters*, vol. viii.–xii.; H. A. Giles, *Introduction to the History of Chinese Pictorial Art*; A. Waley, *Introduction to the Study of Chinese Painting* and *Index of Chinese Artists*; L. Binyon, *Painting in the Far East*; R. Petrucci, *Encyclopédie de la Peinture Chinoise*; F. Hirth, *Scraps from a Collector's Notebook*; J. C. Ferguson, *Chinese Painting*.

WOOD–CARVING

Temples and their Treasures, Dept. of Interior, Japan; F. T. Piggott, *The Decorative Art of Japan* (1910); S. W. Bushell, *Chinese Art* (1904–1909).

SCULPTURE

E. Chavannes, *Mission archéologique dans la Chine septentrionale*, 2 albums of plates, 2 vol. text (1909–15); S. Omura, *History of Chinese Art*; *Sculpture*, 2 albums of plates, 1 vol. text in Japanese (1915); T. Sekino, *Sepulchral Remains of the Han Dynasty in Shantung*, 1 album of plates, text separate in Japanese (1920); S. Taketaro and Nakagawa, *Rock Carvings from Yün Kang Caves*, 1 album of plates without text (1921); S. Tanaka, *T'ien Lung Shan*, 1 album of plates without text (1923); L. Ashton, *Introduction to the Study of Chinese Sculpture* (1924); V. Ségalen, "Premier exposé des résultats archéologiques dans la Chine occidentale par la mission G. de Voisins, J. Lartigue, V. Ségalen," *Journal Asiatique*, tome v₃, vi₂, vii₃; O. Sirén, *Chinese Sculpture from the 5th to the 14th Century*, 3 vol. plates, 1 vol. text (1925), and *Studien zur Chinesischen Plastik der Post-T'ang Zeit* (1927); V. Ségalen, G. de Voisins and J. Lartigue, *Mission Archéologique en Chine*, 2 albums of plates without text (1926); O. Sirén, *A History of Early Chinese Art* (1929).

POTTERY AND PORCELAIN

General: F. Brinkley, *China, Its History, Arts and Literature* (1904); W. Burton and R. L. Hobson, *Marks on Pottery and Porcelain* (1912); S. W. Bushell, *Chinese Art* (2 vols., 1906), *Description of Chinese Pottery and Porcelain* (1910), being a translation of the *T'ao shuo*, *Oriental Ceramic Art* (1899); E. Hannover, *Pottery and Porcelain*, vol. II., *The Far East* (1925); R. L. Hobson, *Chinese Pottery and Porcelain* (2 vols., 1915), *Catalogue*

BIBLIOGRAPHIES

of the Eumorfopoulos Collection (6 vols., 1925–28), *Guide to the Pottery and Porcelain of the Far East* (1924); St. Julien, *Histoire et Fabrication de la Porcelaine Chinoise* (1856), being a translation of the greater part of the *Ching tê chên t'ao lu*, with notes and additions; E. Zimmermann, *Chinesisches Porzellan* (Leipzig, 1923).

Early Periods: J. G. Andersson, *Bulletin of the Geological Survey of China*, No. 5 (1923), *Memoirs of the Geological Survey of China*, Series A, No. 5 (1925); T. J. Arne, *Palaeontologia Sinica* (1925), Series D, vol. I., No. 2; C. Hentze, *Les Figurines de la Céramique Funéraire* (Hellerau, 1927); A. L. Hetherington, *Early Ceramic Wares of China* (abridged ed., 1924); B. Laufer, *Chinese Pottery of the Han Dynasty* (Leyden, 1909), *The Beginnings of Porcelain in China* (Chicago, 1917); O. Rücker Embden, *Chinesische Frühkeran ik* (Leipzig, 1922).

Later Periods: R. L. Hobson, *The Wares of the Ming Dynasty* (1923), *The Later Ceramic Wares of China* (1925); A. E. Hippisley, *Catalogue of the Hippisley Collection*, Smithsonian Institution, Washington (1900).

ENAMEL

F. Brinkley, *Japan and China*, vol. vii. (1904); Brooklyn Museum of the Institute of Arts and Sciences, *The Avery Collection of Ancient Chinese Cloisonnés* (1912); S. W. Bushell, *Chinese Art*, vol. ii. (1919); R. L. Hobson, *Chinese Cloisonné Enamels*, in *Burlington Magazine*, vol. xxi., pp. 137, 202, Ibid. *Canton Enamels*, in *Burlington Magazine*, vol. xxii., p. 165.

JADE

J. Anderson, *Report on the Expedition of Western Yunnan viâ Bhamô* (Calcutta, 1871); S. Blondel, "Le Jade," étude historique, archéologique et littéraire sur la pierre appelée yu par les Chinois (Paris, 1875), trans. by Dr. E. Foreman in the *Annual Report* for 1876 of the Smithsonian Institution (Washington); F. W. Clarke and G. P. Merrill, "On Nephrite and Jadeite," in *Proceedings*, U. S. National Museum, vol. xi. (1888); G. M. Dawson, "On the Occurrence of Jade in British Columbia and its Employment by the Natives," *Canadian Record of Science*, vol. ii. No. 6 (April, 1887); Sir J. Evans, *The Ancient Stone Implements, Weapons and Ornaments of Great Britain* (London, 1872; 2nd ed., 1897); H. Fischer and A. A. Damour, "Notice sur la distribution des hâches et autres objets préhistoriques en jade, néphrite et en jadeite," *Revue Archéologique* (Paris, 1878); B. J. Harrington, "Notes on Specimens of Nephrite from British Columbia," *Transactions* of the Royal Society of Canada, Sect. iii. (1890); J. Hilton, "Remarks on Jade," reprinted from the *Archaeological Journal*, vol. xlv., p. 187 (Exeter, 1888); C. W. King, *Antique Gems and Rings* (London, 1872); G. F. Kunz, *Gems and Precious Stones of North America* (New York, 1890), *The Precious Stones of Mexico* (1907); A. B. Meyer, *Jadeit und Nephrit Objecte*, König. Ethnographisches Museum zu Dresden (Leipzig, 1882); R. Pumpelly, "Geological Researches in China, Mongolia and Japan during the years 1862 to 1865," *Smithsonian Contribution to Knowledge* (Washington, 1866); F. W. Rudler, "On Jade and Kindred Stones," *Popular Science Review* (London, Oct. 1879); E. G. Squier, "Observations on a Collection of Chalchihuitls from Mexico and Central America," *Annals* of the Lyceum of Natural History of New York (1869); H. M. Westropp, "On Jade Implements found in Switzerland," *Journal* of the Anthropological Institute, vol. x. (1880); H. Yule, *The Book of Sen. Marco Polo, concerning the Kingdoms and Marvels of the East* (London, 1871; 2nd ed., 1875).

191

BIBLIOGRAPHIES

IRON

B. Laufer, *Chinese Clay Figures, Part 1, Prolegomena on the History of Defensive Armor* (Chicago, 1914); H. C. Gunsaulus, *Japanese Sword-mounts in the Collection of the Field Museum* (Chicago, 1923); E. Boerschman, "Eisen-und Bronzepagoden in China," *Jahrbuch der Asiatischen Kunst*, pp. 223–235 (1924); B. March, "Iron Pictures: A Chinese Craft," *Chinese Economic Monthly*, vol. iii., pp. 312–313; O. Sirén, *Chinese Sculpture* (1925); G. Soulié de Morant, *Histoire de L'Art Chinois* (1928).

LACQUER

Chinese Lacquer: P. le Bonnani, *Traité de la composition des Vernis* (1723, reprinted 1780); P. d'Incarville, "Mémoire sur le Vernis de Chine" in the *Mémoires* of the Académie Royale des Sciences (Paris, 1760); S. W. Bushell, *Chinese Art*, vol. i. (1904–06; new ed., 1921); O. Muensterberg, *Chinesische Kunstgeschichte*, 2 vol. (Esslingen a. N., 1910–12); W. P. Yetts, *Symbolism in Chinese Art*, publ. by the China Soc. (1912); A. A. Breuer, "Chinese Inlaid Lacquer" and "Chinese Incised Lacquer" in the *Burlington Magazine*, vol. xxv. (1914); E. F. Strange, *Catalogue of Chinese Lacquer in the Victoria and Albert Museum* (1925), and *Chinese Lacquer* (1926).

Chinese and Japanese lacquer: F. Brinkley, *Japan and China*, 12 vol. (1901–02; 2nd ed., 1903–04); Toyei Shuko, *Illustrated Catalogue of the Ancient Imperial Treasury, called Shōsoin* (1909); Omura Seigai, *Record of the Imperial Treasury, Shōsoin* (1910); A. A. Breuer, "Influence of China on Lacquer in Japan," Japan Soc. *Transactions*, vol. xii. (1913–14). *See* also *Kokka*, a monthly journal on Fine Arts, Archaeology, etc. (Tokyo, 1890, etc.).

BRONZE AND BRASS

S. W. Bushell, *Chinese Art* (1904); J. C. Ferguson, "An Examination of Chinese Bronzes," *Annual Report of Smithsonian Institution* (1914); M. Toyoda, *Sumitomo* Part II., "Ancient Mirrors" (1921); Takeuchi Kimpei, "Ancient Chinese Bronze Mirrors" *Burlington Magazine* (Sept. 1911); A. J. Koop, *Early Chinese Bronzes* (1924); Hamada Kosaku, *Explanatory Notes on Sen-oku sei-sho* (*The Collection of Old Bronzes of Baron Sumitomo*) Part I., "Bronze Vases," etc. (1921); R. Petrucci, "L'Epigraphie des Bronzes rituels de la Chine ancienne" in *Jour. Asiatique* (1916); M. Rostovtzeff, *Iranians and Greeks in South Russia* (1922); M. Rostovtzeff, *Inlaid Bronzes of the Han Dynasty in the Collection of C. T. Loo* (Brussels, 1927); E. A. Voretzsch, *Altchinesische Bronzen* (Berlin, 1924); W. P. Yetts, "Bronzes," *Burlington Magazine Monograph* (1925); Otto Kümmel, *Chinesische Bronzen aus der Abteilung für Ostasiatische Kunst an den Staatlichen Museen*, Berlin (1928).

DATE DUE

DEC 1 5 1999	
DEC 1 5 1999	
APR 1 6 2015	

GAYLORD	PRINTED IN U.S.A.